Anonymous

**International Exhibition, 1876, Philadelphia**

Portugese special catalogue. Departments I., II., III., IV., V. Mining and metallurgy;

manufactures; education and science; fine arts; machinery

Anonymous

**International Exhibition, 1876, Philadelphia**
*Portugese special catalogue. Departments I., II., III., IV., V. Mining and metallurgy;
manufactures; education and science; fine arts; machinery*

ISBN/EAN: 9783337291983

Printed in Europe, USA, Canada, Australia, Japan

Cover: Foto ©Suzi / pixelio.de

More available books at **www.hansebooks.com**

# INTERNATIONAL EXHIBITION, 1876

## PHILADELPHIA.

—◆—

# CATALOGUE.

## DEPARTMENTS

### I. II. III. IV. V.

—

MINING & METALLURGY.

—

MANUFACTURES.

—

EDUCATION AND SCIENCE

—

FINE ARTS.

—

MACHINERY.

# PORTUGUESE

# SPECIAL CATALOGUE.

# INTERNATIONAL EXHIBITION, 1876

AT

PHILADELPHIA.

---

# PORTUGUESE
# SPECIAL CATALOGUE.

---

## DEPARTMENTS I., II., III., IV., V.

---

### MINING AND METALLURGY.

### MANUFACTURES.

### EDUCATION AND SCIENCE.

### FINE ARTS.

### MACHINERY.

Ⓥ

# EXECUTIVE COMMITTEES IN PORTUGAL.

## DEPARTMENT I.

*Bureau of Mines.* JOAO BAPTISTA SCHIAPPA D'AZEVEDO, Chief.

### Mining Engineers:

JOAO FERREIRA BRAGA,

LOURENCO MALHEIRO,

FRANCISCO FERREIRA ROQUETTE,

PEDRO VITOR DA COSTA SEQUEIRA.

## DEPARTMENTS II, III, IV, AND V.

*Committee of the Society for the Promotion of the Fabril Industry:*

ANTONIO AUGUSTO D'AGUIAR, Director of the Industrial Institute of Lisbon, President,

DANIEL CORDEIRO FEIO,

JOAQUIM MOREIRA MARQUES,

MANUEL DE CARVALHO RIBEIRO VIANNA,

IZIDORO THOMAZ DE MOURA CARVALHO,

MANUEL GOMES DA SILVA,

JOSE CAETANO D'ALMEIDA NAVARRO,

ANTONIO ADRIANO DA COSTA,

FIRMINO SEIXAS,

FRANCISCO JOSE LOPES FERREIRA,

MATHEUS FERREIRA,

ANTONIO DOS SANTOS MIGUEIS,

JULIO JOSE PIRES,

HENRIQUE PEREIRA TAVEIRA.

### AT OPORTO:

GUSTAVO ADOLPHO GONÇALVES E SOUZA, Director of the Industrial Institute of Oporto.

### AT AZORES ISLANDS:

OFFICIAL COMMISSION OF PONTA DELGADA.

----

## COMMISSION AT PHILADELPHIA.

### INDUSTRIAL DEPARTMENT:

LOURENCO MALHEIRO, *Commissioner.*

### Assistant Commissioners:

ANTONIO JOSE ANTUNES NAVARRO,

JORGE CANDIDO BERKELEY COTTER,

THOMAZ VICTOR DA COSTA SEQUEIRA, Secretary.

# MEASURES OF PORTUGAL.

## LENGTH.

1 metre = 39.37 inches = 3.28 feet.
1 kilometre = 3280 feet = 1093 yards.

## SURFACE.

Hectare = 2.4714 acres.
Are = 1076.43 square feet.
Centare = 1550.06 square inches.

## CAPACITY.

Cubic metre = 1.3047 cubic yards.
Litre = 1.05672 quarts.

## WEIGHT.

Gramme = 15.4323 grains.
Kilogramme = 2.20462 lbs. Avoirdupois.
Ton = 2204.62 lbs. Avoirdupois.

## MONEY.

1 $ 000 = $1.0815 gold.
1 £ English, legal tender in Portugal, = $4.866 gold.

# INDEX.

## DEPARTMENT I.

## MINING AND METALLURGY.

Administrative Board of Ponta
Delgada Artificial Works...... 94
Administrative Board of the Sul-
phurous Baths of Cabeco de
Vide............................... 99
Administration of the Mint and
Stamped Papers................... 99
Agostinho Francisco Velho and
others............................ 58
Alonço Gomez...................... 51
Antonio Martins Henriques & Co. 61
Barreto, Antonio Tavares.......... 81
Bento Rodrigues d'Oliveira........ 80
Bento Rodrigues d'Oliveira and
Simoes A. Guerreiro............ 61
Bernardo Daupias & Co............. 57
Board of Sabicheira Parrish....... 81
Brites, Antonio Pereira........... 98
Bureau of the Districtal Works of
Ponta Delgada..................... 95
Bureau of Mines..............81-112
Carlos Goldbeck and Maximiliano
Schreck........................... 78
Carlos Frederico Blank............ 60
Carvalho, Wenceslau Martins...... 81
Cardozo Junior, José Pereira...... 111
Civil Governor of Portalegre...... 99
Compa. de Mineraçao de S. Pedro
do Sul.......................79-111
Compa. da Mina de Telhadella... 64
Compa. Portuguesa de Mineraçao
de Cobre.......................... 65
Compa. de Mineraçao de Estanho
de Tras-os-Montes.............77-111
Compa. de Mineraçao Transatagana
65-74-113
Compa. Uniao Industrial........... 80
Conde de Farrobo.................. 78
Diederick Mathias Teuerheerd &
Co...........................52-55-111
Direction of Mondego and Figueira
Bar Works........................ 82
Direction of Public Works of the
District of Coimbra............... 86
Direction of Public Works of the
District of Leiria................ 87
Direction of Public Works of the
District of Aveiro................ 87
Direction of Public Works of the
District of Oporto................ 88
Direction of the Public Works of
the District of Vizeu............ 89

Direction of the Public Works of
the District of Braga............. 90
Direction of the Public Works of
the District of Vianna do Cas-
tello............................. 91
Ernesto Deligny................... 75
Extremoz Marble Quarrying Co.. 93
F. A. de Vasconcellos P. Cabral.. 80
F. D. Teuerheerd.................. 76
Ferreira & Souza.................. 111
Fialho & Irmao.................... 100
Freitas, Albino José de........... 100
George Elliot..................... 49
Giron, Don José................... 50
Joao Correa d'Oliveira........78-112
Joao Gonçalves de Moraes........ 60
Lisbon Dyeing and Cotton Print-
ing Co............................ 99
Lourenço Malheiro, Mining En-
gineer............................ 113
Lusitanian Mining Co., limited...56-63
Manilha, Francisco dos Santos ...94-99
Mauricio Kamp..................... 52
Maximiliano Schreck and Mauri-
cio Kamp.......................... 63
Moncorvo Iron Mines............... 50
Monges Iron Co., limited.......... 47
Neuville, Luiz.................... 99
Official Commission of Ponta Del-
gada.............................. 105
Pedras Salgadas Mineral Water
Company........................... 100
Preserverança Co.............61-76-112
Rasca Cement Exploring Com-
pany.............................. 99
Rato, Antonio Moreira............. 96
Sales, Germano Jose de............ 93
Santos, Joaquim Antunes dos...... 97
Silva, S. A. P. da & E. A.Marques 113
Sociedade Descobridora das Minas
de Cortes Pereiras................ 62
Sociedade da Mina da Malhada... 67
The Vallongo State and Marble
Quarries Company, limited ..... 97
Thomaz Sequeira and Eduardo
Carneiro d'Andrade............... 66
Vidago Mineral Waters Company 101
Visconde de Bessone............... 98
Visconde de Freixo................ 59
Visconde Mason de S. Domingos..
67-111-113

# DEPARTMENT II.

## MANUFACTURES.

Albuquerque, Dr. Caetano d'Andrade.....................................27–35
Alcobia, Joao Thomé.................17, 19
Alexandre, Henrigues.............. 42
Almeida, Germano de.............. 46
Almeida, Jacintho Pacheco de... 27
Almeida, e Silva..................... 20
Alves Junior, Antonio............. 64
Andrade, Albano Abilio de......... 63
Anjos & Co..................... 25
Anjos, Cunha, Ferreira & Co..... 26
Antonio Baptista Moreira & Irmao..... 19
Antonio da Camara............... 64
Antunes, Jeronimo José........... 42
Araujo, José Antonio.............. 68
Araujo, Antonio José Barboza de.. 39
Areu, Manuel Joaquin de Silva... 46
Augusta, Maria da Piedade....... 67
Aurificia Company.................. 52
Avellar & Miranda.................. 67
Bahia, Antonio José Rodriguez... 43
Bahia, Custodio José Rodrigues... 44
Bahia & Genro.................22, 27
Balsa Cotton Factory.............. 22
Bandeira, Antonio Souza Brito e Maldonado..... 5
Baptista, Joao Guerreiro............27, 68
Barbosa & Costa.................. 17
Barboza, José Antonio.............. 67
Baroneza de Samora Correa...... 5
Barreiros, Francisco Isidoro...... 46
Beirollas, Antonio Manuel......... 69
Bernardo Daupias & Co............35, 46
Bibianno, Antonio Alves........... 32
Bivar, Jeronimo Coelho d'Almeida de.................... 5, 50
Bolhao Cotton Printing Factory.. 26
Boim & Co...............10, 12, 13
Borges, Joaquim Antonio.......... 13
Borges, Manuel da Cunha.......... 20
Branco, Anna Delfina.............. 5
Brandao, José Marcal............. 38
Braga, Joao José de Souza........ 9
Braga, Manuel José Vieira........ 42
Brum, Caetano de...... ............ 27
Bruno da Silva..................... 20
Cabo Mondego Mining & Industrial Co..................... 16
Calheta, D. Maria Ferreira da.... 43
Camara D. Hermelinda Gago da.. 28

Camara, Manuel da................... 50
Campolini, Miguel .................. 13
Campo-Grande Woolen Fabrics Co....................... 32
Campos Mello & Irmão............. 32
Candido, Coimbra.................... 14
Canto, D. Anna Adelaide do...... 28
Cardozo, Joao Thomas..:.......... 64
Cardozo, José Pereira.............. 59
Cardozo, Manuel Joaquim........ 42
Carneiro, Francisco dos Santos.... 41
Carranquinha, Joaquim Antonio. 14
Carvalho, D. Anna Candida Leonor da Costa...................... 50
Carvalho, D. Isabel Candida Alves 28
Carvalho, Joaquim José........... 46
Carvalho, Manuel de.............. 69
Carvalho, Maria da Conceicao.... 54
Carvalho e Mello, A. J............. 59
Castello Branco, Joao Ferrao da Silva....................... 5
Castro, Joao Vaz Pacheco de...... 28
Cerquinho, Francisco Augusto Vaz 52
Coelho, Francisco.....................11–12
Coelho, José de Souza.............. 41
Collaço, Manuel Matheus.......... 32
Collaço, Manuel Martins........... 28
Conceiçao, Umbelina da............32, 43
Conqueje Manuel................... 14
Constant Burnay..................... 33
Coral, Jaonna Maria Dias.......... 50
Costa, Antonio d'Almeida & Co... 11, 12
Costa Basto & Co.................... 18
Costa Braga & Co.................... 43
Costa and Carvalho................. 33
Costa, Clemente Joaquim............ 36
Costa, Joaquim Soares.............. 7
Costa, José Antonio da............. 42
Costa, Rodrigo de Campos.......... 9
Cooke & Co......................... 6
Coutinho, A. & Filho.............. 53
Coutinho, José Maria da Camara.. 56
Couto, Guilherme do............... 52
Crestuma Spinning Co.............. 22
Creswell & Co....................... 6
Cruz, Joao Maria.................... 66
Cruz, Luiz Ferreira de Souza...... 69
Cuco, José Maria....................11, 12
Cunha, Augusto Mendes........55, 64, 69
Cunha, José Alves................... 14
Custodio & Silva.................... 33

Dabney, R. L..................20, 41
Dabney S. W.............43, 50, 54, 68
David, José d'Azevedo.............. 55
David José da Silva & Filho........ 39
Delaye, Hipolito...................... 49
Deligny Freres....................... 3
Department of Public Works...... 9
Dias, Antonio...................... 46
Dias, Rodrigo Antonio Ferreira...23-28
Diogo, Manuel Antonio............. 55
Direction of Public Works of the
  River Mondego and Figueira
  Bar .................................. 6
Drack Junior, José R. Guimaraes.. 60
Etur, Augusto Frederico............. 26
Esmoriz, Manuel Ferreira de...... 8
Falleiro, D. Barbara Rita Fer-
  nandez............................... 28
Fanfarrao, Joao...................... 14
Ferreira, D. Joanna E....44, 51, 54, 68
Ferreira, José Bento................ 46
Ferreira, Joao José.................. 60
Figueiredo, Joaquim de............. 61
Filippa, Piteira...................... 36
Florencia Serrana.................... 43
Fonseca, Manuel da Motta......... 38
Franco, Pedro Augusto............. 62
Fraternal Association of Weavers
  and correlative arts.............. 23
Freitas, Feliciano Gabriel de...... 57
Galiano, Manuel Aspres de Olive-
  ira............................57, 62
Goes, Francisco Emilio de......... 50
Gomes, F.......................... 47
Gonçalves, Jeromino Ferreira...... 65
Gonçalves, Manuel Joao............ 33
Gonçalves, Ribas & Co............. 55
Guerra, Antonio José de Souza.... 65
Guilherma, Maria.................... 33
Guimaraes, Balthasar José Pere-
  ira.................................. 28
Guimaraes, Custodio José da Silva 41, 47
Guimaraes, Custodio Lopes da
  Silva............................ 41, 47
Guimaraes, Joao Carvalho......... 69
Guimaraes, Joaquim Mendes de... 64
Guimaraes, Manuel Mendes Ribei-
  ro.................................. 29
Gragera, Dr. Antonio Maria Men-
  des.................................. 62
Guerra, Joaquim Baptista da Silva 29, 38
Herdeiros de Manuel Custodio
  Moreira............................ 39
House of Correction................. 47
Jacob Ben-Saude.................... 65
Jeronimo Martins & Filho......... 68
Jesus, Manuel Vicente.............. 62
Joao Antonio.....................12, 14
Joaquim, Maria..................... 67
Joao Rodrigues de Deus & Co..... 26

John Davies.......................... 50
José Gaudencio...................... 67
Jorge, Diogo........................ 49
Juan Domingo....................... 10
Judice, A. J........./............... 6
Lallemant Freres.................... 58
Lamego, Antonio da Costa......... 11
Lança, Francisco Pereira da....... 29
Leandro, Manuel.................... 34
Leite, Francisco de Paula.......... 6
Leite, Tito José..................... 23
Leitao & Irmao..................... 53
Lemos & Antunes................... 65
Lemos, Joao Gonçalves............. 57
Lima, Anna Julia da Conceiçao... 51
Lima, Bernardo de Abreu......... 54
Lima & Carvalho.................... 44
Lima, Guilherme A. E............. 62
Lima, Joao Bernardo d'Abreu.... 54
Lisboa, José Balbino da Silva &
  Co.................................. 57
Lisbon Cotton Dyeing and Print-
  ing Co.............................. 27
Lisbon National Printing Office... 58
Lisbon Spinning and Weaving Co. 23
Lobao & Fereira..................... 53
Lordello Woolen Fabrics Co...... 34
Machado, Julio Rodrigues.......... 41
Machado, Manuel................... 21
Mafra, Manuel Cypriano Gomez
  Mafra.............................. 14
Magalhaes, D. Anna Maria Bar-
  boza............................... 59
Magalhaes, Francisco Thiago...... 29
Maia & Silva, Filho & Gonçalves.. 44
Manuel Antonio da Silva & Filho. 60
Manuel Joaquin de Lima & Filho. 40
Manuel José Ferreira da Silva &
  Filho.............................. 65
Manuel Leite Pereira Irmao....... 15
Manuel Fernandes.................. 37
Manuel Rodrigues Gaspar......... 17
Marçal, Joao Lopes............11-12
Margarido, Manuel d'Oliveira...... 21
Maria Barroga...................... 35
Maria José.......................... 67
Maria da Salga..................... 44
Marinha Grande Royal Glass
  Works.............................. 18
Marques, Joao da Rosa............. 15
Marques, José Antonio............. 55
Marques Junior, Manuel Martins. 53
Martins, Alberto Cypriano.....11, 13, 15
Mattos, Antonio de................. 68
Mattos, F. C. Pereira.............. 21
Melindre, Joaquim de Oliveira..... 21
Meirelles, Antonio Moreira de
  Souza.............................. 6
Mello, A. José Teixeira............
Mello, Gil Travares................. 29

| | | |
|---|---|---|
| Mello, José Carneiro de............24, 29 | Pignatelli, José da Cunha.......... | 36 |
| Mesquita, Pedro José................ | 29 | Pilao e Luzes, Antonio d'Oliveira | |
| Michon, André...................... | 16 | e Joao Gomes Leite.............. | 60 |
| Mira, José Paulo de................11, 13 | Pimentao, Antonio Ayres.......... | 15 |
| Miranda & Filhos................... | 6 | Pimentel & Queiroz............... | 40 |
| Mirrado, José Pedro Mendes...... | 34 | Pinho, Guilhermina d'Oliveira.... | 54 |
| Moedas, José....................11, 13 | Pires, Joao de Jesus.............. | 63 |
| Montes, Manuel Alvares........24, 29, 36 | Pires, Joao Luiz.................. | 7 |
| Moreira, D. Maria José.......... 29, 36 | Ponte, José Caetano da. ........... | 36 |
| Motta, Augusto Antonio da......... | 40 | Portalegre Woolen Mfg. Co....... | 35 |
| Moutinho, Luiz Pinto.............. | 53 | Portuguese Government........... | 15 |
| Moutinho de Souza, F. Successors.. | 53 | Prado Paper Mill Co.............. | 57 |
| Nabinho, José da Fonseca.......... | 51 | Queiroz, José Sequeira Pinto de... | 8 |
| National Rope Yard.............30, 67 | Queiroz, Antonio Gonçalves de.... | 27 |
| National Silk Spinning and Weav- | | Ramalho, José da Cunha.......... | 45 |
| ing Co........................... | 37 | Ramos, Joaquim Antonio.......... | 56 |
| Navarro & Co.... ................ | 8 | Ramires & Ramires.............. | 39 |
| Nepomuceno, Manuel.............. | 59 | Raul Mesnier.................... | 57 |
| Netto, Antonio Eugenio Bello...... | 37 | Rego, A. P...................... | 43 |
| Neuville, Luiz.............10, 12, 13 | Rei, José Joaquim................ | 62 |
| Neves, Balbina das............... | 34 | Resende, D. Barbara ............ | 30 |
| Nobre, José Rodrigues Furtado... | 30 | Resende, Francisca de............ | 36 |
| Nobreza, Frederico Augusto da | | Rio Jr., Joao do................. | 13 |
| Silva............................ | 62 | Rio Vizella Spinning Co.......... | 24 |
| Nogueira, Francisco José.......... | 40 | Rocha, Francisco José da Silva ... | 56 |
| Nogueira, Manuel Augusto......... | 30 | Rodrigues, José Pereira.......... | 63 |
| Oliveira, Balthasar Pinto.......... | 67 | Rosa de Mattos.................. | 30 |
| Oliveira, Gaspar José.............. | 60 | Salgueiro, Nuno Freire Dias...... | 63 |
| Oliveira, J. F. de................. | 51 | Santos, Antonio Marques dos...... | 22 |
| Oliveira, Manuel de............... | 66 | Santos, Ascencio José............ | 31 |
| Official Commission of Ponta Del- | | Santos Brites, Maria Gomes e Rosa | |
| gada........................... | 44 | Gomes dos.................51–58 | |
| Oporto Glove Co................. | 49 | Santos Chaves, Augusto Prudencio | 17 |
| Oporto Industrial Institute........ | 64 | Santos & Irmao.............18–45 | |
| Oporto Spinning Co .............. | 24 | Santos, Joaquim Antunes dos...... | 66 |
| Oliveira, Gaspar José.............. | 60 | Santos, José Marques dos......... | 22 |
| Oliveira, J. Fd.................... | 5_ | Santos, Narcizo José.............. | 77 |
| Oliveira, Manoel de............... | 66 | Santos, Manoel Moreira.......... | 64 |
| Official Commission of Ponta Del- | | Santos, Rocha Moreira............ | 66 |
| gada........................... | 44 | Santo Thirso, Antonio dos Reis.... | 21 |
| Oporto Glove Co................. | 49 | Schalk, H.................19–66–54 | |
| Oporto Industrial Institute........ | 64 | Schofield, John Howarth.......... | 15 |
| Oporto Spinning Co .............. | 24 | Shurman, Adolfo................. | 63 |
| Pacheco, Antonio Vaz ............. | 30 | Seabra, José dos Santos........... | 53 |
| Pacheco, Francisco Gomes......... | 65 | Sericola Egyptianense Co.......... | 37 |
| Pacheco, Francisco Jeronymo...... | 30 | Sequeira, Francisco Pinto.......... | 48 |
| Pacheco, Joao Vaz............30, 36 | Serra, Filippe José................ | 48 |
| Padronello Woolen Fabrics Co.... | 34 | Serzedello & Co................. | 4 |
| Paiva, Manuel Joao................ | 47 | Silva, Antonio Moreira........... | 45 |
| Paixao Jor, Antonio Augusto...... | 43 | Silva, Agostinho Freire da & Co.. | 38 |
| Panada, Joao Luiz ............... | 20 | Silva, Bernaridno Antunes......... | 50 |
| Passos, Augusto Fructuoso......... | 55 | Silva, Diogo Monteiro da.......... | 9 |
| Paula, Antonio José.............. | 44 | Silva e Alves, Antonio José Pe- | |
| Pedro Maralha.................... | 19 | reira.......................... | 38 |
| Pedrosa, D. Maria José Lopes...... | 7 | Silva, Joaquim de................ | 68 |
| Perdigao, Miguel S. R.............. | 35 | Silva, Joao Baptista.............. | 70 |
| Peixoto, José Rodrigo.............. | 65 | Silva, Juao d'Oliveira............. | 70 |
| Pereira, Luiz Maria................ | 47 | Silva, José Francisco da .......... | 35 |
| Pereiras Irmas.................... | 44 | Silva, José Gonçalves.........18–19 | |
| Peres, Joaquim Manuel de Mattos | 8 | Silva, José Pinto da.............. | 31 |

| | | | |
|---|---|---|---|
| Silva, Julio Pereira da............... | 48 | The Portuguese Government....... | |
| Silva, Manuel Dias da............... | 21 | 20-31-44-49-52-54-56-66-68 | |
| Silva, Miguel da...................... | 15 | Thereza de Jesus...................... | 53 |
| Silva, Manuel José Francisco da... | 39 | Thomar Royal Spinning Co........ | 25 |
| Silva, Miguel Manuel da............ | 48 | Torlades O'Neill........................ | 7 |
| Silva, Silverio Augusto Pereira & | | Torres Novas Spinning and Wea- | |
| Antonio Marques Moura......... | 7 | ving Co............................... | 31 |
| Simoes, Clara Rosa................... | 36 | Torres, Feliciano Luiz............... | 10 |
| Soares, José Nogueira............... | 48 | Trindade, Joaquim Antonio....... | 56 |
| Soares, M. E. d'Oliveira............. | 11 | Valença, Domingos Fernandes..... | 45 |
| Souto, Rodrigo Alves Martins..... | 48 | Vasconcellos, José de Souza Pe- | |
| Souza, D. Maria Magdalena de... | 54 | reira...................................... | 40 |
| Souza, José da Cunha Alves de... | 49 | Vianna, Antonio Martins........... | 49 |
| Souza, Luiz Augusto.................. | 70 | Vicencia, Rosa......................... | 35 |
| Souza e Silva, Antonio José........ | 25 | Victoria, José Gonçalves de ....... | 16 |
| Tagus & Sado Lowlands Co........ | 7 | Vieira, Agostinho José.............. | 9 |
| Tavares, Francisco Antonio......... | 59 | Viscount of Alcacer do Sal......... | 7 |
| Tavares, José.......................... | 68 | Vista Alegre Porcelain Manufac- | |
| Tavares, Laureano..................... | 69 | tory...................................... | 16 |
| Tavares, Rita de Jesus............... | 51 | Viuva Burnay...... ................... | 8 |
| Teixeira, Carlota Mathilde......... | 52 | Viuva Barbosa Marinho............. | 31 |
| Teixeira, D. Maria Amalia ........ | 31 | Viuva de A. Roxo.. .................. | 45 |
| Teixeira, José Rodrigues............ | 53 | Viuva Ferreira Campos & Co...... | 41 |
| Tenorio, Francisco Domingos...... | 9 | Xabregas Cotton Manufacturing | |
| Themudo, Maria Eduarda.......... | 52 | Company................................ | 25 |
| The Primary School of Barcellos.. | 52 | | |

# DEPARTMENT III.

# EDUCATION AND SCIENCE.

Administrative Board of Ponta Delgada Artificial Harbor Works... 81
Aranha, Pedro Wenceslau de Brito...................................... 73
Araujo, Joaquim Gomes............. 79
Bayao, F. A. Pinheiro................ 81
Basto, Antonio Pinto................. 79
Cabral, Affonso do Valle Coelho.. 79
Department of Finances............. 74
Direction of Mondego and Figueira Bar Works ................. 81
Ernesto Chardron..................... 74
Ferraz, José Libertador de Magalhaes................................. 74
General Administration of the Mint and Stamped Paper ........ 86
General Direction of the Geodetical, Topographical, Hydrographical, and Geological Labours............. ..................... 82
Godolphin, Costa...................... 73
Lecrenier, Nicolau José.............. 81
Lisbon Industrial Institute.........74–78
Magalhaes e Moniz ................... 74
Mengo, Francisco da Silva.......... 74
Moraes Sarmento, Antonio Evaristo de ............................... 75

Motta, José Maria da................ 79
Observatory of the Infante D. Luiz ... ............................... 76
Oliveira, Justino Gomes de ........ 79
Oporto Industrial Institute.....75–76–82
Pereira Coutinho, D. M. da França..................................... 78
Pereira, Custodio Cardozo........... 80
Pereira, Verissimo Alvares ........ 79
Pery, Gerardo A....................... 82
Portuguese Civil Engineers' Association.............................. 75
Prostes, J. C...... ..................... 75
Queiroz, G. José de ................. 74
Ribeiro, Domingos Candido d'Almeida...................................... 80
Royal Association of the Portuguese Architects and Archeologists..................................... 75
Sanhudo, J. Ferreira................ 80
Silva, Joaquim Possidonio N. da Silva.................................... 75
Silva, Silveiro Augusto Pereira da 81
Society for the Promotion of the Fabril Industry.................... 86

# DEPARTMENT IV.

# FINE ARTS.

Abreu, Severiano José.............. 89
Almeidà, José Joaquim de Aze-
    vedo......... ..................... 89
Aurificia Company................... 94
Braga, Antonio Pereira da Silva.. 92
Brito Aranha, Pedro Wenceslau
    de............................ ........... 91
Biel, E. & F. Bruett.................. 92
Camacho, J. T......................... 93
Commercial Association of Oporto.91–95
Campolini, Miguel................... 89
Costa, Antonio Almeida da & Co.. 89
Cruz, Luis Ferreira da Souza...... 94
Ferreira, Manuel José Souza...... 93
Fonseca, Antonio Correa da........ 93
General Administration of the
    Mint and Stamped Paper.......... 90
General Direction of the Geodeti-

cal, Topographical, Hydrogra-
    phical, and Geological La-
    bours......... ...................... 91
Mendes, Malaquias José............ 90
Mollarinho, J. Arnaldo Nogueira. 90
Nunes, Henrique...................... 93
Rato, Antonio Moreira.............. 90
Reis & Monteiro...................... 92
Relvas, Carlos......................... 93
Rio Junior, Joao do.................. 90
Royal Association of the Portu-
    guese Architects and Archeolo-
    gists............... ..................... 90
Rochini, Francisco................... 94
Sequeira, Thomas..................... 91
Silva & Santos...... .................. 90
Souza Fernandes...................... 93
Venancio, Domingos........ ... ...... 95

# DEPARTMENT V.

# MACHINERY.

Castro, Joao Vaz Pacheco.......... 101
Coutinho, Antonio Ramos da Silva. 100
Cruz, Luiz Ferreira de Souza...... 101
Guerra, Joaquim Baptista da Silva. 100
Joao Goncalves....................... 100

José Lamas & Co...... ............... 100
Oporto Industrial Institute......... 99
Pilao e Luzes, Antonio d'Oliveira
    e Joao Gomes Leite............... 102

# DEPARTMENT I.

# MINING & METALLURGY

## DESCRIPTIVE CATALOGUE

COMPILED BY

LOURENÇO MALHEIRO,

AND

P. V. DA COSTA SEQUEIRA,

MINING ENGINEERS.

# MINERAL RESOURCES OF PORTUGAL.

## I.

## MINING LAW.

**1210** — The most ancient document that is known rélative to mines, is of the year 1210, during the reign of King D. Sancho I., and it had for its object the making of a donation of a tithe of the gold of Adiça to the Order of Santiago.

There did not exist any general law. The mines belonged exclusively to the Crown, and they were worked by the King, or by private parties to whom by a special diploma permission was granted to mine. The concessions thus made to private parties were always regarded as a privilège and a grace, which the King bestowed on his favorites.

The privilege was always temporary, and the miners paid a royalty to the Crown, which generally was at the rate of the "fifth part" of the produce.

**King Duarte's Law (1433-1488.)**—The above regimen lasted until the reign of King D. Duarte (1433-1488), period in which the first mining law of Portugal was promulgated.

By this law every one was allowed to work mines in any place. The miner paid a royalty of "two tithes" of the produce of the mine, whenever the same was located on lands belonging to the Crown; but if it was located on private property, the said impost was equally divided between the proprietor and the King. The miners paid besides that a certain entrance fee in order to obtain the grant, and a fixed annual tax.

This law was not, however, rigorously observed, and the conditions imposed on the concessions were very changeable.

The period of the concession was sometimes fixed, and again its terms were not defined. It seems that the new principle of the proprietor's participation in the profits of the mines was always preserved.

**King D. Manoel's Law, 1516.**—The law of the King D. Duarte remained in force until 1516, the date at which the second decree on mines, known under the title of "Regimento de Ayres do Quental" was promulgated by King D. Manoel. The fundamental principle of King D. Duarte's decree was done away with entirely in this second law; the proprietor remained without any rights at all over the miner's interest ; the mining prerogatives did remain with as much plenitude as in the time of the kings before D. Duarte. The proprietor had the right to demand indemnity for the damages caused to his cultivated fields, but was obliged to allow the cutting down of wood for the foundries, without any redress whatever.

The impost continued to be a "fifth," but the miner was obliged to sell his metals to the King's stores at a fixed price, which was below the market price. Therefore, the imposts paid by the miner were far in excess of 20 per cent. of the production. This law retarded very much the development of mines.

**1557.**—In the year 1557 a new decree was promulgated, which, without altering the fundamental basis of King D. Manoel's law, had the advantage of permitting the free sale of the metals; but later enactments restrained this faculty in regard to certain metals, the others remaining subject to forced sales. The tax continued to be a "fifth," but the fisc invented a new way to raise that impost; whenever a mine was bringing in profits the King could take a fourth himself, contributing towards its workings with proportioned expenses; so that, the miner, besides paying an impost of 20 per cent. on the produce, found himself obliged to give to the King 25 per cent. of the net proceeds. Under such a regimen the mining interests got into such a deplorable state that further regulations promised premiums to any one who should discover any mines, but the demands of the fisc continued so severe that the premium, by itself, was not enough to promote the development of mines.

**1801.**—With the purpose of reanimating this industry, almost extinct, "*A General Superintendence of Mines and Metals of the Kingdom*" was created in 1801, under whose immediate control the mines were explored, the Government defraying all expenses. This new method was by no means productive of any better results, which was a defect of the system. At the end of this regimen there were to be found hardly four mines in operation—two of coal, one of antimony, and one of lead—of which only the coal mine of "S. Pedro da Cova" was able to realize any net profits, which were employed in assisting in the outlay of the others.

The "General Superintendence of Mines and Metals of the Kingdom" did but prove once more how impossible it is for any industry to prosper under the management of any Government.

**1836.**—By an ordinance (potraria) of the 6th of August, 1836, a grant was given to the lead mine of Braçal, and the decree of the 25th of November of the same year, reaffirming said ordinance, put an end to the privilege which the State since the year 1801 had arrogated to itself, of working the mines on its own account.

But the decree of the 25th of November granted only the temporary use of the mines, the State reserving to itself the right of possession; the industry not finding, therefore, in the law sufficient guarantee for its own free development.

**1850.**—The above law was kept in force till the year 1850, and during that period of 14 years only 35 mines had received concessions.

The decree of the 25th of July, 1850, came to promote the creation of the mining property, consecrating the principle of concession for an unlimited period.

The decree of 1836, to a certain extent, became completed by that of 1850; the former, by abolishing the privilege of the State, created the right to the mines; the latter created the mining proprietorship. This law lasted until 1852, and during this period no new grants were made.

**1852.**—The decree of the 31st of December, 1852, adopting the fecund principle of the former and improving some of its regulations, opened a new era of prosperity to the mining industry.

By accepting the basis of the French law of the 21st of April, 1810, this decree regulated the separation of the superficial and subterranean property, circumscribed the rights of the proprietors and of the grantees, and the discovery of mines found, in the decided advantages conceded to the discoverer, a very powerful incentive for its progressive development.

The fundamental principles of the present law are the following:

Every one who should discover a mine has the right to its grant, whether it be located in his soil or not.

The proprietor of the soil is obliged to consent to the working of the mine.

The miner is obliged to give the owner of the soil previous security for the indemnization of the damages he may cause.

All grants are made for an unlimited period.

The general conditions under which ι grant is made, are: To keep the mine in active operation; carry on the labors with safety, and pay the imposts to the Government.

The impost is of 5 per cent. of the net product of the work.

The owner of the land receives half the quantity paid to the Government.

The grant may be set aside, should not the grantee satisfy the conditions under which it was made. In such a case the property remains belonging to the State, and the Government can grant it anew at auction.

The objects of concessions are the deposits of metallic substances and the saline and combustible deposits.

The area granted to the metallic mines is about 500,000 square metres, and for the combustible ones of 100,000.

The law of the 31st of December, 1852, did evidently contribute very much towards the mining progress in Portugal; with all, this law could not fulfill the present requirements of the industry, and placed real impediments in its development.

The mining industry of France is, as yet, being regulated chiefly by the law of the 21st of April, 1810; and, in spite of the administrative regulations that followed in succession, and the laws that have successively improved the original one, the French operators never cease demanding new legislative reforms.

Prussia, which adopted the law of 1810, forced by the pressing demands of the industry, substituted it with the one of June 24, 1865.

England, which has successively reformed several times its law of the 10th of August, 1842, again, on the 10th of August, 1872, promulgated its last law, revoking all former legislation, and introducing all the requirements that the short experience of ten years, counting from the time of the last law, deemed necessary.

Amongst us the experience of twenty years has shown us the defects of the law of 1852, and the necessity of its being reformed.

A simplification of the process for obtaining the concessions; a more complete and much better defined creation of the mining property than at present; a clearer determination of the mutual relations between the concessionists and the land-owners; the organization of safeguards of the mines, clearly defining the administrative power and the relations between the administration and the grantees; the organization, so often asked for, of a new system of imposts, are many reasons for the reformation of the actual law.

All these reforms are objects of a new law, which probably will not be delayed very long, for all those that have any action more or less direct in its promulgation are of accord on the necessity of a reform.

## II.

# MINING INDUSTRY.

## IRON.

The iron deposits are found in great quantities in all the provinces of the Kingdom, and in several geological formations.

The deposits of Mancorvo, without doubt the most important of Portugal, occupy a zone of 10 kilometres long and about 1700 metres wide.

They are constituted by oligist iron, which is found in large masses between the laurentian schists. This deposit will be specially described at the end of this paragraph.

The hematites form the extensive deposit of Quadramil in Tras-os-Montes, which have an extension of 6 to 8 kilometres, with a thickness sometimes of 20 metres.

They crop out between the laurentian schists, stretching N.N.W.*

In Alemtejo are notable the deposits of Monges, Ayres, Zambujal, and S. Bartholomeo.

These deposits form beds between the laurentian schists, altered by the granites that crop out at some four kilometres to the south.

---

*All directions refer to the magnetic meridian, which in Portugal has proximately the direction of N. 20° W., true.

Among these the most important deposit is the one of Monges mountain, whose outcrops follow each other at a distance of about one kilometre, attaining at some places a thickness of 30 metres.

Between S. Thiago do Cacem and Odemira, occupying a zone of 20 kilometres long by 4 wide, there occur several iron lodes associated with manganese, following a general direction of N. 70° E. These lodes show in their outcrops very remarkable thicknesses. The predominant ores are the hematites. The principal gangues are quartz and sulphate of baryta.

The enclosing rocks are the argillous schists of the lower carboniferous period.

The jurassic formations of the province of Extremadura, district of Leiria, contains magnetic iron lodes distributed over a great surface. The deposits of Mendiga, Serro Ventoso, and Arrimal, at the environs of Cabeço do Veodo, are worthy of note, where a bed of jurassic pitcoal exists.

The coal-bed of Chao Preto is cut through by an iron lode.

There exist other deposits of iron which, on account of not being of sufficient importance, we will pass them in silence.

Of all these deposits, the only one working is that of Monges mountain. The ores of this mine are at present all exported.

The fall in the price of iron in England placed the Monges mine in difficult circumstances for the exportation, and the Mining Company thinks of establishing furnaces at Barreiro, landing place in Tejo, and importing the necessary coke for its foundries.

The iron metallurgic industry, whose existence in ancient times is attested by the large piles of rubbish that were found in many mines, disappeared in Portugal with the two furnaces of Foz d'Alge, whose activity lasted since the beginning of this century till 1830.

Yet afterwards the " Portuguese Coal and Iron Company," which owned in the district of Leiria ten coal and iron mines, made a metallurgic attempt, building a furnace at Pedrianes, near to Marinha Grande, where there is a large forestal property of the State with a surface of 10,000 hectaras of maritime pines.

The labors of those mines having commenced in 1865 were totally abandoned in 1868, the attempt having failed.

At present the metallurgic industry does not exist in Portugal, notwithstanding that this country possesses extensive iron deposits.

The resolution adopted by the operators of the iron mine of Monges mountain is, perhaps, the only one.that can possibly take advantage of the large masses of ore that the country possesses, seeing that the coal resources are relatively small. Iron mining in Portugal, only for exportation purposes is, if not impossible, at least, very difficult.

**The Moncorvo Iron Mines.**—The ferriferous region of Moncorvo begins from near the town of *Torre de Moncorvo* to Cabeço da Mua, in an easterly direction, resembling a belt having a length of ten kilometres by about two of width. These mines belong to the " concelho" of Moncorvo, district of Brabança. Almost all the ferriferous region was divided into 33 legal grants. The total surface allotted to these 33 grants was of 1710 *hect.* 54*ar.* 79*cent.*, giving an aggregate surface to each grant of 51 *hect.* 83*ar.* 47*cent.*

The map of these mines is exhibited at the Portuguese Section.

The requisitions for these different grants were made by—

| | | |
|---|---|---|
| Adolpho Leuschener......... ........ 1 | .................................. | No. 1 |
| Francisco J. C. Aulete............... 5 | ...................... | Nos. 2 to 5 |
| Joao Pacheco de Rezende...........21 | Nos. 7 to 11, Nos. 14 & 19 to 22 | |
| Victoriano J. G. da Rocha........... 2 | ..... ................. | Nos. 12 & 13 |
| J. V. de Oliveira..................... 2 | ....................... | Nos. 15 & 17 |
| J. Christiano Keil..................... 1 | .............................. | No. 16 |
| J V. de Carvalho..................... 1 | .............................. | No. 18 |

The culminating summits of the region have an altitude of 950 metres above the level of the sea.

Relatively to the central point of the map (x) these mines are located in Latitude 41° 10′ 11″ North, and in Longitude 2° 10′ 29″ East of Lisbon. The magnetic delineation of the place is 20° 30′ 16″ West.

The distance of the central point of these mines to the river Douro is of 10 kilometres, and their distance to a coast landing in Leichoes, near Oporto, is 173 kilometres.

DESCRIPTION OF THE DEPOSIT.—There are to be found in the ferriferous region of Moncorvo, two kinds of ore entirely distinct as to the manner in which they lay, though they be of the same nature: the *rocky ore* and the *gravel ore.*

The rocky ore is found forming the highest crests of the mountains of *Roboredo, Mindel, Cotovia, Carvalhal, Carvalhosa,* and *Mua,* in the form of lenticular masses of great dimensions, all having a well-defined general direction. Each of these masses is subordinate to the stratification of the argillo-micaceous schists of the locality, which have a general direction of 75° N. to 80° E. in perfect harmony with the general stretch of the deposits. In each of these masses the ore presents itself in compact layers, with its plans of stratification well defined and inclined like the connecting schists, 35 to 45° southward. In its structure the ferrugineous substance yet appears under a schistous form.

The mineral masses of Moncorvo are generally constituted of aligisteiron ore; magnetites are also found, particularly in *Alto do Chapeo,* and hematites in the eastern slope of the *Cabeço da Mua,* and also in *Fragas do Carvalho.*

The assays made with some samples give the following results for metallic iron :

| | | |
|---|---|---|
| *Fragas dos Apriscos.* ......... ...................... | 53.6 | per cent. |
| " " " .............................. | 48.0 | " " |
| " " " .............................. | 43.3 | " " |
| *Alto do Chapeo....* ..... ...................... | 59.2 | " " |
| *Cabeço da Mua.*..................................... | 55.8 | " " |
| " " .............................. | 42.5 | " " |
| " " .............................. | 47.4 | " " |
| " " ...............,.. .............. | 47.0 | " " |
| " " ..................................... | 47.0 | " " |

| | | | | | | |
|---|---|---|---|---|---|---|
| *Cabeço da Mua*............................................. | 39.0 | " | " |
| "      " | ......................................... | 46.0 | " | " |
| "      " | ......................................... | 48.8 | " | " |
| "      " | ......................................... | 53.3 | " | " |
| *Carvalhal e Carvalhosa*............................. | 52.4 | " | " |
| "    "    " | ......................................... | 40.0 | " | " |
| "    "    " | ......................................... | 53.0 | " | " |
| "    "    " | ......................................... | 44.3 | " | " |
| "    "    " | ......................................... | 28.0 | " | " |

A complete assay gave the following results:

| | |
|---|---|
| Magnetic oxyd.... ............................................. | 0.1294 |
| Sesqui-oxyd of iron.......................................... | 0.6585 |
| Lime.............................................................. | 0.0050 |
| Insoluble waste................................................ | 0.1645 |
| Loss by fire.............................................. ...... | { 0.0395 |
| Phosphoric acid.............................................. | { Traces |

| | |
|---|---|
| | 0.9969 |
| Yield in metallic iron...................................... | 0.5495 |

The theory that attributed the formation of this order of deposits to emergent ferruginous springs, is well applied to Moncorvo. Every one of the emanating points of the metalliferous basin converted itself into the centre of a lenticular mass of ore; and as this phenomenon is contemporaneous with the depositing of the sedimentary rocks, the various ferriferous lents shape themselves into the form of an embedded mass in the layers of the schists.

Studying the stratigraphical relations that unite the deposits of Moncorvo to others already known, many remarkable coincidences will be found.

A maximum circle passing through Moncorvo in a parallel line to the Primitive of Land's End of the Pentagonal System adjusts itself exactly to the general direction of these deposits; and the same circle prolonged would pass very near to the north of Sardinia, adjusting itself there in a parallel line with the direction of many iron deposits.

The masses of rocky ore are found at a distance of a kilometre from the granites that crop out in a northerly and easterly direction, being divided by a band of schists which are covered by the gravel-ore.

The granites must have certainly produced a metamorphic action on the mineral mass, contributing probably towards the formation of the magnetic iron that is to be found there.

There are also found the outcrops of various veins of quartz, proximately parallel to each other, crossing the ferruginous deposits and the connecting schists, extending themselves through the granites. These veins are sterile.

Around the ferruginous masses that form the line of the mountain's summit, and at a distance of a kilometre to either of the sides, the soil is covered with a deposit of gravel ore of all sizes.

The meteorological agents operating upon those great pre-existing masses of ore slowly loosened the rock, and the detached blocks rolled down its declivities, thus accumulating in some places deposits of thousands of tons. This phenomenon of denudation, which is yet being produced to this day, gave rise to what we call gravel-ore.

In Moncorvo there are as yet no mining labors going on; therefore, we have no basis on which to make a calculation of the quantity of ore existing there.

The superficial section of some of those masses is very remarkable. Some masses have a length of 500 metres by 200 of width.

Supposing that the depth of these deposits is, at least, equal to its thickness, which is verified in the similar ones of Elba Island, Sardinia, and Mokta-el-Hadid, and is likewise verified in deposits of identical form at all the deposits in mass of manganese and of pyrites of Portugal and Spain; the quantity of ore existing in the 33 grants of Moncorvo, valued at a rough estimate, but sufficient to give an idea of the importance of these mines, is of fifty million tons, at least.

The quantity of gravel-ore disposed over the soil, already out and ready to be loaded in wagons, is from ten to fifteen million tons at least.

MEANS OF COMMUNICATION.—The working of the Moncorvo mines is subject to the existence of economical means of transportation that unites these mines with a landing near the city of Oporto. This communication can be established either by the Douro railroad, or by navigation. This last means appears at first sight as the most economical and easiest of establishing; but it would be necessary to overcome great difficulties and spend large sums to make the Douro river navigable, whose bottom is uneven by numerous falls, and its current generally very impetuous.

As a means truly practical and relatively easier, the Douro railroad, now under construction, is the one to be thought of.

The logical terminus of this railroad is naturally the place where it will connect with the Salamanca railroad in Spain, and to reach said connection it must pass very near the Moncorvo mines, at the mouth of the Sabôr river.

The distance to be travelled in order that the ore may reach a landing-place in Oporto is of 170 kilometres.

ECONOMICAL CONDITIONS.—The working of these mines is of great simplicity and economy. At the beginning, properly speaking, all the working expenses would be reduced to the gathering of the gravel-ore, which is already strewn and which may furnish 10 to 15 million tons.

Later, the cutting of the rocky-ore would also be very easy, because it could be made to a great depth in the open air.

The mountains where the mines are located have a height of about 100 metres above the level of the adjacent valleys, therefore, the establishment of inclined planes will very much facilitate the workings. The utilization of the ores is the most important and difficult question to solve.

Portugal has not enough coal to feed a metallurgic industry in proportion to the Moncorvo mineral resources; it is necessary, therefore, to undertake the working of these mines either *to export the ore*, or *import the combustible, or to do both jointly.*

This last solution seems to us the most convenient and economical. In fact, the yield of Moncorvo ores varies between 45 and 55 per cent. Calculating cautiously all the expenses of a ton of ore from Moncorvo to the English market, it can be assured that all the ore of less yield than 50 per cent. cannot be exported with profit.

Let us suppose, then, that a double transaction could be effected: to export the ore of higher yield than 50 per cent., and to melt near the mine the ore of lesser yield, importing the combustible: by these means the expenses of transportation by railroad and by sea would be reduced to the minimum, because there would be established return trips by both ways. The metallurgy of iron in Moncorvo would bring about the development of the works of the coal mines located in the vicinity of Oporto.

The production of these enormous deposits could supply the markets of importation of Portugal, Spain, and Italy. In conclusion:

1st. The Moncorvo iron mines are sufficient to support in Portugal a large industrial establishment.

2d. The economical problem could be solved as follows: Exporting the ore of higher grade than 50 per cent., and the local metallurgic treatment of the inferior ore.

3d. To carry out the metallurgical treatment, it becomes necessary to import the combustible.

4th. The importation of the combustible corresponding with the exportation of the rich ore, the tariff of the maritime and railroad transportation will be reduced to a minimum.

5th. Under these conditions the Moncorvo iron mines could be the basis of large iron industry in Portugal.

---

## MANGANESE AND IRON.

The manganese and iron deposits follow each other in their plentifulness.

The more characterized and distinct region occurs in the district of Beja, occupying a large area in the " concello" of Odemira. These deposits occur under three different forms; in lodes, superficial layers of schists impregnated by oxyd of iron, and in superficial layers, resulting from the cementation of the tertiary soil, which covers the subcarboniferous schists, with the oxyds of iron, presenting, therefore, the aspect of a ferruginous sandstone.

The lodes are numerous enough, and very thick. The principal gangues are quartz, which are found in great masses, and baryta.

The ores which compose the deposits are hematites and pyrolusite, either separate or intimately mixed. At several points these lodes have a thickness of 30 metres, and their outcrops are visible for a great distance. The deposits in layers are very numerous, but in general of small extension and little depth; the ore is, besides that, of low yield. The ferruginous sandstone occurs in small deposits, with an average depth of 2 or 3 metres, and occupying a small area.

From all this region the deposits in lodes are the ones that seem to offer more guarantees.

## MANGANESE.

The manganese deposits occur principally in Baixo-Alemtejo, irregularly distributed within a strip of land of about 40 kilometres wide, and in the direction of a line that passes through Mertola and Grandola.

These deposits accompany very near, as well in Portugal as in Spain, the pyritous masses of both countries, and occupy about the same width of ground. They occur in masses of lenticular form, and always intercalated in the stratification of the slates, which belong in part to the silurian, and part to the subcarboniferous schists. Its general direction is N. 40° W., inclined to the E.

They all belong to the same period in regard to the formation, and are entirely similar in their forms and prevailing features. Their almost constant characteristic is the existence of a bed of quartzites, more or less reddish, as a part of the deposit.

The ore occurs either in the top or in the foot-wall of this bed; it also often occurs between its own quartzites in veins or pockets.

These quartzites seem to be owing to a special effect of metamorphism acted on the enclosing slates.

The gangues of these deposits are the clays of the enclosing slates and the quartzites and quartz. Sometimes there also occurs the oligist iron and the baryta, but in small quantity.

The species that forms almost the total production of the manganese is the pyrolusite. The more general yield of these ores varies between 65° and 70° chlorometric.

The manganese mines are in general of very little depth. As a very singular instance, the Lagoas do Paço mine may be cited, which reached a depth of 36 metres. The thickness of these deposits is hardly in general of a few metres, but their length may reach proportions relatively large.

The labors are generally carried on in the open air, and few are the mines that need be worked by subterraneous labor.

Its production is generally small, but the work is easy and demands small capital; for that reason this industry has given important results. The ores are almost all exported to England.

## LEAD.

Lead is found in Portugal in as great an abundance as copper, occupying also very distinct zones.

The most important lead regions are found in the districts of Villa Real, Vizeu, Aveiro, Portalegre, and Beja.

Near the borders of the Douro, embracing the "concelhos" of Armamar, Taboaço, and S. Joao da Pesqueira in the district of Vizeu, and the "concelho" of Sabroza in the district of Villa Real, there is found a very extensive lead region, which has been made already the object of a great number of concessions. These deposits are at present an object of researches.

The enclosing rocks of this region are the macliferous slates of the Cambrian system.

The lodes, which are a great many, seem to belong to three distinct groups characterized by their directions.

Lodes N.W. to 15° E.
Lodes N. 30 to 50° E.
Lodes N. 75° E.

The lodes are almost vertical, inclining a little to the N.W. those of the third system, and a little to the S.E. those of the others.

The lodes of the third system occur metallized; on the contrary, the first and second are rather little, as verified in the Facuca mine; but we do not think that the labors so far made are sufficient to establish a general law.

At the sides of Marao mountain, in the "concelho" of Villa Real, there occur some lead deposits. The labors that have there been done recently seem to reveal important lead deposits very argentiferous.

The region of the district of Aveiro is to-day the most important; it embraces the "concelhos" of Sever do Vouga and Castello de Paiva. There belong to these regions the lead mines of Braçal, Malhada, and Coval da Mó, in working operation, employing establishments for the mechanical preparation and metallurgical treatment, and likewise the one of Ribeiro da Lomba, which is commencing work and which shows already great importance on account of the yield of its argentiferous galenas and the constancy of its metallization. Some other lodes are being known in this zone, which seem to belong to the same system.

The deposits of this district may be referred in a general way to two very different systems, on account of their directions; the lodes comprehended between N.E. and E.W., part of which have already a work ancient enough, and the lodes comprehended between N.N.W. and N.W.

There occurs yet another lead region between the "concelhos" of Arronches and Elvas, with small works.

At the shores of the Guadiana, in the "concelho" of Mertola, district of Beja, there occurs also a zone of lead deposits, actually in pickings.

There occur there numerous lodes with several directions, being the E.W. the most constant. Their outcrops are found distributed in a zone of 6 kilometres long by 2 wide. The enclosing rocks of these deposits belong to the lower carboniferous.

# ANTIMONY.

The sulphurets of antimony are found in Portugal in three distinct regions, and in different geological formations.

Following the order of its antiquity, we first have to speak about the deposit of antimony in the "concelho" of Monte Mor, district of Evora, which occurs as a contact lode between the paleozoic schists and the granites. This deposit has a very irregular form, but occurs very much metallized.

The principal antimonial region is found in the district of Oporto, in the "concelhos" of Gondomar, Vallongo, and Paredes. The deposits of this region seem all to belong to two distinct systems, characterized by their directions.

Lodes N. 10 to 20° W. perfectly agreeing with the stratification of the schists and the lodes N. 30 to 60° E. They crop out between the schists of the silurian age.

In the "concelho" of Alcoutim, district of Faro, there occurs a deposit of antimony formed by two lodes, one of which has the direction E.W. and the other that of N.W., agreeing with the stratification of the schists, and the only one in work. This deposit crops out between the argillaceous schists and grauwacks of possidonomiæ of lower carboniferous age.

The labors so far advanced show a great irregularity in the distribution of the ore in the interior of the deposits.

Among all, the Mont Alto mine is that whose metallization has been more constant. The ore occurs sometimes in concentrations very important and very pure.

# COPPER.

The copper ores appear in Portugal in deposits of several forms. Deposits in veins; deposits in mass; deposits of contact.

DEPOSITS IN VEINS.—These deposits are very numerous throughout the country, and are found in soils of geological nature and age very different.

In the district of Bragança the copper region occurs in the "concelho" of Vimioso. These deposits occur enclosed in metamorphic schists adjacent to the granites that are noticed to the east of Vimioso. None are acutally found in operation.

In the district of Aveiro the copper mines occupy principally the "concelhos" of Albergaria and Oliveira de Azemeis. They occur in the metamorphic paleozoic schists. To the east of this mine occur also the granites.

The Palhal, Telhadella, and Moinho do Pintor mines, now in active operation, belong to this group.

In the district of Evora the copper region occurs principally between the granites, or in the proximities of the contact of the granites with the schists. This region comprises a great number of deposits, very few of which have up to this day been hardly worked.

It seems that the deposits of this region can be classified in two distinct systems; one with a direction of about E.W., and the other with about the direction of N.E.–S.W. This division is made according to the direction, and shown also by the nature of the enclosing veins of each of these systems.

In the first predominates the gangues of carbonate of iron, accompanied with the quartz and calcite.

In the second predominates the quartz accompanied by calcite and carbonate of iron in small quantity.

The common ores are the pyrite, accompanied with oxyds and carbonates of copper. In the second system the pyrites occur more frequently than in the first.

To the first system belong the mines of Commenda and Pecena, Alkala and Alkalaim, and Alpedreira; to the second, those of Sobral and S. Manços. These veins, above all those of the first system, sometimes acquire large thickness, which in some places reach 11 metres. These deposits yet preserve vestiges of large ancient labor.

In the district of Portalegre the copper veins occur principally in the "concelhos" of Extremos, Villa Vicosa, and Alandroal. To this group belong the mines of Mostardeira and Bogalho, now in operation. To this region also belongs the mine of Azambujeira, whose labors were abandoned. All the others have hardly beginning labors.

These deposits crop out between the laurentian schists and limestones. The veins seem to belong to three distinct systems by their direction and character. They observe the directions of N.S., N.E., and E.W. The veins N.S. have in general very irregular thickness, and some that have been experimented have shown themselves sterile; and such are the mine of Cobres e Vieiros, Almagrera, and a vein N. S. of Bogalho mine.

The veins E.W. are more regular, but the copper pyrites occur extremely disseminated in the body of the vein and mixed with the arsenical pyrite; therefore, its advantage is extremely difficult to get. To this system belongs the Mostardeira mine.

The veins N.E. are of less thickness, and contain richer ore. To this system belongs the vein worked in the Bogalho mine.

To the south of Alemtejo, in the "concelho" of Almodovar, occurs another cupriferous region, now beginning labors. These deposits are enclosed by schists and grauwacks of the subcarboniferous period, and follow two distinct directions, N. 30° to 35° E., and N. 65° to 70° W.

In the district of Faro, in the "concelho" of Alcoutim, occur veins whose directions are N. 60° to 65° E., and E.W. proximately.

DEPOSITS IN MASS.—These deposits are represented in Portugal by the mines of Chança, S. Domingos, Aljustrel, and Serra da Caveira. They belong to an extensive metalliferous strip which, with a width of 30 kilometres approximately, follows a general direction of N. 40° W. from Castillo de las Guardias, in Spain, to Grandola, in Portugal, a distance of 200 kilometres. Within this strip occur all the deposits in mass of pyrites in Spain and Portugal.

This phenomenon is entirely isolated, and the only one in the Peninsula.

All these deposits have entirely identical characters, and belong to the same formation. They all have the form of a lenticular mass intercalated in the stratification of the schists, which in Portugal all belong to the silurian age. All their outcrops are very characteristic, and nothing is easier than to find the existence of a deposit of this order by their exterior features.

In an area that corresponds approximately to that which is limited by the walls of the mass, occur large blocks of a rock of a brecciaform aspect, formed by oligist iron and fragments of schists; in many places the schists are reduced to quartzites colored red by the oxyds of iron, limiting the walls of the mass.

In the adjoining valleys occur very much a yellow rock, which in Spain they call it by the name of *toba*, and which is a breccia in which the oxyds of iron form a cement which wraps fragments of schists and rolling gravel. The waters taken out of the mine have with them dissolved a large quantity of sulphate of iron, which, by the decomposition in coming in contact with the atmospheric air, is transformed in subsulphate, and, in time, in oxyds of iron, constituting the cement of the *toba*. This rock is entirely different from that which composes the outcrops of these masses.

The soil that is over the masses and which covers the large blocks of ferruginous schists occur very much decomposed, with a color pronouncedly red, owing to the quantity of oxyds of iron that they contain.

In contact with the masses, in the vicinity of the deposits, occur almost always the pophyrs in mass, or the schists metamorphized by them. These deposits become also easy of discovery on account of the vestiges of ancient labors that they almost all contain, and above all, by the enormous piles of rubbish that are found in their vicinity.

These works are principally attributed to the Romans, and the coins and other objects found in the course of work confirm this fact.

In some mines, however, the workings cannot refer all to the period of the Roman domination, and it is supposed that formerly there must have been Phœnician workings. This fact is revealed by the piles of the same rubbish, which in many places are laid in two layers, separated from each other by a layer of vegetable soil, as was entirely verified in Tharsis and Rio Tinto.

The ore occurs, in general, compact and with an aspect of great homogenity; accidentally ores occur of great yield, but in small quantity, and in limited zones.

The ore shows from space to space plans of separation, a species of plans of cleavage, which cross each other in angles very much open.

Slippery movements, posterior to the formation of the deposit, exercised under a strong pressure on the surfaces of contact, leave in some places a specular polish very charactersitic.

The mines of pyrites of Portugal and Spain are to-day prepared for a total work of 800 to 1,000,000 tons.

The pyrites were at the beginning used in commerce for sulphur and copper. The ores, after being burnt to manufacture sulphuric acid, were handed to the copper founders, who used them as flux in the melting of quartziferous minerals. All the iron was lost. To these pyrites, afterwards, the wet way was applied, and by these means the sulphur, copper, and iron came to be utilized.

It can be said in a general way that these ores contain: Sulphur, 45 to 50 per cent.; copper, 2 to 3 per cent.; iron, 40 to 45 per cent.

Deposits of Contact.—In the province of Algarve there appears a narrow zone of triassic soil. It extended along the littoral, following the sides of the mountains of Monchique and S. Barnabe.

There lays immediately over that soil the limestone and clay of the jurassic period, which extend to the south till near the coast.

In the contact the copper ores occur, whose outcrops can be followed from Silves to Alte, a distance of 30 kilometres, with a direction N.E. to S.W. The places where, up to to-day, the greatest concentration of ore have been found, were in St. Estevam, near Silves, and in Alte, where there are also found ancient labors.

The diorites and serpentines break through the jurassic rocks, producing deep metamorphisms.

The magnetic oxyd of iron occurs in large concentrations, either in layers or in veins, accompanied by the copper ores. The red oxyd of copper, gray copper, and the carbonate of copper occur commonly.

The native copper also occurs in thin leaves between the jurassic clays. The distribution of the ores is extremely irregular.

By their geognostic and mineralogic characters these deposits have a very remarkable resemblance to the ones of Traversella and Monte Catini in Toscana. Some attempts to work them were made, which were hurriedly abandoned.

## TIN.

The working of tin in Portugal dates from the first period of the monarchy, and it was, after the washings of gold of Adiça, the object of the greatest cupidity for the ancient miners.

The oxyd of tin occurs in form of stockwerk between the granites, or in veins, more or less thick, between the chrystalline schists, or in alluvium.

Between the porphyritic granite which predominates in the province of Minho, there is found in Rebordosa, in the district of Oporto, an elliptic mass of a granite of a finer grain, very feldsparic, containing amphibole, having a maximum length of 65 metres in the direction of N.N.W., and a thickness of 30 metres.

It is between this granitic mass that the oxyd of tin occurs in the form of stockwerk. The ore occurs distributed very irregularly in concentrations, in veins, or disseminated in the granite mass.

The stanniferous alluviums are found in the district of Bragança, but the principal deposits, as well in this district as in those of Villa

Real and Vizeu, occur in veins, cutting the paleozoic metamorphical schists. In different regions these deposits occur always at a short distance from the granites in the schistous zone altered by those rocks. That zone is formed of macliferous and amphibolic schists.

In the district of Bragança the tin region comprises a great number of lodes of very variable directions comprehended between N. 43° E. and N. 74° E.

In the Codeço mine there is found a crossing sterile lode with the direction N. 31° 30′ W.; there occurs also a lode with the direction N. 7° W.

In the district of Villa Real there is found also a region of parallel lodes with the direction about N.E., and another with lodes of direction N.S.

In the district of Vizeu the tin lodes go towards N. 10° W.

The grade of metallization and the distribution of the ore, as well as the form of the fracture, are very irregular and various in the several deposits.

The labors so far advanced are not sufficient to discover a law of useful direction, if it exists. Hardly as a note, and not as a law of practical application to follow, we will add some observations relative to the application of the Pentagonal system as criterion for the determination of that direction.

The useful angle for tin is comprehended in Cornwall, between E. 6° S. and E. 54° N.; the bissecting line of this angle stretches E. 24° N., coinciding approximately with the system of Finisterre, which is there stretched E. 21° 46′ N., true directions.

The lodes of Bragança are in general comprehended between E. 16° to 47° N. magnetic, or E. 36° to 67° N. true.

The system of Finisterre transported to a point in Portugal, where upon the Primitive of Lisbon four bissecting circles cross each other, there stretches E. 23° 58′ N. true.

The amplitude of the useful angle of tin, transported to the same point, will be comprehended between E. 56° 12′ N. and E. 3° 48′ S.

Some of the lodes of Bragança are comprehended within these limits; there are, however, others that go outside of them.

In the districts of Vizeu and Villa Real also, the deposits of tin are not within those limits.

About these facts, however, we cannot meanwhile arrive at any conclusion; it would be withal very curious to verify as far as where the influence of the parallelism in the metallization of the deposits can be extended, and with what assurance can be accepted a law of useful directions known in a region transported parallel to another region very distant.

## SUNDRY ORES.

There are found yet other qualities of ores, like nickel, cobalt, argentiferous zinc, and, more accidentally, red and native silver. The production of nickel and cobalt ores are supplied from the copper mines of Telhadella and Palhal, and in this last one there has been found small quantity of red silver, as likewise argentiferous zinc. The native silver occurs in the lead mine of Varzea de Trevoes.

---

# COAL.

**Carboniferous Formation.**—The coal measures have in Portugal a small development. There are hardly known three areas : in Vallongo, Bussaco, and Moiuho de Ordem, all belonging to the carboniferous period.

The carboniferous area of Vallougo occurs in the form of a narrow belt, which occupies an extension of about five kilometres to the N. W. of Vallongo and 52 kilometres to the S. E. as far as Gafanhao, crossing the river Douro. This belt has a general direction of N. 35° W.

The coal area rests to the North in all its extension over the lower silurian formation, which occurs also in the form of a belt, always very narrow in all the extension of its development on the left of the river Douro, and after passing hardly near to Vallongo it takes a breadth of about four kilometres.

This belt has been worked at several places, withal the most important basin so far kuown is the one of S. Pedro da Cova.

There occur two beds of coal, reduced to a state of anthracite by a special metamorphism, owing perhaps to the presence of the diorites that there crop out, and of the granites that occur in all the extension of the coal measures at an average distance of some seven kilometres on either side.

The coal measures of Bussaco have hardly a longitudinal extension of 16 kilometres in a belt that has a general direction of N. 10° E.

The coal measures of Bussaco rest on the E. side, on the Cambrian formation, and on the silurian formation to the S.E, and gets under the Trias to the S.W. and N.W.

The pickings made so far are insufficient to determine whether there exists a coal basin that can be advantageously worked. At present, labors are commenced for this purpose, which already leave no doubt of the existence of coal.

The carboniferous formation is represented in Moinho de Ordem, near Alcacer, but a deposit of very small dimensions, where there have not yet been discovered any vestiges of a coal-bed.

**Jurassic Formation.**—There exist beds of coal that can be worked, belonging to the jurassic period.

The more prominent deposits are those of Cabo Mondego, near Buarcos, and those of the district of Leiria.

The deposit of Cabo Mondego is composed of five beds, only one of which, with a thickness of one metre, can be worked : this bed crops out at the border of the sea, in the cape of Mondego, with an inclination of 25° to the S. E., and goes on to the summit of the Buarcos mountain, disappearing at a distance of three kilometres under the cretaceous formation.

The works performed at the beginning of this century demonstrated the continuation of this bed under the sea, but an inundation impeded the continuation of the labors.

At present, this mine is worked for the consumption of a glass factory and one of ceramic products, belonging to the same mining company.

This coal produces a large quantity of gas and gives a very light coke, but resistent: by its characters it can be considered as a lignite passing to bituminous coal.

The same geological formation in the district of Leiria contains several known beds of coal, but not worked at present.

The outcrops of a bed that is found in Cabeço de Veado and Arrimalde can be followed in the distance of four kilometres. It has an average thickness of one metre, and inclines 35° to the S. 60° E. This bed was anciently worked.

In Chao Preto, near the Mosteiro da Batalha, a coal-bed is also known, with a thickness of one metre, following an approximate direction N. S.

**Cretaceous Formation.**—There is found in the district of Leiria bituminous gres, forming beds, sometimes very thick and of sufficient richness, at the point of turning semi-fluid.

They are very well known in Granja, Marrazes, Pedras Negras, and Canto de Azeche. They have not been regularly worked, and are at present without being operated.

There is found yet near Marrazes a bed of fossil wood of 2.50 metres, which has not yet been conveniently worked.

**Recent Formations.**—Peat is found in the country, with important development at Comporta, opposite to Setubal, near the river Sado; it forms there a bed of one metre in thickness approximately, and occupying a large superficial extension. It has not yet been worked.

------

## STATISTIC.

The statistical tables which follow were organized by the Bureau of Mines.

Table I. refers to the movement of the granting of mines, distributed by districts and by years.

The statistic is organized for two distinct periods; a period previous to the 31st of December, 1852, date of the promulgation of the present mining law, and a posterior one, up to 1875.

For the comprehension of this table, it is important to know that the Government, when any mine is discovered, orders the verification of its existence and the drawing up of plans of the ground.

By the informations obtained, the Government gives to the discoverer a diploma of legal discovery, in which the area that the grant might have is determined, as also the necessary capital for the work.

Proving that he has the necessary capital for the work, a title of "provisory concession" is given him, in which will be specified all the conditions imposed on the grant.

Having satisfied all the requisites of the law the "Definitive grant" is given by a decree. For that reason the statistic in Table I. designates the mines that had diploma of legal discovery, and of those that had definitive grant.

  The granteé loses the right to the grant whenever he does not comply with the conditions under which it was given him, among which the principal one is to have the mine always in active operation.

The statistic under designation "Definitive concessions forfeited," gives the number of grants that have been forfeited. The forfeited grants are put at auction by the Government, and thus these mines may be granted anew. It is to these new grants to which refers the designation "Definitive concessions anew."

Table II. designates the mines by the qualities of the ore, with the area of grant and the state of the mining labors. It designates also the movement of the processes for the concessions of mines and their progress.

Table III. designates the mining expenses and production of the mines from 1853 to 1874 inclusive. The expenses are indicated in two columns. "In reference to imposts" are those which are counted for the determination of the impost, which are lower than the true ones, because for this determination some are afterwards excluded.

As mines are exempt from imposts for two years, and as no account is made of the expenses of pickings, the expenses referring to the impost are yet for this reason lower than the total ones.

The figures relating to "Total calculated or known" result from informations directly collected, or from a calculation made on the labors executed.

22

**I.**

| DISTRICTS | FIRST PERIOD. Concessions made prior to the 31st of December, 1852. | | | | | | | | | | | | Diploma of general discovery from 1853 to 1875 inclusive. | SECOND PERIOD. Definitive concessions from 1853 to 1875. | | | | | | | | | | | | | | | | | | | | | General total of the definitive concessions. | Definitive concessions forfeited. | Renewed definitive concessions. | Definitive concessions valid on the 31st of December, 1875. |
|---|---|---|---|---|---|---|---|---|---|---|---|---|---|---|---|---|---|---|---|---|---|---|---|---|---|---|---|---|---|---|---|---|---|---|---|---|---|---|---|
| | 1836 | 1839 | 1842 | 1843 | 1844 | 1845 | 1846 | 1847 | 1848 | 1849 | 1850 | Total | | 1855 | 1856 | 1858 | 1859 | 1860 | 1861 | 1862 | 1863 | 1864 | 1865 | 1866 | 1867 | 1868 | 1869 | 1870 | 1871 | 1872 | 1873 | 1874 | 1875 | Total | | | | |
| Bragança | | | | 3 | 3 | 2 | | | | | | 6 | 30 | 2 | | | 2 | | | | | | | | 2 | 2 | 2 | | 1 | 1 | | 1 | 3 | 8 | 14 | 8 | 3 | 9 |
| Villa Real | | 4 | | 1 | 1 | | 1 | | | | 1 | 8 | 19 | | 2 | 1 | | | 2 | | | | | | 2 | | | | 1 | | 3 | 2 | 7 | 7 | | | 7 |
| Braga | 1 | | | | | | | 1 | 1 | 3 | 1 | 8 | 3 | 2 | | | | | 4 | 4 | | | 1 | | | 2 | | 1 | | 1 | 1 | | | 18 | 26 | 7 | 2 | 21 |
| Vianna | | | | | 1 | | | 1 | | 3 | 1 | 6 | 29 | | | | | 2 | 1 | | | | | 1 | 1 | 2 | 1 | | 3 | 1 | 10 | 7 | 4 | 16 | 19 | 3 | 1 | 16 |
| Oporto | | | 1 | | | | | | | | | | 27 | | | | 1 | | | | | | | | 1 | 2 | 1 | 1 | 3 | 1 | 3 | 2 | 1 | 12 | 6 | 6 | 3 | 1 |
| Aveiro | | | | | | | | | | | | | | | | | | | | | | | | | | | | | | | | | | | 12 | 3 | | 12 |
| Coimbra | | | | | | | 1 | 1 | | | 1 | | 16 | | | | | | | | | 2 | | | | | | | 1 | | | | | 8 | 3 | 1 | | 2 |
| Vizeu | | | | | | | | | | | | | 15 | | | | | | | | | | | | | | 1 | | | | | | | 3 | 2 | 1 | | 1 |
| Guarda | | | | | | 1 | | | | | | 1 | 5 | | | | | | | | | | | | 1 | 1 | | | | | 1 | 1 | | 1 | 16 | 4 | 1 | 12 |
| Castello Branco | | | | | | | | | | | | | 7 | | | | | | | | | | | | | | | | | | | | | | 1 | 1 | | |
| Leiria | | | | | | | | | | | | | 16 | | | | | | | | | | | | | | | | | | | | | | | | | 26 |
| Santarem | | | | | | | | | | | | | 4 | | | | | | | | | | | | | | 1 | | | | | | | 11 | 27 | 2 | | 9 |
| Lisbon | | | | | | | | | | | | | 42 | | | | 1 | 2 | 2 | 4 | 1 | | 2 | 3 | 2 | 9 | 23 | 14 | 3 | 7 | 7 | 2 | 3 | 25 | | 2 | (a)4 | 26 |
| Portalegre | | | | | | | | | | | | | 20 | | | | | | | | | | | | | | 1 | 1 | | | 1 | | | 9 | 9 | 2 | 1 | 9 |
| Evora | | | | | | | | | | | | | 36 | | | | 1 | | | 4 | | | | | 2 | 1 | 1 | 1 | 1 | 11 | 1 | 24 | 15 | 24 | 25 | 22 | | 1 |
| Beja | | | | | | | | | | | | | 242 | | | | | | | | | | 2 | | | | 1 | | | | | 24 | 15 | 136 | 138 | 2 | | .5 |
| Faro | | | | | | | | | 1 | | | | 12 | | | | | | | | 4 | | | | | | 1 | | | | 1 | | | 4 | 5 | 1 | | |
| **Total** | 1 | 4 | 1 | 5 | 6 | 4 | 2 | 4 | 1 | 5 | 2 | 35 | 512 | 2 | 2 | 1 | 5 | 4 | 8 | 6 | 12 | 3 | 8 | 7 | 13 | 22 | 26 | 21 | 17 | 14 | 37 | 37 | 29 | 275 | 310 | 61 | 15 | 262 |

(a). Two of these concessions were forfeited anew.

## II.

| DISTRICTS | Mines with definitive concessions valid on the 31st of December, 1875. | | | | | | | | | | | | | State of mining labors in 1875. | | | | | | | | | | | | | | Processes under way on the 31st December, 1876. | | | | | |
|---|---|---|---|---|---|---|---|---|---|---|---|---|---|---|---|---|---|---|---|---|---|---|---|---|---|---|---|---|---|---|---|---|---|---|
| | Copper | Lead | Copper and lead | Antimony | Tin | Iron | Manganese | Iron and manganese | Coal | Coal and iron | Asphaltum | Total | Area in hectares | Mines commencing labors | Copper | Lead | Antimony | Tin | Iron | Manganese | Iron and manganese | Coal | Asphaltum | Total | Mines under labors, little active | Mines under labors, very little active | Mines in which there is no labors | Of legal discovery | Of provisory concession | Of definitive occession | At auction | Of change in proprietorship | Total |
| Braganca | 1 | | | | 7 | 1 | | | | | | 9 | 1,711.8165 | | | | | | | | | | | | | | | 36 | 2 | 1 | | | 39 |
| Villa Real | | 5 | | | 2 | | | | | | | 7 | 396.5890 | | | | | | | | | | | | | | | 7 | | 6 | | | 13 |
| Braga | | | | | | | | | | | | | | | | | | | | | | | | | | | | 2 | | | | | 2 |
| Vianna | | | | | | | | | | | | | | | | | | | | | | | | | | | | | | 1 | | | 5 |
| Oporto | 6 | 2 | | 6 | | 3 | | | 4 | | | 21 | 1,812.6760 | | | | | | | | | | | | | | | 23 | 3 | | | | 28 |
| Aveiro | | 8 | 1 | | | | | | 2 | 5 | | 16 | 2,840.7531 | | | | | | | | | | | | | | | 15 | 3 | | | 1 | 18 |
| Coimbra | | | | | | | | | 1 | | | 1 | 340.5760 | | | | | | | | | | | | | | | 9 | | | | | 9 |
| Vizeu | | 9 | | | | 3 | | | | | | 12 | 609.5517 | | | | | | | | | | | | | | | 2 | | 2 | | | 2 |
| Guarda | | 1 | | | | 1 | | | | | | 2 | 119.8750 | | | | | | | | | | | | | | | 3 | | | | | 3 |
| Castello Branco | | 1 | | | | | | | | | | 1 | 43.0000 | | | | | | | | | | | | | | | 1 | | 2 | | | 7 |
| Leiria | | | | | | 7 | | | 2 | | 2 | 12 | 21,342.3560 | | | | | | | | | | | | | | | 1 | | 2 | | | 2 |
| Santarem | | | | | | | | | | | | | | | | | | | | | | | | | | | | 1 | | 1 | | | 2 |
| Lisbon | 14 | 4 | | 2 | | 6 | | | | | | 26 | 1,483.8845 | | | | | | | | | | | | | | | 8 | 4 | 10 | | | 18 |
| Portalegre | | | | | | | | 9 | | | | 9 | 587.2170 | | | | | | | | | | | | | | | | | 1 | | | 2 |
| Evora | 7 | 5 | | | | 1 | 10 | | | | | 23 | 1,998.6600 | | | | | | | | | | | | | | | 11 | 1 | 2 | | | 15 |
| Beja | 8 | 5 | | | 2 | | 72 | 31 | | | | 118 | 6,510.3711 | | | | | | | | | | | | | | | 25 | 4 | 34 | | 2 | 64 |
| Faro | | | | 1 | 1 | 1 | | | | | | 5 | 518.8575 | | | | | | | | | | | | | | | 2 | | 4 | 1 | 2 | 6 |
| **Total** | 36 | 40 | 1 | 9 | 16 | 22 | 82 | 40 | 9 | 5 | 2 | 262 | 40,466.4824 | 48 | 9 | 3 | 2 | 2 | 1 | 12 | 2 | 3 | 1 | 35 | 55 | 62 | 62 | 145 | 17 | 66 | 1 | 6 | 235 |

III.

| DISTRICTS | Quality of the ore | No. of mines | NAMES OF MINES | Area in hectares | WORKING EXPENSES | | Production in metrical tons | Value of the ore at the mouth of the mine | Total of imposts paid | |
|---|---|---|---|---|---|---|---|---|---|---|
| | | | | | In reference to imposts | Total calculated or known | | | | |
| Aveiro | Lead | 1 | Bracal e Malhada | 467,9423 | 420,367 $ 454 | 696,688 $ 185 | 23,064,513 | 996,513 $ 378 | 8,076 $ 692 | a |
| | | 1 | Carvalhal | 263,0600 | 143,842 " 581 | 144,272 " 581 | 1,781,814 | 90,900 " 135 | 92 " 787 | b |
| | | 1 | Moinho da Penn | 370,0000 | 15,232 " 425 | 16,072 " 425 | 352,671 | 4,410 " 766 | 98 " 318 | |
| | | 1 | Coval da Mo... | 368,9000 | 114,490 " 893 | 117,670 " 104 | 1,857,210 | 62,725 " 766 | 84 " 129 | |
| | | 4 | Valuga, Ferral, Mte. Meao e Ribeiro da Lomha | 243,2000 | 18,319 " 695 | 29,205 " 085 | ? | 912,594 " 186 | 29 " 039 | c |
| | Copper | 1 | Palhal | 437,2220 | 735,580 " 975 | 735,580 " 975 | 21,844,981 | | 9,722 " 656 | d |
| | | 1 | Telhadella | 102,8000 | 182,268 " 245 | 194,066 " 445 | 1,767,718 | 61,556 " 663 | 23 " 865 | |
| | | 2 | Pindello e Moino do Pintor | 251,9000 | 6,362 " 910 | 19,744 " 773 | 45,000 | | 37 " 086 | |
| | Lead and copper | 1 | Arieiro (abandoned) | 138,0000 | | ? | no yield | | 4 " 838 | |
| | | 1 | Cova de Pigeiros (abandoned) | 53,2500 | | 12,505 " 995 | ditto | | 5 " 807 | |
| | Coal (anthra.) | 1 | Fijao | 136,5000 | 4,935 " 385 | 5,103 " 385 | 66,100 | 168 " 625 | 21 " 888 | |
| | | 1 | Povoa | 90,0000 | 2,281 " 804 | 7,933 " 510 | 260. | 1,382 " 305 | 6 " 984 | |
| | Total | 16 | | | | | 1851.349,035 | 7,912,449 " 177 | 281,409 " 510 | e |
| Beja | Copper | 1 | S. Domingos | 79,9000 | 247,648 " 581 | 181,095 " 190 | 7,896,541 | | 6,455 " 036 | e |
| | | 1 | S. Joao do Dezerto e Algares, (2 grants) | 278,5542 | | | | | | |
| | | 3 | Cova da Moura, Ruy Gomes e Arradinha (abandoued) | 329,0000 | | 21,800 " 000 | | | 52 " 340 | |
| | Lead | 1 | Corrego da Vinha (abandoued) | 94,0000 | | | no yield ditto | | 3 " 769 | |
| | | 56 | Several | 619,0000 | 223,446 " 002 | | 32,797,913 | 350,846 " 995 | 28 " 070 | |
| | Manganese | 17 | Several (abandoned) | 2645.1588 | | | | | 7,778 " 103 | |
| | | 2 | Cerros Aitos e da Roch e Ouro e Boa-Vista (abandoned twice) | 825,0935 | | 26,370 " 740 | 5,474,148 | 62,741 -- 480 | 4,381 " 453 | |
| | Total | 86 | | 131,6150 | | | | | | |
| Braganca | Copper | 1 | Villa Mean | 72,1000 | | ? | | | 4 " 138 | |
| | Tin | 6 | Cudeco, Raposo, Riheira, Chaira, da Cruz, Raia, e S. Martinho | 1527,0340 | | 58,593 " 957 | 119,566 | 20,312 " 025 | 156 " 066 | |
| | Iron | 1 | Folgueira | 37,4825 | | 1,350 " 000 | 175,000 | ? | 4 " 618 | g |
| | Total | 8 | | | | | | | | |

## III. (Continued.)

| District | Mineral | No. | Mine | | | | | | |
|---|---|---|---|---|---|---|---|---|---|
| Castello Branco | Lead | 1 | Rabacinha | 43,0000 340,3760 | 94,905 $ 205 | 3,000 " 000 | 6,000 17,164,125 | 210 " 000 63,573 " 285 | 346 $ 706 |
| Coimbra | Coal | 1 | Mostardeira | 167,0050 | 246,819 " 066 | 275,000 " 000 | 813,074 | 17,745 " 795 | 30 " 793 |
| | | 1 | Bogalho | 167,5000 | | 443,822 " 156 | 1938,184 | 97,309 " 102 | 19 " 910 |
| | | 1 | Azambujeira | 55,2000 | 23,505 " 938 | 135,383 " 448 | 318,117 | 23,010 " 230 | 6 " 228 |
| | Copper | 2 | Sobral e Alpedreira | | | 141,870 " 495 | | | 8 " 065 |
| | | 3 | Algares, Pacena e Commenda | | | 43,857 " 360 | | | 59 " 411 |
| Evora | | 4 | Cacharroeira-Cherez — He. do Castello e Serra das Correias | 976,6960 | | | | | 82 " 822 |
| | Antimony | 1 | Alcala e Alcaiaim (abandoned) | 95,0000 | | 26,223 " 877 | 63,296,157 | | 17 " 690 |
| | Iron | 2 | He. da Prais e He. das Palmas | 81,3000 | 29,216 " 735 | | | | 5 " 808 |
| | | 1 | Serra dos Monges | | | | | | |
| | Total | 16 | | | | | | | |
| Faro | Copper | 2 | Alte 6 Cova dos Mouros | 300,0000 | 26,672 " 361 | 8,420 " 000 | ? | 23,283 " 096 | 40 " 791 |
| | Antimony | 1 | Cortes Pereiras | 1123,6750 | | ? | 495,429 | | 53 " 396 |
| | Manganese | 1 | Murraçao | 45,0000 | | ? | | | 3 " 282 |
| | Total | 4 | | | | | | | |
| Guarda | Lead | 1 | Gracies | 69,8750 | | | | | 2 " 162 |
| Leiria | Iron Coal and Iron | 10 | Mines of the Coal and Iron Company | 20886,4000 | 2,217 " 600 | | 1,000,000 | 3,220 " 500 | 966 " 544 |
| | Coal | 1 | Azeche | 404,0000 | ?-? | ? ? | 177,684 | 1,549 " 387 | 543 " 748 |
| | Asphaltum | 1 | Barroca (Granja) | 52,4560 | | | | | 5 " 409 |
| | Total | 12 | | | | | | | |
| Lisbon | Copper | 1 | Serra da Caveira | 150,00 | 28,627 " 000 | ? | 200 | ? | 24 " 470 |
| | Lead | 4 | Reboleda, Vargem, Canafezaes, He. das Minas | 230,80 | | ? | | | ? |
| | Manganese | 3 | Montinho, Penedo do Frade Saramaga | 124,50 | | 5,900 " 000 | 250 | 4,500 " 000 | 3 " 630 |
| | Total | 8 | | | | | | | |
| Portalegre | Lead | 4 | Balouco, Lobatos, Olival das Freiras e Tapada do Olival | 275,30 | | 5,649 " 443 | | | 15 " 981 |
| | Manganese | 1 | Souto Queimado | 55,4070 | | | | | 2 " 592 |
| | Total | 5 | | | | | | | |

III. (Continued.)

| DISTRICTS. | Quality of the ore. | No. of mines. | NAMES OF MINES. | Area in hectares. | WORKING EXPENSES. In reference to imposts. | WORKING EXPENSES. Total calculated or known | Production in metrical tons. | Value of the ore at the mouth of the mine. | Total of imposts paid. |
|---|---|---|---|---|---|---|---|---|---|
| | Lead | 1 | Serradela | 96,0000 | | ? | ? | ? | 13 $ 715 |
| | Antimony | 2 { | Valle d'Ache e Ribeiro da Igreja | 5000,0000 | 31,736 $ 741 | 25,130 " 828 | 400,075 | 24,850 " 735 | 78 " 241  n |
| | | 1 | Mont-Alto | 98,0000 | | | 518,113 | 37,228 " 579 | 326 " 815  o |
| | | 1 | Rebordoza | 2500,0000 | | 4,231 " 113 | 16,074 | 4,822 " 200 | |
| Oporto | Tin | 3 { | Bodas do Marao, Ramalhoso e Gaiva | 415,7500 | | | 3,556 | 889 " 000 | 71 " 620  p |
| | | 1 | S. Pedro da Cova | 123,0870 | 8,393 " 324 | 357,516 " 981 | 171,035,698 | 682,535 " 970 | 15,457 " 611 |
| | Coal (anthra.) | 1 | Gens, Midoes e Covello | 280,0000 | 1,999 " 695 | 7,097 " 935 | 843,205 | 2,987 " 580 | 1 " 039  q  r |
| | | 1 | Barral | 117,9275 | | 393 " 350 | | | |
| | | 1 | Valle de Deao (abandoned) | 19,5000 | | 183 " 565 | 58,500 | 97 " 689 | |
| | Total | 12 | | | | | | | |
| | Lead | 1 | Fonte Nova | 50,0000 | | | | | 937 |
| Villa Real | Tin | 1 | Serrinha da Cascalheira | 50,0000 | | 55,566 " 000 | 38,391 | 8,278 " 843 | 937 |
| | Total | 2 | | | | | | | |
| | | 1 | Trevoes | 130,0000 | 33,735 " 260 | | 139,195 | 9,123 " 425 | 18 " 066  s  t |
| | Lead | 2 { | Adorigo e Portella dos Corvos | 138,9950 | | | | | 17 " 995 |
| Vizeu | | 3 { | Albergan, Zambulhal e Sta. Leocadia | 195,4337 | | 418 " 560 | | | |
| | Tin | 1 | Sto. Adriao | 73,2113 | | | | 512 " 099 | 5 " 426  u |
| | | 1 | Outeiro dos Hujos | 69,6000 | | | | | 4 " 447 |
| | Total | 8 | | | | | | | |

## REMARKS.

a.  Production, 1836 to 1852, 937.700 tons.  Expenses, 50,000 $ 000.  Production zinc ore in 1869–70–72, 7.694 tons.

b.  Without any mining since 1869.

c.  Production, 1862, 46 tons.  Production nickel ore, 1867 to 1870, 18.703 tons.  Lead ore, 1858–69, 139.309 tons.

d.  Production, 1867–74, nickel ore, 9.511 tons.  Lead ore, 178.420 tons.

e.  Two concessions paying a fixed rate of 800 reis per ton of utilized ore.

f.  They paid, 1872–73 and 1873–74, the annual fixed rent of 1,083.500 each.

g.  Expenses and production up to 1872.

h.  Production, 1802 to 1821, 1,740 tons.  Value, 44,490 $ 510.  Expenses, 60,718 $ 887.

i.  In pickings.  Expenses of Castello mine, 13,000 $ 000.

j.  Mining suspended since 1868.

k.  Without any mining since 1862.

l.  Expenses, 1866–68.  Production, 1864.

m.  Without mining.

n.  Before 1853, production, 136.582 tons.

o.  Concessions previous to 1853.  Production, 1851–52, 32.376 tons.

p.  Since 1803 till 1853, known production, 27,275,288 kilogrammes.  Value 74,374 $ 930.

q.  Expenses and imposts, 1874.

r.  Expenses and production, 1858.

s.  Expenses and production, 1867–69.

t.  Expenses, 1867–68.

u.  Production, 1867–69.

## III.

# QUARRYING.

Portugal possesses a great variety of building and ornamentation materials.

**Granites.**—They occupy a great area in the northern provinces —Minho, Beira, and Traz-os-Montes—breaking through the extensive regions of laurentian, cambrian, or silurian schists.

Mr. Schiappa d'Azevedo, Mining Engineer, determined there four varieties of granite of different characters and geological ages, which we will enumerate, following the order of age that he assigns them.

The common granite of two micas, white quartz transparent and orthoclase. It constitutes a belt of 9 kilometres wide, which crosses the Douro by one side, and by the other it stretches in a direction NN.W.

The porphyritic granite, only with black mica, gray quartz semi-translucent, two feldspar generally and accidentally crystals of bright white talc, containing large crystals of orthoclase, at times with more than 0.1m of length. It is characterized by the orbicular structure and by the facility of the crumbling out on the surface.

This granite predominates in the province of Minho, occupying the central part from North to South, in a zone of 60 kilometres wide, taken on a parallel that passes some kilometres to the north of Braga, which narrows to the North.

Granite with white mica, albite feldspar and vitreous quartz, containing as characteristic element the amphibole.

This rock forms a narrow belt of 5 kilometres wide at the east of Oporto; it is also found to the N.N.W. of Barcellos, to the W. of Villa Flor, and in other points.

Granite of very fine grain is found in the surroundings of Villa Pouca de Aguiar, and to the north of Guimaraes.

In these provinces the large buildings are all executed with granite, this rock being also employed in sculpture.

The works of ornamentation executed to-day in the building of the Commercial Association of Oporto are very remarkable by their extreme delicacy.

There is employed in the pavements of the streets of Oporto a very hard granite from Canellas, cut in prisms, with the dimensions of 18x 16x10 centimetres.

To the north of Alemtejo there are also found some large areas of granite, principally in the districts of Portalegre and Evora, there being also found small spots in the Beja district.

There are found in some places granites of bright colors, that would make a fine effect were they polished; nevertheless, this industry does not yet exist.

The volcanic rocks are found on the continent in the suburbs of Lisbon, where they are employed in the paving of streets alone, combined with white limestone in design of a very fine effect. In the Azores these rocks are employed in all constructions.

**Slates.**—The slates are worked principally in Vallongo, district of Oporto, and produce slabs of great size, very resistent, adapted to large billiard tables, offering likewise very thin layers, being very much adapted for covering roofs.

The quarries belonging to the " Vallongo Slate and Marble Company" are worked at present on a large scale. These rocks belong to the silurian age.

**Sandstones.**—The sandstones, susceptible of being employed as building materials, belong to the triassic period and are found in distinct regions.

To the east of Aveiro there is found a small area of sandstone; in the district of Coimbra, a narrow belt stretching to the north up to Arco de·Anadia, and to the south down to Thomar, which rests on the east side upon the carboniferous rocks of Bussaco and upon schists of laurentian and cambrian period, and to the west side supports the jurassic and cretaceous rocks. In Algarve there is found also a belt narrower yet of triassic rocks, having a general direction E.W., in contact at the north side with the schists of the lower carboniferous age, and at the southern side with the jurassic limestone.

**Marbles and Limestone.**—There is found a zone of chrystalline marbles which takes its greatest importance in Extremoz, Borba, and Villa Viçosa. There exist layers of pure white, and more or less colored in flesh and yellow, especially in Extremoz and Borba; and layers of gray marbles—"bardilho"—at times almost black, or gray with white veins, which are found in Montes-Claros.

These marbles may acquire a fine polish, and the quarries are susceptible of furnishing large monoliths. They belong to the laurentian period, and follow a direction of N. 35° W. In Vianna, Alvito, and Portel there are found marbles with the same characters, embedded in metamorphic schists of the same period.

In the mountain of Ficalho there is found also a zone of chrystalline marbles of the same geological period.

The rocks of the jurassic period furnish a large quantity of building and ornamenting stone. A little to the west of Coimbra an extensive zone of jurassic rocks commences, which on the oriental side rests on the belt of the triassic rocks which pass Coimbra, and whose occidental line passes up to Pombal, following afterwards a little to the west of Thomar, stretching towards Batalha, Aljubarrota, and coming to wind up in triassic soil a little to the west of Rio Maior. To the west of Coimbra there is found also a small zone of jurassic rocks, comprehended by a line which passes by Ançan, Portunhos and Outil. These limestones also exist near to Figueira da Foz.

Bearing on the jurassic rocks there is found the limestone and marl of the cretaceous period, which occupy a large area to the east of Leiria, and a less extensive area to the north of Torres Vedras. The ground limited by a line which commences at 5 kilometres to the north of Ericeira and terminates in Alhandra, following by Tejo and the sea-coast, is constituted by the cretaceous rocks, which are interrupted by the basalts to the east; by the granites between Cintra and the Cape of Roca; and by the jurassic zone placed to the east of those granites.

The jurassic and cretaceous rocks furnish limestones of very varied and bright colors, as likewise extremely pure white; they are generally soft, and for that reason the most delicate and capricious ornamentations can be executed on these; but in some places, by effect of local metamorphism, these rocks were transformed in perfect marbles.

This phenomenon turns to be very remarkable in the limestones of Cintra, belonging to the jurassic period and metamorphized by the granites adjoining, and the limestones of Pero Pinheiro, belonging to the cretaceous, and likewise metamorphized by the volcanic rocks of the suburbs of Lisbon.

The marbles of Cintra have the white and black, almost pure or more or less mixed.

With the marbles of Pero Pinheiro all the buildings of Lisbon are built. They are easily worked, at the same time that they resist the action of the weather.

In Arrabida mountain the breccia marbles are found of very bright colors; they acquire a fine polish and are of a fine effect, above all in indoor ornamentation.

In the province of Algarve there is found also a narrow belt of jurassic calcareous stone stretching from E. to W., and which also furnishes ordinary limestone and marbles.

**Clays.**—These rocks are found very frequently. The porcelain manufacture of Vista Allegre uses the clays of Feira (Aveiro.) The clays of Abrigada are employed there in the ceramical products factory. The refractory clays of the district of Leiria from "Casal dos Ovos" and "Valle de Lobos" have been for a long time used.

The Cabo de Mondego Mining Co., which has a glass factory in Buarcos "Concelho da Figueira da Foz," has there also a ceramical products factory, where there are manufactured the refractory materials used in said factory.

**Statistic.**—There is not an exact statistic of the number of quarries and their production. By inquiry made by the Bureau of Mines, there were gathered 802 quarries in operation, distributed as follows:

| | | | |
|---|---|---|---|
| District of Aveiro | 67 | quarries. |
| " " Beja | 61 | " |
| " " Braga | 33 | " |
| " " Castello Branco | 15 | " |
| " " Coimbra | 20 | " |
| " " Evora | 46 | " |
| " " Faro | 9 | " |

District of Leiria.................................... 18 quarries.
"    "  Lisbon.................................... 105    " '
"    "  Portalegre............................. 9    "
"    "  Santarem............................... 37    "
"    "  Vianna do Castello.................. 74    "
"    "  Vizeu.................................... 103    "
"    "  Villa Real............................,.............. 89    "
Açores: Angra........................................ ▶ 27    "
        Horta....................................... 16    "
        Pouta Dellgada....................... 73    "

                               802

It is difficult to find out the production of these quarries; there are many that have yet accidental labors. From a great number of those that are represented at the Exposition, the particular production is known, but of many others we have no data.

The movement of importation and exportation of earthy substances in 1872 was as follows:

| Materials. | Importation. Reis. | Exportation. Reis. |
|---|---|---|
| Marble.................. | 3,999 $ 000 | 2,814 $ 000 |
| Millstones............. | 490 $ 000 | 1,326 $ 000 |
| Stones ................. | 2,471 $ 000 | 29,897 $ 000 |
| Flintstone............. | .................. | 398 $ 000 |
| Chalk................... | 8,099 $ 000 | 447 $ 000 |
| Lime.................... | 4,575 $ 000 | 12,626 $ 000 |
| Clay and sand........ | .................. | 439 $ 000 |
| Cement................. | 12,444 $ 000 | 143 $ 000 |
| Total........ ......... | 32,078 $ 000 | 48,090 $ 090 |

The movement of importation and exportation of earthy substances in 1873 was as follows:

| Materials. | Importation. | | Exportation. | |
|---|---|---|---|---|
| | Kilograms. | Value. Reis. | Kilograms. | Value. Reis. |
| Sand............................... | ............ | ............ | 39,708 | 132 $ 000 |
| Clay............................... | 47,809 | 326 $ 000 | ........ | ............ |
| Lime.............................. | 883,983 | 2,880 $ 000 | 1,345,916 | 11,191 $ 000 |
| Cement...... ................... | 736,492 | 12,858 $ 000 | 204,000 | 620 $ 000 |
| Chalk............................. | 261,160 | 2,714 $ 000 | 40,000 | 60 $ 000 |
| Emery............................ | 892 | 159 $ 000 | ............ | ............ |
| Gems............................. | 54,864 | 9,277 $ 000 | ............ | ......•.... |
| Gypsum.......................... | 2,571,442 | 9,429 $ 000 | 33,944 | 1,038 $ 000 |
| Jasper............................ | 3,586 | 903 $ 000 | ............ | ............ |
| Marble........................... | 223,907 | 17,144 $ 000 | 18,447 | 667 $ 000 |
| Whetstone....................... | 79,090 | 2,831 $ 000 | 490 | 15 $ 000 |
| Stones...,....................... | 92,905 | 3,103 $ 000 | 5,742,000 | 36,807 $ 000 |
| Sulphate of Baryta............ | 144,584 | 1,955 $ 000 | ............ | ............ |
| Ochres........................... | 154,651 | 5,737 $ 000 | 9,066 | 14 $ 000 |
| Flint stone...................... | ............ | ............ | 4,377 | 283 $ 000 |
| Total......................... | 5,255,465 | 69,016 $ 000 | 2,446,948 | 50,827 $ 000 |

IV.

# MINERAL WATERS.

From a report written in 1867, by Mr. J. B. Schiappa de Azevedo, Mining Engineer, as member of a commission of which Dr. Thomas de Carvalho, Physician, and Dr. Agostinho Vicente Lourenço, Chemist, also formed part, we extract the following data:

The number of groups of mineral springs known in Portugal reach 81, and are distributed in the following manner:

| | |
|---|---:|
| Province of Minho | 13 |
| " " Tras-os-Montes | 11 |
| " " Beira | 26 |
| " " Extremadura | 17 |
| " " Alemtejo | 14 |
| " " Algarve | 3 |
| Total | 81 |

| There are: | | |
|---|---|---:|
| | Sulphurous | 58 |
| | Gaseous alkaline | 3 |
| | Gaseous | 5 |
| | Salines of various basis | 4 |
| | Simple thermæ | 5 |
| | Metallic ferro-cupriferous | 2 |
| | Chlorurated | 3 |
| | Not determined | 1 |
| | Total | 81 |

In relation to temperature:

| | |
|---|---:|
| Cold (up to 20° Centg. = 68° Far.) | 30 |
| Fresh (up to 25° Centg. = 77° Far.) | 6 |
| Temperate (up to 32° Centg. = 89°.6 Far.) | 10 |
| Hot (up to 38° Centg. = 100°.4 Far.) | 17 |
| Very hot (over 38° Centg., or 100°.4 Far.) | 10 |
| Not ascertained | 8 |
| Total | 81 |

The hottest spring known on the continent is that of S. Pedro da Cova, in the province of Beira, whose temperature observed near the opening is of 68°.75 Centg. = 155°.75 Far.

In the same report of Mr. Schiappa de Azevedo, he states the following conclusions:

1st—That in Portugal the greatest frequency of the mineral springs are found principally in the regions most remote from basaltic and trachytic rocks, which are in the vicinity of Lisbon the representatives of volcanoes of a geological period previous to the present.

2d—That the mineral waters spring in greater abundance in mountainous grounds than in flat.

3d—That in more uneven soils the springs that gush from granite are more numerous, and these almost always in the contact of the granitic with other sedimentary rock, or at least of different nature and origin.

The following tables comprise an account of the more notable mineral waters of Portugal, as likewise the general result of the analysis made by Dr. Agostinho Vicente Lourenço.

I.

| NAMES | Temperature. ° Cent. | Sulphydric acid. | Solid residue obtained by the evaporation of 1,000 grammes of water. | Salts which they contain. |
|---|---|---|---|---|
| **PROVINCE OF MINHO.** | | | | |
| Caldas de Vizella { Mourisco | 36°.5 | 0.00862 | 0.331 | Alkaline silicates and chlorides, and small quantities of calcareous and magnesian salts. |
| Lameira | 32°.5 | 0.00913 | 0.3415 | |
| Medico | 37°.5 | 0.00987 | 0.3475 | |
| Taipas | 29° to 30° | 0.00242 | 0.2085 | Exactly the same salts as those above. |
| Lijó e Gallegos | 19° | | 0.473 | Alkaline sulphates and chlorides of lime and magnesia, and very small quantities of iron, alumina and silica. |
| Caldelas de Rendufe | 32°.5 | 0.00801 | 11.467 | Alkaline sulphates and chlorides, calcareous and magnesian, and silica. |
| Monsão { Banho brando (weak bath) | 31°.75 | | | Mainly of alkaline and calcareous chlorides and sulphates, and silica. |
| Contra forte (medium) | 39° | | 0.4615 | |
| Forte (strong) | 43°.5 | | | |
| Gerez { Banho forte (strong) | 45° to 48° | | | Mainly of alkaline and calcareous silicates and chlorides. |
| Contra forte (medium) | 49° | | 0.2675 | |
| Da Bica | 42° to 42°.5 | | | |
| **PROVINCE OF BEIRA.** | | | | |
| Alcafache spring | 49° | 0.00026 | 0.304 | Mainly of alkaline chlorides and sulphates of magnesia and lime, and silica. |
| Felgueira | 32°.5 to 35° | | 0.34467 | Mainly of alkaline sulphates and chlorides of lime and magnesia, silica and small quantities of alumina and iron. |
| Moledo { Banhos contra fortes (medium baths) | 42° | 0.00425 | 0.25167 | Mainly of alkaline chlorides and silicates of lime and magnesia, with very small portions of iron and alumina. |
| Estrada springs | 39° at opening 37° at spring 35° at baths | 0.00061 | 0.267 | |
| S. Pedro do Sul | 69° | 0.0014 | 0.315 | Mainly of sulphates, alkaline chlorides and silicates of lime and magnesia and small quantities of iron and alumina. |
| Entre Rios | Cold | 0.0018 | 0.321 | Mainly of silica, alkaline sulphates and chlorides of lime and magnesia, as well as a small portion of alumina. |
| Aregos | 57° | 0.00235 | 0.290 | Silica, alkaline sulphates and chlorides, calcareous and magnesian salts, and very small quantities of iron and alumina. |
| Bussaco | Cold. | | 0.1134 | Alkaline sulphates and chlorides, silica, phosphate of iron and alumina, and calcareous and magnesian salts. |
| Luso | 25° | | 0.05917 | Silica, alkaline chlorides, calcareous and magnesian salts, and very small quantities of alumina and iron. |

II.

| NAMES. | Temperature Cent. | Sulphydric Acid. | Solid residue obtained by the evaporation of 1,000 grammes of water. | Salts which they contain. |
|---|---|---|---|---|
| PROVINCE OF TRAS-OS-MONTES. | | | | |
| Vidago | Cold. | | 4.405 | Carbonates of soda, potassa, lime, magnesia and iron, chloride of potassium, silicum acid, vestiges of sulphuric acid, alumina and organic matter and great quantity of carbonic acid free. |
| Villarelho da Rais | 16°.4 | | 1.8996 | Same as above only more minute proportions. |
| Caldas de Chaves | 50° to 56° | | 1.7645 | Same as above with the exception of carbonate of soda. |
| PROVINCE OF EXTREMADURA. | | | | |
| Casaes Springs { Estoril | 28° | | 3.57 | Chlorides of sodium, potassium, magnesium and calcium, sulphate of lime, carbonates of lime and magnesia, and silica. |
| Poça | 27° | | 3.111 | The same exactly as above. |
| St. Antonio do Estoril | Of the air. | | 1.174 | Chlorides of sodium, potassium and calcium. sulphate of lime, carbonates of lime and magnesia, and silica. |
| Waters of the Navy-yard well | 22°.5 | 0.021026 to 0.042612 | 26.2963 to 28.2139 | Chlorides of sodium, potassium and magnesium, bromide of potassium, sulphates of lime and magnesia, iron, alumina, and silica. |
| Alcagarias do Duque | 34° | | 0.7128 | Chloride of sodium, sulphates of lime, soda and potass, carbonates of lime and magnesia, and silica. |
| Alcagarias de D. Clara | 33° | | 0.7275 | Same as above, exactly. |
| Fountain of El-Rei | 29° | | 0.6442 | Chloride of sodium, sulphates of potass and lime, and carbonates of lime, magnesia and protocide of iron. |
| Waters of "Doutor" | 26°.5 | | 0.5423 | Chloride of sodium, sulphates of potassa and lime, carbonates of lime and magnesia, and silica. |
| Fountain of "Andaluz" | 22° | | | Same as above, exactly. |
| Cucos Springs | 32° | | 3.457 | Chlorides of sodium, potassium, caicium and magnesium, sulphate of lime, carbonates of lime and magnesia, silica, etc. |
| Torres Vedras Spring | 21° | | 2.442 | Chlorides of sodium and magnesium, sulphates of potass, lime and magnesia, and carbonates of lime and magnesia. |
| Vimieiro Springs | 24° | | 0.826 | Chlorides of sodium and magnesium, sulphates of potass, lime and magnesia, and silica. |
| Caldas de Rainha | 33°.8 | 0.0085 | 2.785 | Chloride of sodium, sulphates of lime, magnesia, soda and potassa, carbonates of lime and magnesia, silica, etc. |
| Caldas de Gayeiras | 33°.8 | 0.006657 | 2.2766 | Same as above, exactly. |
| Obidos | 27°.4 | 0.004465 | 2.7325 | Chloride of sodium, sulphates of soda, potassa, lime and magnesia, carbonates of lime and magnesia, silica, etc. |
| Arrabidos Spring | 29°.2 | 0.004169 | 2.564 | Same as above exactly. |
| Aguas Santas | Cold. | | 0.219 | Chlorides of sodium and magnesium, sulphates of potassa, soda, lime and magnesia, carbonates of lime, magnesia and iron, and silica. |

III.

| NAMES. | Temperature °Cent. | Sulphydric Acid. | Solid residue obtained by the evaporation of 1,000 grammes of water. | Salts which they contain. |
|---|---|---|---|---|
| **PROVINCE OF ALEMTEJO.** | | | | |
| Aljustrel { Exterior Spring | Cold. | | 7.151 | Mainly of sulphate of protoxide of iron, sulphate of copper, alkaline chlorides, sulphates of lime, magnesia, alumina and zinc, and silica and arsenic that give to 0.00169 per 1,000. |
| Interior Spring | | | 0.831 | Exactly the same as above. |
| Cabeço de Vide { External use | 25° to 25°.5 | 0.00693 | 0.3225 | Alkaline chlorides and carbonates of lime, magnesia and soda, silica, etc. |
| Internal use | 26° to 25°.5 | 0.00455 | 0.23 | The same as above only in lesser proportions. |
| Ouguella | Cold. | | 0.7849 | Chloride of sodium, sulphate of soda, nitrates of soda and lime, carbonates of soda and magnesia, and silica. |
| **PROVINCE OF ALGARVE.** | | | | |
| St. Antonio de Tavira | 26° | | 0.490 | Alkaline sulphates and chlorides, carbonates of lime and magnesia, silica and small quantities of iron and alumina. |
| Monchique | 31°.5 to 34° | | 0.2848 | Mainly of silica, alkaline sulphates and chlorides, carbonates of lime and magnesia, and small quantities of iron. |

V.

# MINING ENGINEERING.

In order to grant the mines, the Government orders an examination of the deposit to be made, and a surveyed plan of the grounds also, on which to determine, in relation to the direction, inclination and extension of the deposit, the limit of the area of the grant within which the miner may carry on his labors.

The plans are drawn in the scale of 1-10,000, and referred to fixed points on the ground.

The granted area is generally delineated by a rectangular of 1000 metres long by 500 wide. These plans are surveyed with all the accurateness possible, whose failure, besides other inconveniences, would be the origin of questions and law-suits between neighboring grantees.

Fortunately, the superior administration of mines in Portugal is made in such a way that the law-suits regarding the grant of property are not only rare, but have always had a very rapid decision, whereas the industry never has suffered any by these means which, in other countries constitute one of the greatest difficulties for its development.

The plan of the Moncorvo iron mines, exhibited by the Bureau of Mines (Repartição de Minas), gives an idea of the way in which these labors are executed in Portugal. These plans, accompanied by the determination of the mineral nature of the soil comprised, serve as a basis for the execution of the mineral map, work initiated by the Chief of the Bureau of Mines, J. B. Schiappa d'Azevedo, Mining Engineer, and which at present is under way.

The *Mineral map* will be executed upon the chorographical map of the country, in the scale of 1-100,000. This map will contain a delineation of the different species of rocks which constitute the soil of the country, the position of the different metallic deposits determined accurately, their nature, direction and inclination, the direction and inclination of the sedimentary layers, the fractures and other geological features, the position of the quarries worked in the country, and that of the mineral springs.

This map will be the only base of the rational study of the condition of the metallic deposits of the country and their relations among each other, having in view to arrive at the knowledge of their laws of distribution and of their wealth.

The Bureau of Mines exhibits also some plans of operations, which the grantees are obliged to send annually to the Ministry of Public Works. This administrative requirement has in view the fiscalization of the conditions in which the mining labors are carried on, and at the same time serves for the study of the conditions of the bearing of the lode, and of the distribution of the ore in each deposit.

# The Pentagonal System in Spain and Portugal

## AND

# The Pentagonal System in Portugal.

### BY LOURENÇO MALHEIRO, MINING ENGINEER.

These two maps, exhibited at the Portuguese mineral section, contain the graphical representation of several circles of the pentagonal system that pass through Portugal and Spain.

In the first one these circles are traced on a geographical map of Spain and Portugal; in the second one the circles that pass through Portugal are traced on a geological map of Portugal in the scale of 1-500,000.

These maps are the base of an application of the Pentagonal System of Elie de Beaumont, which will be made in the execution of the mineral map of Portugal, now in course of preparation.

We have not as yet sufficient data to determine all the importance of those circles in the study of geological lineations of Portugal, with all we will already cite some facts which show some remarkable coincidences. The only Primitive circle which passes through Portugal is the Primitive Circle of Lisbon. It starts from a point T in Burgos, Spain, and enters into Portugal by the eastern side at the point where the river Douro, having traversed all the country in a direction proximately E. to W., suddenly turns to the N. E., following parallel with that circle. From this point the primitive circle of Lisbon passes with extreme precision over the summit line of all the chain of the mountain of Estrella, and follows to the western coast of Portugal, going out at a point to the north of Ericeira. In the western extreme this circle passes along the slopes of the mountain of Cintra parallel with the direction of that mountain.

The most important line of mountains of Portugal runs from the Cape of S. Vicente to the turn of the river Douro in the Spanish frontier, and this line coincides very approximately with the primitive circle of Lisbon.

The Diametral $D a c$, which Pouyanne proposed to substitute for the Hundsruck system of Elie de Beaumont, and which in these maps was definitely adopted, lineates with the principal hydrographical lines of Northern Portugal and Galicia in Spain, passing to the north of the river Minho.

The trapezohedral circle $T T b b c$ (system of Saucerrois) enters into Portugal to the north of Cape S. Vicente, and follows proximately by the summit of Monchique mountain in the point of Foya, lineating itself there with a notable part of that mountain.

The diametral $D a c$ (system of Cote d'Or) enters into Portugal by the South, passing next to Faro, and follows from there up to near

Alcoutim, fitting in its passage to some remarkable features of the mountain of Algarve.

Four bissectors cut each other in Portugal on the primitive circle of Lisbon, some of which adjust themselves to orographical and hydrographical features important enough in Portugal and Spain.

Two hexatetrahedral circles H $a\,a$ cut each other at the Primitive of Lisbon in a point whose longitude is of 12° 18′ 34″.66, and latitude 38° 31′ 21″.53, one of which steering at this point N. 5° 14′ 6″.71 and the other E. 20° 46′ 22″.17 S.

This circle that follows near the western coast of Portugal, to which is proximately parallel, has a position very remarkable in relation to the geographical configuration of Europe.

This circle passes the eastern coast of Greenland, goes on, touching Iceland along its eastern coast, and there afterwards lineates itself parallel to the general coast of Europe; it enters into the African continent at the mouth of Tensift, between Safi and the Mogador, traversing the great Desert, and goes on to cross proximately the mountains that divide the waters of the Senegal and the Niger, leaving this continent by the Cape of Palmas.

The other hexatetrahedral circle H $a\,a$ traverses Portugal in a direction very proximately E. to W. in relation with several remarkable geographical features, and with a direction of several metalliferous deposits; it determines the maximum circle that unites two very notable and symmetrical capes of Portugal and Spain, Cabo da Roca, to the west of Lisbon, and Cabo de la Nao, to the north of Alicante, It goes on, passing afterwards a little to the south of Tunis, the most boreal point of the African continent, in Dernah, near Cairo, going to unite to point H in the coast of the Red Sea.

In the map of the Pentagonal system in Portugal there is traced a compass of the directions of the systems of mountains, transported parallel to the crossing point of the bisectors with the primitive circle of Lisbon.

The influence of these several systems in Portugal is not yet studied, therefore we cannot now give especial indications.

The application made by Moissenet and Chancourtois of the Pentagonal system to the study of the metalliferous deposits will be followed in the execution of the mineral map above mentioned.

Unfortunately these studies are nevertheless circumscribed to small regions, and they are not of an order that can be generalized easily. Of its general application to the several surveyed mining regions could perhaps be deduced laws very useful to the mining industry, and within the Pentagonal system there would perhaps be found a *metalliferous system* in intimate connection with that one, that would contribute powerfully to make disappear a great part of the emperism that reigns yet in the previous estimation of the wealth of a deposit.

The circles of the Pentagonal system were determined calculating the geographic co-ordinates of the crossing points of several circles among each other.

Following we give a table of the data that determine them geographically in Portugal and Spain.

*Table of the Data determining the intersections of the various Circles of the Pentagonal System which pass through Spain and Portugal.*

## INTERSECTIONS WITH THE PRIMITIVE CIRCLE OF LISBON.

| Circles. | Notations. | Systems. | Point of inters'n | Latitude. | Longitude. | Azimuth of the Prim. Circle of Lisbon. | Azimuth of the Circles. |
|---|---|---|---|---|---|---|---|
| Octahedral | | Pyrenées | T | 40° 44′ 24″.29 N. | 6° 38′ 05″.62 W | N. 47° 28′ 05″.93 E. | N. 77° 47′ 45″.88 W |
| Octahedral | | Mulehacen | T | 42 44 24 .29 N. | 6 38 05 .62 W | N. 47 28 05 .93 E. | N. 7 16 02 .26 W |
| Rhomboidal dodecahedral | | | T | 42 44 24 .29 N. | 6 38 05 .62 W | N. 47 28 05 .93 E. | N. 42 31 54 .07 W |
| Bisector | D H | | | 39 36 56 .51 N. | 10 56 18 .79 W | N. 44 37 58 .82 E. | N. 20 11 44 .67 W |
| Bisector | I H | | | 39 36 56 .51 N. | 10 56 18 .79 W | N. 44 37 58 .82 E. | N. 39 02 11 .28 W |
| Bisector | I H | | | 39 36 56 .51 N. | 10 56 18 .79 W | N. 44 37 58 .82 E. | N. 51 41 51 .08 W |
| Bisector | D H | | | 39 36 56 .51 N. | 10 56 18 .79 W | N. 44 37 58 .82 E. | N. 70 32 17 .69 W |
| Hexatetrahedral | H a a | | | 38 31 21 .53 N. | 12 18 34 .66 W | N. 43 46 07 .73 E. | N. 5 14 06 .71 W |
| Hexatetrahedral | H a a | | | 38 31 21 .53 N. | 12 18 34 .66 W | N. 13 46 07 .73 E. | N. 87 13 37 .88 W |

## INTERSECTIONS WITH THE PRIMITIVE CIRCLE OF NOVA ZEMBLA.

| Circles. | Notations. | Systems. | Point of inters'n | Latitude. | Longitude. | Azimuth of the Prim. Circle of Nova Zembla. | Azimuth of the Circles. |
|---|---|---|---|---|---|---|---|
| Octahedral | | Pyrynees | a | 40° 39′ 14″.55 N. | 3° 23′ 04″.36 E. | N. 18° 52′ 45″.83 E. | N. 71° 07′ 14″.17 W |
| Diametral | D a e | Forez | a | 40 39 14 .55 N. | 3 23 04 .36 E. | N. 18 52 45 .83 E. | N. 14 36 30 .93 W |
| Hexatetrahedral | M b a n b | Noutron | a | 40 39 14 .55 N. | 3 23 04 .36 E. | N. 18 52 45 .83 E. | N. 35 36 26 .06 W |
| Hexatetrahedral | H b a n b | Alpes principales | | 40 39 14 .55 N. | 3 23 04 .36 E. | N. 18 52 45 .83 E. | N. 73 21 57 .72 E. |
| Hexatetrahedral | H a T t a | Erymanthe et Mermoucha | a | 40 39 14 .55 N. | 3 23 04 .36 E. | N. 18 52 45 .83 E. | N. 59 46 22 .09 E. |
| Diagonal | I b | Mont Serrat | | 39 08 30 .88 N. | 2 43 07 .52 E. | N. 18 27 08 .24 E. | N. 40 02 09 .19 W |
| Trapezohedral | T b· | Veodée | | 38 18 43 .87 N. | 2 21 58 .16 E. | N. 13 13 54 .09 E. | N. 18 30 36 .37 W |
| Rhomboidal dedocahedral | | | | 35 28 18 .57 N. | 1 13 12 .25 E. | N. 17 32 36 .43 E. | N. 37 33 40 .80 W |
| Rhomboidal dedocahedral | | Axe volcanique | | 35 28 18 .67 N. | 1 13 12 .25 E. | N. 17 32 36 .43 E. | N. 72 38 57 .66 E. |
| Bisector | D H | | | 35 28 18 .57 N. | 1 13 12 .25 E. | N. 17 32 36 .43 E. | N. 63 06 24 .62 E. |
| Bisector | D H | | | 35 28 18 .57 N. | 1 13 12 .25 E. | N. 17 32 36 .43 E. | N. 81 48 22 .53 W |

* All the points are referred to the meridian of Paris—Lat. 11° 25′ 56″.925 of Lisbon.

## INTERSECTIONS WITH THE OCTÁHEDRAL CIRCLE OF MOUNT SINAI (S. PYRÉNÉES).

| Circles. | Notations | Systems. | Points of intersec'n | Latitude. | Longitude. | Azimuth of the Octahedral Circle. | Azimuth of the Circles. |
|---|---|---|---|---|---|---|---|
| Bisector | D H | | y4 | N. 43°33' 23".45 N. | 12°56' 45".34 W | N. 82°06' 52".33 W | N. 21°31' 44".37 W |
| Diametral | D a c | | | N. 43 08 21.04 N. | 9 22 10.25 W | N. 79 39 13.24 W | N. 52 03 22.41 E. |
| Diametral | D a c | Cote de Or | | N. 42 20 58.29 N. | 2 20 08.12 W | N. 76 14 28.27 W | N. 42 32 34.48 E. |
| Trapezohedral | T a b c | Longmynd | | N. 41 56 55.44 N. | 2 14 23.61 W | N. 74 50 05.29 W | N. 24 56 20.63 E. |
| Bisector | D H | Monte Seny | y5 | N. 41 41 56.74 N. | 1 02 14.28 W | N. 74 01 58.22 W | N. 33 38 13.11 E. |
| Trapezohedral | T T b b c | Sancerrois | y5 | N. 41 41 56.74 N. | 1 02 14.28 W | N. 74 01 58.22 W | N. 63 28 40.67 E. |
| Diagonal | I b | Mont Serrat | | N. 41 26 58.40 N. | 0 06 00.63 E. | N. 73 16 40.72 W | N. 43 43 47.65 W |
| Trapezohedral | T b | Vendee | | N. 41 13 38.20 N. | 1 03 57.37 E. | N. 72 38 24.41 W | N. 19 20 31.91 W |
| Diametral | D a c | Alpes occidentales | | N. 41 08 33.92 N. | 1 25 21.26 E. | N. 72 24 18.94 W | N. 25 42 52.78 E. |

## INTERSECTIONS WITH OCTAHEDRAL CIRCLE OF MULEHACEN.

| Circles. | Notations | Systems. | Points of intersec'n | Latitude. | Longitude. | Azimuth of the Octahedral Circle. | Azimuth of the Circles. |
|---|---|---|---|---|---|---|---|
| Diametral | D a c | | | N. 44°27' 50".76 N. | 6°56' 34".71 W | N. 7°28' 47".54 W | N. 58°44' 09".71 E. |
| Diametral | D a c | Côte d'Or | | N. 40 42 53.12 N. | 17 39 56 W... | N. 7 02 45.96 W | N. 41 14 38.39 E. |
| Trapezohedral | T T b b c | Sancerrois | | N. 39 37 54.92 N. | 6 07 14.52 W | N. 6 55 42.81 W | N. 60 09 49.04 E. |
| Bisector | D a c | | y4 | N. 38 06 00.23 N. | 5 53 03.19 W | N. 6 46 48.62 W | N. 67 21 56.58 W. |
| Hexatetrahedral | H b a a b | Alpes principales | y4 | N. 38 06 00.23 N. | 5 53 03.19 W | N. 6 46 48.62 W | N. 29 35 35.83 E. |
| Bisector | D H | Mont Seny | y | N. 36 04 21.71 N. | 5 35 10.01 W | N. 6 36 01.24 W | N. 30 46 37.26 E. |
| Bisector | I H | | y | N. 36 04 21.71 N. | 5 35 10.91 W | N. 6 36 01.24 W | N. 43 24 38.46 W. |
| Bisector | D H | | y | N. 36 04 21.71 N. | 5 35 10.01 W | N. 6 36 01.24 W | N. 85 47 16.96 W. |
| Hexatetrahedral | H a T T a | Erymanthe et Mermoucba | y | N. 36 04 21.71 N. | 5 35 10.01 W | N. 6 36 01.24 W | N. 54 11 37.54 E. |
| Trapezohedral | T a b c | Longmynd | y | N. 36 04 21.71 N. | 5 35 10.01 W | N. 6 36 01.24 W | N. 22 49 46.73 E. |

## INTERSECTIONS WITH THE RHOMBOIDAL DODECAHEDRAL CIRCLE.

| Circles. | Notations | Systems. | Points of Intersec'n | Latitude. | Longitude. | Azimuth of Rhomb. Dodec. Circle. | Azimuth of the Circles. |
|---|---|---|---|---|---|---|---|
| Bisector | D H | Belle-Ile | | N. 45°48' 50".27 N. | 10°46' 31".22 W | N. 45°25' 26".22 W | N. 62°04' 43".45 E. |
| Diametral | D a c | | | N. 43 51 39.95 N. | 8 04 20.79 W | N. 43 31 04.13 W | N. 52 56 56.82 E. |
| Diametral | D a c | Côte d'Or | | N. 41 36 06.31 N. | 8 14 55.75 W | N. 41 36 03.44 W | N. 41 55 55.61 E. |
| Trapezohedral | T T b b c | Longmynd | | N. 41 32 00.57 N. | 4 00 31.55 W | N. 40 38 10.62 W | N. 61 31 25.02 E. |
| Trapezohedral | T a b c | Sancerrois | | N. 40 00 19.58 N. | 3 24 56.61 W | N. 40 24 10.94 W | N. 10 04 04.61 E. |
| Bisector | D H | Mont Seny | | N. 39 31 52.91 N. | 2 53 37.79 W | N. 40 04 09.02 W | N. 39 25 41.31 E. |
| Hexatetrahedral | H b a a b | Alpes principales | | N. 39 08 48.02 N. | 2 28 38.63 W | N. 39 46 18.75 W | N. 32 36 12.96 E. |
| Hexatetrahedral | H a T T a | Erymanthe et Mermoucha | | N. 38 17 00.18 N. | 1 33 53.06 W | N. 39 14 03.07 W | N. 56 37 29.54 E. |
| Diametral | D a c | Alpes occidentales | | N. 37 30 29.83 N. | 0 46 10.72 W | N. 38 44 45.48 W | N. 24 19 28.54 E. |
| Prim. of Nova Zembla | D a c | Rhin | θ2 | | | | |

INTERSECTIONS WITH THE BISECTORS I H. (2)

| Circles. | Notations | Systems. | Point of intersection. | Latitude. | Longitude. | Azimuth of the Bisectors (I H). | Azimuth of the Circles. |
|---|---|---|---|---|---|---|---|
| Diametral | D a c | | | 41° 10' 86".17 N. | 12° 57' 59".36 W. | N. 40° 08' 05".41 W. | N. 49° 51' 54".59 E. |
| Primitive of Lisbon | | | | 39 36 56 .51 N. | 10 56 18 .79 W. | N. 39 02 11 .29 W. | N. 44 37 58 .82 E. |
| Trapezohedral | T T b b c | Sancerrois | | 38 06 27 .79 N. | 9 23 43 .31 W. | N. 38 04 04 .92 W. | N. 58 06 29 .08 E. |
| Diametral | D a c | Côte d'Or | | 37 59 29 .20 N. | 9 16 47 .40 W. | N. 37 59 48 .88 W. | N. 30 21 00 .36 E. |
| Hexatetrah-dral | H b a a b | Alpes principales | | 37 12 12 .91 N. | 8 30 34 .64 N. | N. 37 31 37 .18 W. | N. 65 52 21 .43 E. |
| Bisector | D H | | | 36 12 02 .95 N. | 7 31 57 .35 W. | N. 36 56 35 .47 W. | N. 86 56 08 .09 W. |
| Diametral | D a c | | | 40 52 57 .30 N. | 13 05 35 .28 W. | N. 33 65 23 .13 W. | N. 49 33 47 .63 E. |
| Primitive of Lisbon | | | | 39 36 56 .51 N. | 10 56 18 .79 W. | N. 51 41 51 .08 W. | N. 44 37 58 .82 E. |
| Diametral | D a c | Côte d'Or | | 38 29 33 .38 N. | 8 54 43 .57 W. | N. 50 25 21 .53 W. | N. 39 34 38 .47 E. |
| Trapezohedral | T T b b c | Sancerrois | | 38 20 33 .38 N. | 8 54 43 .57 W. | N. 50 25 21 .53 W. | N. 58 24 25 .38 E. |
| Hexatetrah-dral | H b a a b | Alpes principales | | 37 30 24 .12 N. | 7 38 51 .90 W. | N. 49 38 44 .01 W. | N. 66 23 44 .04 E. |
| Hexatetrahedral | H a T T a | Erymanthe et Mermoucha | y | 36 04 21 .71 N. | 5 35 10 .01 W. | N. 48 24 38 .46 W. | N. 54 11 37 .54 E. |

## INTERSECTIONS WITH THE BISECTORS D H (4)

| Circles. | Notations. | Systems. | Point of intersection. | Latitude. | Longitude. | Azimuth of the Bisectors (D H). | Azimuth of the Circles. |
|---|---|---|---|---|---|---|---|
| Octahedral | D a c | Pyrennees | y4 | 43° 33' 23".45 N. | 12° 56' 45".34 W. | N. 21° 31' 44".37 W. | N. 82° 06' 52".33 W. |
| Diametral | | | | 41 37 11 .60 N. | 11 55 35 .64 W. | N. 20 50 35 .63 W. | N. 50 19 56 .76 E. |
| Primitive of Lisbon | | | | 39 36 56 .51 N. | 10 56 18 .79 W. | N. 20 11 41 .67 W. | N. 44 37 68 .82 E. |
| Trapezohedral | T T b b c | Sancerrois | | 37 45 18 .27 N. | 10 04 24 .22 W. | N. 19 33 34 .22 W. | N. 57 41 12 .25 E. |
| Diametral | D a c | Cote d'Or | | 37 22 55 .39 N. | 9 54 24 .90 W. | N. 19 38 12 .34 W. | N. 38 58 00 .20 E. |
| Hexatetrahedral | H b a a b | Alpes Principales | | 36 47 27 .33 N. | 9 38 41 .67 W. | N. 19 23 43 .98 W. | N. 65 11 21 .89 E. |
| Bisector | D H | | | 36 14 20 .22 N. | 9 24 14 .63 W. | N. 19 15 07 .59 W. | N. 88 02 26 .02 E. |
| Diametral | D a c | | | 40 22 12 .66 N. | 13 52 41 .65 W. | N. 72 25 40 .20 W. | N. 49 03 07 .26 E. |
| Primitive of Lisbon | | | | 39 36 56 .51 N. | 10 56 18 .79 W. | N. 70 52 17 .69 W. | N. 44 37 58 .82 E. |
| Diametral | D a c | Cote d'Or | y4 | 38 52 25 .59 N. | 8 20 48 .55 W. | N. 68 53 54 .06 W. | N. 39 55 48 .55 E. |
| Trapezohedral | T T b b c | Sancerrois | | 38 46 18 .88 N. | 8 00 34 .69 W. | N. 68 41 13 .34 W. | N. 58 58 10 .58 E. |
| Hexatetrahedral | H b a a b | Alpes Principales | | 38 06 00 .23 N. | 5 53 03 .19 W. | N. 67 21 56 .58 W. | N. 67 28 25 .83 E. |
| Trapezohedral | T a b c | Longuynd | | 37 42 29 .76 N. | 4 42 51 .36 W. | N. 66 38 48 .95 W. | N. 23 21 11 .05 E. |
| Bisector | D H | Mont Seny | | 37 36 34 .33 N. | 4 25 35 .82 W. | N. 66 26 16 .19 W. | N. 31 28 21 .23 E. |
| Hexatetrahedral | H a T T a | Erymanthe et Mermoncha. | | 37 16 20 .03 N. | 3 27 51 .30 W. | N. 65 53 09 .74 W. | N. 55 27 40 .04 E. |
| Diametral | D a c | Alpes Occidentales | | 36 29 21 .87 N. | 1 20 30 .17 W. | N. 64 36 42 .12 W. | N. 23 56 49 .13 E. |
| Prim. of Nova Zembla | | Rhin | | 35 28 18 .57 N. | 1 13 12 .25 E. | N. 63 06 24 .62 W. | N. 17 32 36 .43 E. |
| Trapezohedral | T b | Vendee | | 43 02 35 .92 N. | 0 35 49 .98 W. | N. 34 27 56 .47 E. | N. 19 55 42 .23 W. |
| Diagonal | I b | Mont Serrat | | 42 05 47 .11 N. | 0 11 32 .08 E. | N. 33 52 30 .81 E. | N. 42 15 19 .21 W. |
| Trapezohedral | T T b b c | Sancerrois | y5 | 41 41 56 .14 N. | 2 40 14 .26 W. | N. 33 35 13 .11 E. | N. 63 28 40 .67 E. |
| Rhomboidaldodecahedral | | | | 39 31 52 .91 N. | 3 53 37 .78 W. | N. 33 25 41 .31 E. | N. 40 04 09 .02 W. |
| Hexatetrahedral | H b a a b | Alpes Principales | | 38 51 54 .38 N. | 3 26 11 .10 W. | N. 32 05 06 .77 E. | N. 68 59 59 .96 E. |
| Bisector | | | y | 37 36 34 .33 N. | 4 25 35 .82 W. | N. 30 46 37 .26 E. | N. 28 28 16 .19 W. |
| Hexatetrahedral | H a T T a | Erymanthe et Mermouche. | | 36 04 21 .71 N. | 5 35 10 .01 W. | N. 88 59 37 .20 W. | N. 54 11 37 .54 E. |
| Diametral | D a c | Cote d'Or | | 36 16 21 .25 N. | 11 00 53 .03 W. | N. 88 59 37 .20 W. | N. 31 18 09 .51 E. |
| Hexatetrahedral | H b a a b | Alpes Principales | | 36 14 20 .22 N. | 11 00 53 .03 W. | N. 86 02 28 .02 W. | N. 64 22 26 .30 E. |
| Bisector | D H | | | 36 12 02 .95 N. | 9 21 28 .02 W. | N. 88 56 08 .09 W. | N. 19 15 07 .59 W. |
| Bisector | I H | | y | 36 04 21 .71 N. | 7 21 14 .63 W. | N. 85 47 16 .96 W. | N. 36 36 35 .47 W. |
| Diametral | I H | | | 36 46 50 .60 N. | 5 57 57 .35 W. | N. 83 31 29 .63 W. | N. 48 24 38 .46 W. |
| Prim. of Nova Zembla | D a c | Alpes Occidentales | | 35 28 18 .57 N. | 1 13 12 .25 E. | N. 81 48 22 .52 W. | N. 36 32 04 .77 W. |

## TABLE OF THE DIRECTION OF THE SYSTEMS OF MOUNTAINS TRANSPORTED TO A POINT(*) IN PORTUGAL.

| SYSTEMS. | Corresponding circle of the Pentagonal System. | Notations of the Circles. | Direction in the point (*) |
|---|---|---|---|
| Pyrennees | Octahedral | T D b | N. 80° 42' 53".26 W. |
| Finisterre | Trapezohedral | D a c | N. 66 02 55 .15 E. |
| Pays-Bas | Diametral | T D b | N. 72 48 16 .84 E. |
| Marhihan | Trapezohedral | T I a | N. 87 08 41 .25 W. |
| Alpes principales | Trapezohedral | H b a a b | N. 55 13 53 .99 W. |
| Mount Serrat | Hextetrahedral | I b | N. 64 22 54 .17 E. |
| Rhin | Diagonal | | N. 59 12 45 .62 W. |
| Longmyad | Primitive | | N. 9 57 22 .48 E. |
| Mount Serry | Trapezohedral | T a b s | N. 19 23 14 .19 E. |
| Tenare | Bisector | D H | N. 27 26 27 .93 E. |
| Thuringerwald | Primitive | | N. 26 31 34 .59 W. |
| Land's End | Primitive | | N. 64 12 27 .77 W. |
| Axe Volcanique | Primitive | | N. 79 18 35 .16 E. |
| Mont Viso | Rhomboidal Dodecahedral | | N. 65 41 59 .02 E. |
| Forez | Trapezohedral | I T | N. 33 17 22 .42 W. |
| Tatra | Diametral | D a c | N. 24 07 05 .05 W. |
| Erymanthe et Mermonche | Trapezohedral | T b | N. 66 01 04 .86 E. |
| Alpes occidentales | Hextetrahedal | H a T T a | N. 50 57 48 .79 E. |
| Vercors | Diametral | D c | N. 18 02 23 .11 E. |
| Nord d' Angleterre | Trapezohedral | T a | N. 1 47 13 .82 W. |
| Corse et Sardaigne | Bisector | D H | N. 8 01 24 .97 W. |
| Vendée | Trapezohedral | T D b | N. 12 29 15 .42 W. |
| Sancerrois | Trapezohedral | T b | N. 27 18 45 .58 W. |
| Primitive of Lisbon | Prapezohedral | T T b b c | N. 57 08 35 .48 E. |
| Octahedral of Mulehacen | Primitive | | N. 44 37 58 .82 E. |
| | Trimitive | | N. 10 01 09 .10 W. |

* This point is situated at Longitude 39° 36' 55".51, Latitude 10° 56' 18."79 of Paris, 0° 29' 38".135 of Lisbon.

# CATALOGUE.

# DEPARTMENT I.---MINING AND METAL-LURGY.

*Locotion*—MAIN BUILDING.

## MINERALS, ORES, BUILDING STONES AND MINING PRODUCTS.

CLASS 100.—Minerals, ores, etc. Metallic and non-metallic minerals, exclusive of coal and oil. Collections of minerals systematically arranged; collections of ores and associated minerals; geological collections.

CLASS 101.—Mineral combustibles. Coal, anthracite, semi-bituminous and bituminous, coal-waste and pressed coal; albertite, asphalt and asphaltic limestone; bitumen, mineral tar, crude petroleum.

CLASS 102.—Building stones, marbles, slates, etc. Rough, hewn, sawn or polished, for buildings, bridges, walls or other constructions, or for interior decoration, or for furniture.

Marble—white, black or coloured—used in building, decoration, statnary, monuments or furniture, in blocks or slabs not manufactured.

CLASS 103.—Lime, cement, and hydraulic cement, raw and burned, accompanied by specimens of the crude rock or material used, also artificial stone, concrete, beton.

Specimens of lime mortar and mixtures, with illustrations of the processes of mixing, etc. Hydraulic and other cement.

Beton mixtures and results, with illustrations of the processes.

Artificial stone for building purposes, building blocks, cornices, etc.

Artificial stone mixtures, for pavements, walls, or ceilings.

Plasters, mastics, etc.

CLASS 104.—Clays, kaolin, silex, and other materials for the manufacture of porcelain, faïence, and of glass, bricks, terra-cotta and tiles, and fire brick. Refractory stones for lining furnaces, sandstone, steatite, etc., and refractory furnace materials.

CLASS 105.—Graphite, crude and refined; for polishing purposes; for lubricating, electrotyping, photography, pencils, etc.

CLASS 106.—Lithographic stones, hones, whetstones, grindstones, grinding and polishing materials, sand quartz, garnet, crude topaz, diamond, corondum, emery in the rock and pulverized, and in assorted sizes and grades.

CLASS 107.—Mineral waters, artesian well water, natural brines, saline and alkaline efflorescences and solutions. Mineral fertilizing substances, gypsum, phosphate of lime, marls, shells, coprolites, etc., not manufactured.

---

### 1.—Mine of "Monges."—Iron.

Location—" Freguesia," of Santiago do Escoural, "Concelho," of Monte-mor-o-Novo, District of Evora.

Legal Grantee.—Visconde do Cartaxo, Street & Co.

Operator.—Monges Iron Company, limited, Exhibitor.

Commencement of labors.—By the present company, in 1873.

Area—81 hect. 31 ar. 00 cent.

No. of hands in 1875—250 to 350, Wages $\begin{cases} \text{Men, } 300 \text{ to } 380 \text{ reis.} \\ \text{Boys, } 160 \text{ to } 240 \text{ reis.} \end{cases}$

Production:

Tons.
```
1869—  1,127.970
1870—    106.520
1871—    145.740
1872—  4,639.333
1873—15,173.787
1874—40,496.000
```

Total ..61,689.350

Labors in open air.—Three automatic inclined planes.
Enclosing rocks.—Laurentian slates and limestones.
"         "          Direction N. W.
"         "          Inclination 70° S. W.
Number of deposits ascertained.—5 layers and 3 masses.
Strike of the layers.—N. W. to S. E.
Dip      "          "      45° N. E.

The Mongos deposit is constituted by hematites and magnetites accompanied with pyrites.

Among the 5 mineral layers ascertained only one is worked, which has a maximum thickness of 11 metres.

The iron ore of these deposits seems to be owing to a decomposition of the pyrites, because at the depth of about 23 metres the pyrites almost substitute the oxyds of iron.

Besides the layers, there exist three masses which seem to be superficial deposits.

Several analysis of the mining engineer, Joao Pacheco de Rezende, give:

|  | SAMPLING PLACES. | | |
|---|---|---|---|
|  | No. 7. | St. George's Cuttings. | English Cuttings. |
| Water and Carbonic Acid. | 12.2 | 7.2 | 3.3 |
| Lime | 2.7 | Traces. | 2.2 |
| Magnesia | 1.2 | 1.5 | 0.8 |
| Oxyd of Magnetic Iron | 10.6 | 62.9 | 81.9 |
| Peroxyd of Iron | 57.5 | 00.0 | 00.0 |
| Bioxyd of Manganese | 1.1 | 10.8 | 2.8 |
| Alumina | 2.0 | 3.5 | 1.1 |
| Insoluble Residue | 11.7 | 14.5 | 8.5 |
| Sulphuric Acid | 1.0 | Traces. | Traces. |
| Phosphoric Acid | Traces. | Traces. | Traces. |
|  | 100.0 | 100.4 | 100.6 |
| Yield. |  |  |  |
| Metallic Iron | 47.88 p. c. | 46.4 p. c. | 60.50 p. c. |
| Manganese | 0.696 p. c. | 6.8 p. c. | 1.77 p. c. |

| | SAMPLING PLACES. | | |
| --- | --- | --- | --- |
| | Pyramid. | D. Fernando. | Old Roman Gallery. |
| Water.......................... | 9.00 | 7.90 | 1.70 |
| Protoxyd of Iron............ | 7.06 | 8.99 | 6.42 |
| Sesquioxyd of Iron......... | 77.82 | 67.33 | 67.28 |
| Lime............... | 1.52 | Traces. | 0.79 |
| Magnesia...................... | 1.12 | Traces. | 1.04 |
| Alumina...................... | 0.25 | 0.75 | 3.35 |
| Bioxyd of Manganese...... | 0.23 | 2.37 | 2.37 |
| Insoluble Residue ........... | 2.70 | 13.00 | 17.00 |
| Sulphuric Acid............... | 0.30 | Traces. | 0.00 |
| Phosphoric Acid............ | 0.00 | 0.00 | 0.00 |
| | 100.00 | 100.34 | 99.95 |
| Yield. | | | |
| Metallic Iron.................. | 60 p. c. | 54.15 p. c. | 52.12 p. c. |
| Manganese..................... | 0.15 p. c. | 1.05 p. c. | 1.05 p. c. |

In order to utilize a great quantity of ore which occurs in dust, bricks are made out of this ferruginous earth with lime water.

Up to the present time all the ore is exported to England.

Samples, Class 100.
1. Oligiste Iron.
2. " "
3. " " earthy, } ferruginous earth for the manufacture of
4. " " earthy, } bricks.
5. " " products of mechanical dressing—bricks.
6. " " " " " "
7. Limestone—enclosing rock.

2.—Mine of " Zambujal,"
3.—Mine of " Ayres," } Iron.
4.—Mine of " S. Bartholomeu," 

Location—" Freguesia," of Villa Nova da Baronia, " Concelho" of Alvito, District of Beja.

Legal Grantee—José Hygino Ferreira Castello.

**Operator.—George Elliot, Exhibitor.**

Area—Zambujal 66 hect. 00 ar. 00 cent.
Ayres, 56 hect. 00 ar. 00 cent.
S. Bartholomeu, 60 hect. 00 ar. 00 cent.

These three deposits constitute with the Monges Mine a mettalliferous system stretched parallel to the limit line of the laurentian slates, with the granites which outcrop 5 kilometres to the South.

The labors to the present time have been very little.
The production of these mines was, in

*Tons.*
1873—3946.44
1874—1038.97
———————
4975.41

Samples, Class 100.
1. Oligiste Iron.
2. " "
3. " "
4. " "
5. " "
6. " "

## 5.—Moncorvo Iron Mines.—Iron,

Location—"Freguesia," of Moncorvo and Felgar, " Concelho," of Moncorvo, District of Bragança.
These mines were the object of special reference—see page 7.
Samples, Class 100.
1. Oligiste Iron (Fragas dos Apriscos).
2. " " " Facho).
3. Magnetite Iron (Alto do Chapeo).
4. Oligiste Iron (Alto do Mindel).
5. " " (Alto da Cotovia).
6. " " (Fragas do Carvalhal).
7. " " (Fragas da Carvalhosa).
8. " " (Carvalhosinha).
9. " " (Alto da Mua).
10. Schist (enclosing rock).
11. Granite—1000 m. to the N. of the deposits.

## 6—Mine of "Lagoas do Paco."—Manganese.

Location—"Freguesia" and "Concelho" of Ferreira, District of Beja.
Legal Grantee—James Lloyd.

**Director of Works—Don Jose Giron, Exhibitor.**

Commencement of labors—In 1867.
Area—50 hect. 00 ar. 00 cent.
Number of hands in 1875—60.
Production in 1875—812 tons.
The ore occurs as a deposit between the strata of the talc schists and quartzites of the laurentian age, having the same direction and inclination as the enclosing rocks.
Direction—N. 35° W.
Inclination—S.E.
Thickness—0.60 metres to 1.00 metres.

Samples—Class 100 :
1. Pyrolusite.
2. Pyrolusite.

### 7.—Mine of " Paraiso "—Manganese.

Location—"Freguesia" and "Concelho" of Aljustrel, District of Beja'
**Legal Grantee—Alonco Gomez, Exhibitor.**
**Operator,**      "            "
Commencement of labors—In 1869.
Area—49 hect. 00 ar. 00 cent.
The ore occurs in a bed between the argilaceous slates of the silurean age, which have the direction of N. 25° W., and an inclination of 70° to the east.
This mine has been very important. Its thickness is irregular, but it has reached 10 metres.
Samples—Class 100 :
1. Pyrolusite.
2. Pyrolusite.

### 8.—Mine of " Ferragudo "—Manganese.

Location—" Freguesia " and " Concelho " of Castro Verde, District of Beja
**Legal Grantee—Alonco Gomez, Exhibitor.**
**Operator,**      "            "
Commencement of labors—In 1875.
Area—38 hect. 48 ar. 00 cent.
The ore occurs in a bed between the silurian slates, having the direction of N. 50° W., and inclination to the E.
This deposit is one of the most important of the manganesian region of Alemtejo on account of the amount of the ore and by its richness.
The yield is, on an average, 70 per cent. chlorometric. Its thickness was, in the surface, of 12 metres.
Samples—Class 100.
1. Pyrolusite.          •

### 9.—Mine of " Valle de Calvo "—Manganese.

Location—" Freguesia " of Ervidel, "Concelho" of Aljustrel, District of Beja.
**Legal Grantee—Alonco Gomez, Exhibitor.**
**Operator,**      "            "
Commencement of labors—In 1869.
Area—50 hect. 00 ar. 00 cent.
The ore occurs in a bed between the silurian slates.
Direction—N.W.
Inclination—Towards the E.

Samples—Class 100.
  .1. Pyrolusite.
  2. Pyrolusite.
  3. Red quartzite (outcrops).

### 10.—Mine of "Pinhal do Cunha"—Manganese.

Location—"Freguesia" of Avintes, "Concelho" of Villa Nova de Gaya,
  District of Oporto.

**Legal Grantee—Mauricio Kamp, Exhibitor.**
**Operator,** " "

Commencemeut of labors—In 1873.
Area—50 hect. 00 ar. 00 cent.
The formation where the mine occurs is a layer which covers the
laurentian slates, constituted by sand and clay, formed on account of
the decomposition of the next granites, and the ore forms a bed of
this layer, being mixed with the sand of the same and contemporaneous with that formation, constituting a manganiferous sandstone.
This deposit is entirely different from the ones in Alemtejo.
The mineral is not of a good quality.

Samples—Class 100.
  1. Oxyds of Manganese.
  2. Oxyds of Manganese.
  3. Oxyds of Manganese.

### 11.—Mines of "Bracal" and "Malhada"—Lead.

Location—"Freguesia" and "Concelho," of Sever do Vouga, District of
  Aveiro.

**Legal Grantee—Diederick Mathias Fewerheerd & Co,, Exhibitor.**
**Operator,** " " "

Commencement of labors—In 1836.
Area of the two grants—467 hect. 49 ar. 28 cent.
No. of hands in 1874–431. Wages  { Men, - 240 to 1000 reis.
  { Boys, - 60 to 180 reis.
  { Women and Girls, 70 to 160 reis.
Production in 1874—71,600 tons of 1st quality; 197.576 tons of the sec-
  ond, and 1532 tons of the third : Total, 1801.176.
Price per ton at the mouth of the mine :
  First quality : 54$000 reis.
  Second " 47$000 reis.
  Third " 34$000 reis.
Depth of the work in the mine of Malhada—218.6 metres.
Motors employed : 6 hydraulic wheels for the extraction, pumping,
  washing, movement of the debris; 2 steam engines, one of 16

horse power that works during the dry season to extract the ore; from the German factory of A. Richard Herman de Aachen, and the other one of 14 horse power, from the English factory of Robey & Co., of London, to assist the mechanical preparation and transportation of the debris.

Enclosing rocks—Laurentian argillaceous talc schists.

Direction—N. S.

Inclination—Very changeable almost vertical.

Number of lodes ascertained—In the Mine of Malhada, 2.

Lode of Malta—E. W.

Main Lode—N. 80° E., varying between E.N.E. and E.S.E.

Inclination—70° to S. 10° W.

Thickness—Varying between 0.001 metres and 6.00 metres.

This last lode is the most important.

Let it be observed that the lode becomes poor in the direction E.N.E., and rich when it changes to E.S.E.

The principal ore is galena, being accompanied by blend, pyrite, calcareous spar and quartz.

The galena contains 0.08 grammes of silver per kilogram.

Price of cubic metre pulled out:

    Soft   rock,   800 to 1300 reis.

    Hard   "    1300 to 2000 reis.

Number of hours of labor of the miner—8.

The richest ores are exported and the third quality ones are smelted.

There is at the mechanical dressing shop the following apparatuses:

    5 sets of stampers.

    1 mill with two crushing rollers.

    7 classifiers.

    4 washing-boxes, Rutlinger's system.

    1     "            "

    1      "     Sievers' system.

    2      "     Freiberg's system.

    2 rundheerd.

    2 "debourbage" cases.

At the foundry shop there are as motors:

    1 hydraulic wheel.

    1 steam engine of 8 horse power of Robey & Co., of London.

As apparatuses:

    1 blasting engine.

    1 crushing machine.

    3 reverberatory furnaces.

    2 small blast furnaces.

    1 apparatus for the operation of "zincage;" each boiler has a capacity for 10 tons.

    1 oven for the sublimation of zinc.

    1 cupel-furnace.

Number of hands at the foundry—24. Wages, 320 to 460 reis.

The mines are situated at the shores of the river Mau; an affluent of the Vouga; they communicate with the navigable part of this river by a tramway of 9 kilometres long.

| Years. | Working Expenses. Reis. | Production, Tons. | Imposts. | Remarks. |
|---|---|---|---|---|
| 1837 to 1839<br>1840 to 1850 | } 35000$000 | 700.922 | { From 1836 to 1849 inclusive, 869$000 reis. 1850...? | The product from 1836 to 1839 inclusive, is supposed to have been of 8813 tons. |
| 1851—1852 | 12,000$000 | 236.777 | | |
| | 47,000$000 | 937.699 | | |
| 1853—1855 | 44,086$032 | 1,013.472 | { Exempt from imposts from 1854 to 1863. | It does not pay any fixed impost on account of having been granted previous to 1852. |
| 1856—1860 | 133,891$979 | 3,136.677 | | |
| 1861—1865 | 139,541$715 | 4,253.895 | } From 1864 to 1874 inclusive, 8.076$292 | |
| 1866—1870 | 166,104$739 | 7,424.814 | | |
| 1871—1874 | 213,063$720 | 7,135.655 | | |
| | 696,688$185 | 23,064.513 | 8,076$292 | The foundry of D. Fernando commenced in 1842. The mining of Malhada cemmenced in 1851. |

The labors of the mine of Braçal are at present suspended.

Samples, Class 100 :
1. Galena.
1. Schist, enclosing rock.
2. Schist,      "      "
3. Quartz.
4. Iron pyrite.
5. Calcareous spar.
6. Schistous gangue.
7. Quartz and iron pryites.
8. Calcareous spar.
9. Galena.
10. Galena.
11. Antimoniferous galena.
12. Galena in chrystals.
13. Galena in chrystals.
14. Blende with schistous gangue.
15. Blende.
16. Orbicular blende.
Products of mechanical dressing :
17. Galena and schist (mixture).
18. Sterile schist.
19. Sterile iron pyrites.
20. Galena, sieves size 32 to 22 mil.
21.    "         "     22 to 12  "
22.    "         "     16 to 12  "

23. Galena, sieves size 12 to 10   "
24.      "       "    10 to  8   "
25.      "       "     8 to  6   "
26.      "       "     6 to  4   "
27.      "       "     4 to  3   "
28.      "       "     3 to  2   "
29.      "       "     2 to  1   "
30.      "       "     1 mil.
31.      "       "     ½    "
32. Rund-heerd.
33. Lead in bar, Class 113.

### 12.—Mine of "Coval da Mo"—Lead.

Location—"Freguesia" and "Concelho," of Severdo Vouga, District of Aveiro.

**Legal Grantee—Diederick Mathias Fewerheerd & Co., Exhibitors.**
**Operator,**         "         "         "         "

Commencement of labors—In 1860.
Area—368 hect. 90 ar. 00 cent.
No. of hands in 1874–119. Wages ⎰ Men, 200 to 600 reis.
                               ⎱ Boys, 120 reis.
                                 Women and girls, 100 to 120 reis.
Production in 1874—35 tons of second quality; 307,832 of the third; total, 342,832 tons.
Price per ton at the mouth of the mine—second quality, 45$000 reis; third quality, 34$000 reis.
Depth of labors—140 metres.
Motors employed—A turbine, Schwammkrug's make; theoretical power, 167 horse power; useful power, 100 horse power; minimum, 30 horse power; making 90 revolutions per minute.
The power is divided as follows:
45 horse power for pumping purpose.
15    '    "      "   extraction.
25         "      "   mechanical dressing.
The balance of power for sawing.
The turbine is placed at the shore of the Villarinho river, 880.513 metres distant from the main shaft.
Difference of level between the turbine and the mouth of the main shaft.................................... ......... 111.248 m.
Difference of level between the mouth of the main shaft and the highest point in the ground where the wire rope passes.......................................... ......... 73.023 m.
Difference of level between this point and the turbine, 184.271 m.
The transmission of power is made by means of wire ropes, Hirn's make, of 36 wires. The pulleys are placed at distances shorter than 100 metres.
Vertical fall of the water, 43 metres.
Useful fall of the water, 42 metres.
Inside diameter of the pipes, 0.57 metres.

Diameter of the wheel, 3.50 metres.

Works with water from 100 to 300 litres.

A steam engine of Robey & Co., of Lincoln, of 16 horse-power, which substitutes the turbine during the dry season.

The apparatuses of mechauical dressing are the same as those of the Malhada mine:

4 Ruttlinger's boxes.
1 Sievers' box.
2 boxes for washing off the mud.
2 boxes for washiug (débourbage).
6 classifiers.

Hours of labor of the miners—8 hours.

The enclosing rocks of the lode are the laurentian talc schists.

Direction—N. 10° E.

Number of lodes ascertained—two.

Direction—1 lode, N. 60° to 65° E., the main one.

Direction—1 lode, E.W.

The ores found in this mine are like those of Malhada, and the collection exhibited by the mine of Malhada represents also the Mine of Coval da Mo.

| Years. | Working Expenses. Reis. | Production Tons. | Imposts. Reis. |
|---|---|---|---|
| 1860 | 1,126$300 | 3.000 | |
| 1861 to 1865 | 12,765$270 | 30.349 | |
| 1866 tó 1870 | 54,981$535 | 1,328.609 | } 84.129 |
| 1871 to 1874 | 48,796$999 | 495.252 | |
| Total....... | 117,670$104 | 1,857.210 | 84,129 |

### 13.—Mine of "Carvalhal."—Lead.

Location—" Freguesia " of Ribeira da Fraguas, " Concelho " d'Albergaria-a-Velha, District of Aveiro.

Legal Grantee.—José Maria Pinto Basto and F. Andrewes.

**Operator.—Lusitanian Mining Company, limited, Exhibitor.**

Commencement of labors—In 1856.

Area—263 hect. 06 ar. 00 cent.

The labors are very little active at present.

Production iu 1875—10 English tons.

Price per ton at the mouth of the mine—£17. 7s. 0p.

Depth of works—123,76 metres (a main shaft that follows the dip of the main lode.)

Motors employed—3 hydraulic wheels from 20 to 35 hose-power, and 1 kevel (malacate).

Enclosing rocks—Gneiss.

Number of lodes ascertained—Great, Copper, Valle and Caunter, lodes.

Direction } Group, E. to W.
{ Group S.E. to N.W.

Principal lode ——
Direction—E.W.
Inclination—52°·to the N.
Thickness—From 0.07 metres to 1.00 metres.

| Years. | Working Expenses in Reis. | Production Tons. | Imposts. |
|---|---|---|---|
| 1858 | 430$000 | None. | |
| 1859 to 1860 | 1,781$495 | 6,250 | From 1859 to 1874, 92$787 |
| 1861 to 1865 | 30,227$873 | 108,304 | |
| 1866 to 1870 | 71,134$466 | 1,016,760 | |
| 1371 to 1874 | 40,698$747 | 650,500 | |
| | 143,842$581 | 1,781,814 | 92$787 |

Apparatuses of mechanical dressing:
    8 English sieves.
    2 crushing rollers.
    1 round buddle.
    Several boxes and labyrinths.
This mine is situated on the shores of the river Caina, affluent of Vouga. Communicates by a good highway, with a station on the Northern Railroad called Estarreja, from where it is about 12 kilometres.
    The Caunter lode, second in importance, has :
Thickness—From 0.07 metres to 1.00 metres.
Direction—N. 35° W.
Inclination—60° N.
Samples—Class 100.
    1. Galena, iron pyrite.
    2. Blende.

### 14.—Mine of "Pego."—Lead.

Location—" Freguesia " of Adorigo, " Conceho " of Taboaço, District of Vizeu.
Legal Grantee—Ladislas Zarzecki.
Operator.—Bernardo Daupias & Co., Exhibitor.

Commencement of labors—In 1874.
Area—51 hect. 03 ar. 67 cent.
Number of hands in 1875—70.  Wages, 300 to 360 reis.
Production in 1875—45 tons.
Average price per ton at the mouth of the mine—57 $ 400 reis.

Depth of works in 1875—45 metres.
Motor employed—1 kevel (malacate) and washing apparatus worked
by hand.
Enclosing rocks—Cambrian slates.
Strike—N. 75° E.
Dip—N.W. (almost vertical.)
Thickness—1.00 metres approximately.

This mine is situated on the shores of the Douro river, hardly
navigable, and is about 15 kilometres from Villa do Peso da Regoa.
Samples, Class 100.
1. Galena (sample showing the thickness of the vein).
Products of mechanical dressing.
2. ⎫
3. ⎪
4. ⎬ Galena.
5. ⎪
6. ⎪
7. ⎭

### 15.—Mine of "Facuca."—Lead and Zinc.

Location—"Freguesia" of Villa Cova, "Concelho" and District of
Villa Real.

**Legal Grantee.—Agostinho Francisco Velho and others, Exhibitors.**
**Operator.—**          "          "          "          "          "

Commencement of labors—In 1872.
Area—50 hect. 00 ar. 00 cent.
Number of hands in 1875—16 to 21.
Enclosing rocks—Cambrian argillaceous slates.
Direction—N.W.
Inclination—S.W.
Number of lodes ascertained—One.
Direction—N. 20° W.
Inclination—45° to the N.E., varying to 80°. .
Thickness—0.40 metres.
Samples, Class 100.
1. Galena and gangue (iron pyrite and quartz).
2. Galena and gangue (iron pyrite and slate.
3. Galena and quartz.
4. Galena and gangue, blende iron pyrite and quartz.
5. Galena and oxydized products of lead.
6. Galena and gangue.
7. Galena and gangue.
8. Oxydized products of lead.
9. Galena and gangue.
10. Oxydized products of lead and enclosing rock.
11. Galena and gangue.
12. Pyritous slate.

### 16.—Mine of "Ribeira de Loriz."—Lead.

Location—"Freguesia" of S. Martinho do Campo, "Concelho" of
V llongo, District of Oporto.

**Legal Grantee.—Bento Rodrigues de Oliveira, Exhibitor.**
**Operator.—**      "      "      "      "

Commencement of labors—In researches.
Area—50 hect. 80 ar. 00 cent.
Enclosing rocks—Argillaceous slates.
Number of lodes ascertained—Two.
Direction—N. 25° to 30° W.
Inclination—0.44 metre.
  Samples, Class 100.
    1. Galena, iron pyrite and quartz.

### 17.—Mine os "Ribeiro da Lomba."—Lead.

Location "Freguesia" of Raiva, "Concelho" of Castello de Paiva,
District of Aveiro.

**Legal Grantee.—Visconde de Treixo, Exhibitor.**
**Operator.—**      "      "      "

Commencement of labors—In 1872.
Area—50 hect. 00 ar. 00 cent.
Depth of works—48 metres.
Motors employed—Windlasses moved by hand.
Enclosing rocks—Metamorphic slates.
Direction—N. 30° W.
Main lode.
Direction—N. 75° E.
Inclination—76° to the S.

| Years. | Working Expenses. | Production. | Imposts (Fixed). | Observations. |
|---|---|---|---|---|
| 1873 | 10,886 $ 390 | } Without | 875 reis. | } Work sus- |
| 1874 | 14,092 $ 960 | } production. | | } pended. |
| Total.. | 24,979 $ 350 | | 875 reis. | |

Samples, Class 100.
  1. Argentiferous galena, 0.3 per cent. of silver.
  2. Samples of the lode and enclosing rock containing argentifer-
    ous galena, sulphate of baryta, blende, quartz, copper pyrite,
    and argilaceous slate.

### 18.—Mine of "Castanheira."—Lead.

Location—"Freguesia" of Raiva, "Concelho" of Castello de Paiva,
District of Aveiro.

**Legal Grantee.—Visconde de Freixo, Exhibitor.**
**Operator.—**      "      "      "

Commencement of labors—In researches.

Area.—50 hect. 00 ar. 00 cent.
Enclosing rocks.—Metamorphic slates.
Direction } Very changeable.
Inclination }
Number of lodes ascertained.—Three, two only being metallized.
Direction of the metallized lodes—N.E.
Thickness—0.40 metres.
　　The workings of this mine are temporarily suspended.
　　Samples.　Class 100.
　　　　1. Argentiferous galena.　0.3 per cent of silver.
　　　　2. Samples of the lode and enclosing rock.

### 19.—Mine of " Torre Trigueiros."

**Exhibitor.—Jose Goncalves de Moraes.**

　　This mine has not yet being officially granted.
　　Samples, Class 100.
　　　　1. Galena.

### 20.—Mine of "Herdade da Prata."—Antimony.

Location—" Freguesia " of S. Thiago do Escoural, "Concelho" of
　　Montomor-o-Novo, District of Evora.
Legal Grantee—José Hygino Ferreira Castello.

**Operator—Carlos Frederico Blanck, Exhibitor.**

Commencement of labors—In 1871.
Area—50 hect. 00 ar. 00 cent.
Number of hands in 1875—Work interrupted, recommenced in 1876.
Depth of works—20 metres.
Motor employed—1 kevel ("malacate") moved by hand.
Enclosing rocks—Granite and laurentian slates.
Number of lodes ascertained—One.
Direction—N. 30° W.
Inclination—To the W.
　　This deposit is situated 200 metres from the Southeastern Railroad,
and about 1,000 metres from the "Casa Branca" station of the said
road.　This deposit has an irregular form showing itself in the contact
of the granites and laurentian slates of the region.　"Casa Branca"
station is situated 90 kilometres from a port of landing in Tagus in
the town of Barreiro.
　　Samples, Class 100.
　　　　1. Stibine.
　　　　2. Stibine.
　　　　3. Stibine.
　　　　4. Stibine.
　　　　5. Stibine and quartz.
　　　　6. Stibine and quartz.

**21.—Mine of "Ribeiro da Igreja" and "Valle d'Ache."—Antimony.**

Location—" Concelho " of Vallongo, District of Oporto.

**Legal Grantee.—" Perseveranca Company," Exhibitor.**
**Operator.—** " "

Commencement of labors—In 1832.
Enclosing rocks—Silurian slates with trilobites.
Direction of enclosing rocks—N. 10° W. magn.
Number of lodes—Two.
Direction of lode No. 1—N. 10° W. magn.
Direction of lode No. 2—N. 65° E. magn.
Direction of the lode of Valle d'Ache—N. 30° E.
These mines are situated 10 kilometres to the N. E. of the city of Oporto.
Samples, Class 100.
1. Stibine.

**22.—Mine of "Visinhanca."—Antimony.**

Location---" Freguesia " of S. Martinho do Campo, "Concelho" of Vallongo, District of Oporto.
**Legal Grantee.—Bento Rodrigues de Oliveira and Simao A. Guerreiro Exhibitor.**
**Operator.—** " " " " " " " "
Commencement of labors--This mine is hardly in researches.
Enclosing rocks---Argillaceous silurian slates.
Number of lodes---One.
Thickness---0.40 m. to 0.50 m.
Samples, Class 100.
1. Stibine and quartz.

**23.—Mine of "Mont Alto"—Antimony.**

Location.—" Freguesia " of Covéllo, "Concelho " of Gondomar, District of Oporto.

**Legal Grantee.—Antonio Martins Henriques & Co., Exhibitor.**
**Operator.—** " " " "
Commencement of labors—In 1865.
Area—98 hect. 00 ar. 00 cent.
Number of hands in 1875—150.   Wages, 100 to 1$200 reis.
Production in 1875—400 tons.
Price per ton at the mouth of the mine—76$000 reis.
Depth of works—55 metres.
Motors employed—A hydraulic wheel of 30 horse-power and a steam-engine of 15.
Enclosing rocks—Silurian argillaceous slates.
Direction—N.N.W.
Inclination—E.S.E.
Number of lodes—One working.

Direction—N.E.

Inclination—Almost vertical.

This lode forms, without doubt, part of a system of antimony lodes of Vallongo, that have a direction to the N.E. and outcrops between the same geological formation.

Samples, Class 100.

1. Stibine.
2. Stibine with quartz.
3. Enclosing rock, argillaceous slate.
4. Stibine (dressed ore).
5. Stibine (dressed ore).
6. Stibine (dressed ore).
7. Stibine (dressed ore).

## 24.—Mine of "Cortes Pereiras"—Antimony.

Location—" Freguesia " and " Concelho " of Alcoutim, District of Faro.

**Legal Grantee.—Sociedade Descobridora das Minas de Cortes Pereiras, Exhibitor.**
**Operator.—**              "              "         "      "     "     "        "

Commencement of labors—In 1865.

Area—112 hect. 35 ar. 75 cent.

Number of hands in 1875—20.   Wages, 240 to 500 reis.

Production in 1875—4 tons.

Price per ton at the mouth of the mine—36$000 reis.

Depth of works—60 metres.

Motors employed—2 kevels (" malacate ")

Enclosing rocks—Slates and grauwacks of the lower carboniferous.

Direction—N. 50° W.

Inclination—50° to 75 E°.

Number of lodes ascertained—2, of which one is hardly worked.

Direction of lode worked—N.W.

Inclinasion of lode worked—73° W.

Medium thickness of the lode worked—1 metre.

The unexplored lode has a direction of E.W.

The mine is a short distance from the landing place of Alcoutim, in Guadiana, about 5 kilometres.

This mine exported up to 1875, 325.113 tons.   At present there is very little labor carried on.

Samples, Class 100.

1. Stibine.
2. Stibine.
3. Gangue, schist and quartz.
4. Enclosing rock, slates.
5. Enclosing rock, slates with possidonomiæ.
6. Enclosing rock, slates with possidonomiæ.

### 25.—Mine of "Campo Redondo."—Antimony,

**Operator.—Maximiliano Schreck and Mauricio Kamp, Exhibitors.**

Commencement of labors—In researches.
Enclosing rocks—Argillaceous slates.
This mine is not officially recognized.
Samples, Class 100.
1. Stibine.
2. Stebine.
3. Enclosing rocks, slates.
4. Stibine and enclosing rock.

### 26.—Mine of "Palhal."—Copper.

Location—" Freguesia " of Ribeira de Fraguas, " Concelho " d'Albergaria a Velha, District of Aveiro.
Legal Grantee—José Ferreira Pinto Basto.

**Operator.—Lusitanian Mining Company, limited -Exhibitor.**

Commencement of labors—In 1864.
Area—437 hect. 22 ar. 20 cent.
Number of hands in 1875—324.   Wages, 50 to 450 reis.
Production in 1875—932,688 tons of copper ore.
Price per ton at the mouth of the mine—40$000 reis.
Depth of works—365.82 m. (of the main shaft that follows the dip of the principal lode).
Motors employed—8 hydraulic wheels and 3 kevels ("malacates").
Enclosing rocks—Gneiss and slates of the laurentian age.
Number of lodes ascertained—8.   Bastos, Branch, Mill, Bridge, Counter, House, Great Counter and Slide lodes.
Direction of main lode—E. W.   Bastos.
Inclination—70° to the N.
Thickness—1 metre.
Apparatuses of meccanical dressing: 17 English sieves, 3 round-buddles, 2 crushing rollers and 1 classifier.
This mine is situated 10 kilometers from the Estarreja railroad station, having a good means of communication.
It produces besides pyrites of copper, galena, blende, nickel ore and cobalt ore.

| Years. | Working expenses. reis. | Production. Tons. | Imports. reis. | Remarks. |
|---|---|---|---|---|
| Up to 1852 | | 48.000 | | |
| 1853 to 1855 | 21,463 $ 750 | 678.350 | | It comenced paying fixed imposts in 1858. |
| 1856 to 1860 | 129,746 $ 033 | 4,431.964 | | |
| 1861 to 1865 | 211,782 $ 426 | 6,798.255 | 9,722 $ 656 | |
| 1866 to 1870 | 223,202 $ 690 | 6,439.572 | | |
| 1871 to 1874 | 149,386 $ 076 | 3,596.840 | | |
| | 735,580 $ 975 | 21,944.981 | | |

Samples. Class 100.
1. Chalkopyrite.
2. Chalkopyrite from mechanical dressing of No, 1.
3. Chalkopyrite and quartz.
4. Chalkopyrite and quartz from mechanical dressing of No. 2.
5. Chalkopyrite.
6. Gray copper and iron pyrite, containing silver.
7. Nickeline and chalkopyrite.
8. Cobaltine, erythrine and chalkopyrite.
9. Iron pyrite.
10. Iron pyrite.
11. Gneiss, enclosing rock.
12. Gangues—quartz and calcareous spar.

There also occurs some galena with $60\frac{1}{2}$ per cent. of lead and 0.114 per cent. of silver.

### 27.—Mine of "Telhadella"—Copper.

Location—" Freguesia " of Ribeira de Fraguas, " Concelho " of Albergaria a Velha, District of Aveiro.

**Legal Grantee.—Companhia da Mina da Telhadella, Exhibitor.**
**Operator.—** " " " " "

Commencement of labors—In 1861.
Area—102 hect. 80 ar. 00 cent.
Number of hands in 1875—114 Wages, 60 to 700 reis.
Production in 1875, { Copper 97,855 kilograms } Total production,
{ Lead 46,514 kilograms } 144,369 kilograms
Depth of works—140.0 metres (in the main shaft, vertical).
Motors employed—2 hydraulic wheels.
Enclosing rocks—Gneiss and talc schists of the laurentian age.
Direction—N.S.
Inclination—E.
Number of lodes ascertained—Two : " Bocage" and " Machado."
Direction—E.W.
Inclination—60 to the N. 60 to the N.
Thickness— 0.8 metre. 0.7 metre.
Apparatuses of mechanical dressing—1 stone-breaker of the American
system of Huet & Geyler ; 2 crushing rollers ; 4 classifiers ; 3
sieves, movable ; 8 fixed sieves, system of Sievers ; 2 rund-heerd,
2 washing boxes (debourbage).

This mine is situated on the shores of the river Caima, affluent of the Vouga. It communicates by a good highway with the town of Estarreja (being 11 kilometres from it) a station of the Northern Railroad, 45 kilometres from the city of Oporto. It produces besides copper pyrites, galena, blende, and nickel ore.

Samples, Class 100.
1. Chalkopyrite, with gangue of quartz.
2. Chalkopyrite, without gangue.
3. Chalkopyrite, of mechanical dressing.

4. Galena, with quartzous gangue.
5. Galena, without gangue.
6. Galena, of mechanical dressing.
7. Blende, with gneiss gangue.
8. Blende, without gangue.
9. Blende, of mechanical dressing.
10. Nicheline, with gneiss gangue.
11. Nickeline, without gangue.
12. Nickeline, of mechanical dressing.

### 28.—Mine of "Bogalho"—Copper.

Location—" Fregusia" of S. Braz de Mattos, "Concelho" of Alandroal, District of Evora.
Legal Grantee—José Rodrigues Tocha.
**Operator.—" Companhia Portugueza de Mineracao de Cobre," Exhibitor.**
Commencement of labors—In 1866, by this Company.
Area—167 hect. 50 ar.
Number of h auds in 1875—225 ; wages, 120 to 1200 reis.
Production in 1875—250 tons.
Motors employed—A steam-engine of Wolf's system, of 50-horse power ; 2 kevels (malacates) ; 3 pumps ; 1 crusher, and 20 separating sieves.
Enclosing rocks—Laurentian talcschists.
Direction—N. 50° W. to S. 30° E.
There are three lodes, of which one is mainly worked, and has the direction of N. 50° E., and the inclination of 80° to the N.W. The other two lodes have the direction of N.S. This deposit is remarkable on account of the great yield of the ore. The thickness of this deposit reaches sometimes to six metres.
The principal gangues are the carbonates of iron, quartz, and clay.
This mine is located at 25 kilometres from the Eastern railroad.
This mine possesses an establishment of dressing ore. The extraction and pumping is made by a steam engine.
Samples, Class 100.

1. Chalkopyrite.
2.     "
3.     "
4.     "    and gangue.
5.     "     "     "
6.     "    product of mechanical dressing, selected by hand.
7.     "     "     "     "   ore washed in sieves.
8.     "     "     "     "     "     "
9.     "     "     "     "   extracted from mud.

### 29.—Mine of "Sobral," Copper.

Location—" Freguesia " of S. Bento de Pomares, Concelho and District of Evora.
**Legal Grantee.—Companhia de Mineracao Transtagana, Exhibitor.**
**Operator.—**     "     "     "

Commencement of labors—In 1863.

Area—48 hect. 00 ar. 00 cent.

Enclosing rocks are in part the granite, and in part the talc and amphibolic schists.

Direction—N. 51° W.

Inclination—N.E.

Tnis deposit has the direction of E.N.E.

The continuation of this deposit makes the object of the grant of Alpedreira mine, belonging to the same company.

This last mine is entirely enclosed in the granites, and its direction is approximately E.W.

To the west of the Sobral grant outcrop amphibolic rocks. The outcrops of these two grants can be followed a distance of 4 kilometres. The main ore is the chalkopyrite accomponied by gangues of quartz, carbonates of lime and carbonates of iron.

It is located at a distance of about 10 kilometres from the Southwestern Railroad and possesses an establishment of mechanical dressing, very complete, whose motive power is furnished by a steam engine of 10 horse power. The extraction is made by another steam engine.

Samples, Class 100.

1. Chalcopyrite.
2.    "                                                 .
3. Granite, enclosing rock to the east and west of the lode.
4.    "     with veins of quartz (region of the hanging wall of the lode).
5. Chalcopyrite (20 per cent.), product of mechanical dressing.
6.    "     (8 per cent.),    "          "          "
7.    "     and gangue·
8.    "          "     "
9.    "          "     "
10. Enclosing metamorphic schist of the lode.

### 30.—Mine of "Juliana."—Copper.

Location—" Freguesia " of Sta. Victorio, " Concelho " and District of Beja.

**Legal Grantee—Thomas Sequeira and Eduardo Carneiro de Andrade, Exhibitor.**

**Operator—**        "        "          "          "          "

Commencement of labors—In 1872.

Area—50 hect. 00 ar. 00 cent.

Depth of works—40 meters.

Motors employed—1 kevel ("malacate") and windlasses moved by men.

Enclosing rocks—Silurian slates.

Direction—N. 20° W.

Number af lodes ascetained—One.

Direction—N. 70° W.

Inclination—65° to the N. 20° W.

Average thickness—1.00 m. to 1.40 m.

The principal ores are the gray copper, sulphuret of copper and variegated copper pyrites. The gangues are mainly the carbonate of lime.

Samples, Class 100.

1. Gray copper and copper glance, with gangue of carbonate of lime.
2. Gray copper, variegated copper pyrites, copper glance and gangue of carbonate of lime.
3. Products of dressing.

### 31.—Mine of "Forrg Merendas," Copper.

Location—"Freguesia" of Vaqueiros, "Concelho" of Alcoutim, District of Faro.

Legal Grantee.—Luis Diogo da Silva.

**Operator.—Sociedade da Mina da Malhada, Exhibitor.**

Commencement of labors—1874.

Area—51 hect. 74 ar. 25 cent.

Number of hands in 1875—19. Wages, 240 to 500 reis.

Enclosing rocks—Grauwackes and argillaceous slates of the lower carboniferous.

Direction—N. 30° W.

Number of lodes ascertained—4.

Average direction. $\begin{cases} 2 \text{ to the North—N. } 62° \text{ W.} \\ 3 \text{ to the South—N. } 86° 30' \text{ W.} \end{cases}$

Inclination—75° to the N.E.

This mine is situated at 15 kilometres from the mouth of the river Odeleite, in Gaudiana, the road being somewhat difficult.

Samples, Class 100 :

1. Chalkopyrite.
2. Chalkopyrite with gangue of carbonate of lime, quartz and grauwack.
3. Chalkopyrite.
4.      "
5.      "

### 32.—Mine of "S. Domingos"—Cupreous Pyrites.

Location—"Freguesia" of Sta. Anna de Cambas, "Concelho" of Mertola, District of Beja.

Legal Grantee—Ernesto Deligny and others (Sabina Company).

**Operator.—Visconde de Mason de S. Domingos, Exhibitor.**

Commencement of labors  In 1859.

The mine of S. Domingos is situated at a distance of 14 kilometres from the Guadiana river and about 50 kilometres from the coast. This deposit is a compact mass of lenticular form, resembling perfectly a *ship;* having in the section, taken at 47 metres below the surface, its widest extension, 600 metres long and 60 metres on an average ; this extension goes on diminishing as it goes down. The general direction of this deposit is W.N.W., to E.S.E., following precisely in inclination and direction the stratification of the schists, which belong to the silurian age. The ore contains an average of 2.75 per cent. of copper and 45 to 50 per cent of sulphur dry way.

The richness in copper with all varies a little. An analysis of Pattison gives the following composition to the S. Domingoes pyrites:

| | |
|---|---:|
| Sulphur | 49.30 |
| Iron | 41.41 |
| Copper | 5.81 |
| Lead | .66 |
| Zinc | Traces. |
| Thallium | Traces. |
| Lime | .14 |
| Magnesia | Traces. |
| Arsenic | .31 |
| Oxygen | .25 |
| Gangue | 2.00 |
| Moisture | .05 |
| | 99.93 |

The S. Domingos cupreous pyrites, after being burnt to get out the sulphur, are handed over to the founders for copper and iron.

Comparative analysis of an average of a great many assays of S. Domingos cupreous pyrites and burnt copper ore give:

| | Cupreous pyrites. | Burnt Copper Ore. |
|---|---:|---:|
| Sulphur | 48.90 | 2.77 |
| Iron | 43.90 | 57.60 |
| Copper | 2.46 | 2.80 |
| Lead | .98 | 1.16 |
| Zinc | .44 | .50 |
| Arsenic | .55 | .25 |
| Silica | .70 | 5.20 |
| Oxygen | 1.12 | 27.20 |
| Lime | .20 | .25 |
| Moisture | .75 | 2.27 |
| | 100.00 | 100.00 |

The cupreous pyrites of Spain and Portugal contain a small portion of gold and silver, which the most minute analysis value them at. 0020 to .0028 per cent., or 20 to 28 grammes of precious metals in one metric ton of the residue of the pyrites burnt to manufacture sulphuric acid.

Claudet & Philipps discovered an advantageous process to extract the gold and silver. This process is based in the property that the ioduret of silver has of being almost insoluble in a solution of chloride of sodium at an ordinary temperature.

The ore is burnt, with the addition of chloride of sodium, and afterwards washed with water acidulated with chloridric acid.

These waters are treated by the ioduret of potassium, resulting in a deposit composed of sulphate of lead and ioduret of silver and gold

as, likewise, different ceramic objects, such as tiles and bricks, and large pots with handles and round bottoms. There were also found and copper salts; these are separated by being washed with chloridric acid, obtaining afterwards the cement copper by precipitation over metallic iron. The deposit is afterwards decomposed by the metallic zinc and water, resulting in soluble ioduret of zinc, that is separated by filtration, and a rich deposit in silver and gold, whose composition is as follows:

| | |
|---|---:|
| Silver | 5.95 |
| Gold | 0.06 |
| Lead | 62.28 |
| Copper | .60 |
| Oxyd of Zinc | 15.46 |
| Oxyd of Iron | 1.50 |
| Lime | 1.10 |
| Sulphuric Acid | 7.68 |
| Insoluble Residue | 1.75 |
| Oxygen and Loss | 3.62 |
| | 100.00 |

The precious metals are separated by the ordinary process.

The application of this treatment in the manufactory at Widnes, in Liverpool for the year 1871 gave over 16,300 tons of burnt ore: silver, 333.242 grammes; gold, 3.172 grammes; being worth $15,715.60. The special cost of separation, deducting charges for refining, was $2,022.80. According, however, to the samples exhibited the production for 500 tons of crude ore is:

Silver, 204 ounces, valued at $237.94
Gold, 3 " " 63.13

$301.07

This does not seem much, but if we think that England consumes an enormous quantity of pyrites, this process applied to 500,000 tons would produce a value of $301,070, which is not to be despised.

ARCHEOLOGY.—In this mine, as in many others in Portugal and Spain, we find traces of having been extensively worked by the Romans. The coins found while working show that the working of it by them must have taken place from the ending of the reign of Augustus or the accession of Tiberius until the division of the empire under Theodosius; a period of about three and a half centuries. There were found in this place traces of a population which, in all probability, belonged to the date assigned to the Roman exploration. Parts of foundations and other debris of habitation are very abundant; capitals, sockels, and fragments of columns are also found, but in very small quantities and without artistic labor on them.

There was found also alongside of the valley where the drain of the mine empties, a row of graves made with slab slates containing the remains of bones; and yet lately, in the excavations made for some buildings, they came across signs of cremation in cinerary urns:

copper objects, such as wild-boar heads, and a statuette. Among the signs of ancient labors the more worthy of mention are without doubt the large wooden wheels that, as the Tharsis mine of Spain, were found in good state of preservation, and which were used to pump the water.

·These wheels, exclusively of wood, were placed in successive steps, and the water ascended from one to the other. They were ten in number, all covered with troughs in their circumferences, having eight of them a diameter of 16 English feet, and the other two, 12. A gallery was met with made by the ancients for the draining of water, which, after being elongated, served for the modern workings. The Roman works descended more than 20 metres below this gallery. They, being only in search of the richer ores in copper, left to one side those that they considered inferior. From this we find a great irregularity in the works, which has created for the modern operators many difficulties and an increase of expenses in timbering the mine.

ACTUAL MINING.—The working of the mine is carried on in three different stories ; the first at 12 metres from the top of the mineral mass, this depth corresponding with the drain gallery. The second story is 16 metres below the first, and the third 24 metres under the second. The ground on the top of the surface of the mass of ore has a thickness of 32 metres. The principal galleries and ways of transport were made following the greatest length. They also follow the walls N. and S. of the mass. The other excavations have been made by the method of crossways. There are besides several wells that served for the extraction of the ore, and now are only used for ventilation and for direct communication between the different stories.

The principal excavations in the ore have the following dimensions: Longitudinal galleries, 2.00 m. × 2.00 m. to 7.50 m. × 8,00. Cross galleries, 1.80 m. × 1.20 m. to 4.00 m. × 6.00 m. The dimensions of the walls are of 2.20 m. × 1.10 m. in the sterile earth on the top of the ore, and 2.00 m. × 2.50 inside of the ore. The total extraction of the ore up the end of the year 1875 is represented by the following figures :
Ancient excavations caculated approximately, 150,000 cubic meters. Modern excavations, 537,086 cubic meters. Total, 687,086 cubic meters, 3,085,510 tons. The excavating is done by contract at so much per cubic meter ; the tools, gunpowder and other necessary materials are supplied to the miners by the enterprise at cost price.

The enterprise has, at the same time, for the making and repairing of the tools, a certain number of blacksmiths, by contract, to charge a fixed price for each article made or repaired ; this price comprises only the actual labor, the enterprise furnishing the work-shop, coal and other implements. The labor on the miners' tools is paid by themselves.

To diminish the cost and facilitate the mining ; to be able to increase rapidly the prodcution, if necessary, and to allow the pulling out of all the ore with less danger for the miners, it was undertaken in the year 1867, the cutting away of the sterile earth covering the mass to the depth of 32 metres. This project was quickly put in execution, and is to-day very much ahead; the surface of the ore has been already reached, and the work is at present carried on in the open air. The walls of the excavation were made in steps communicating with the surface by tunnels, and by these means the work is being carried on in different steps at the same time, and there are employed locomotives of 20 to 30 horse-power to bring out the dirt. The volume of earth taken out up to the end of 1875 is 2,134,772 cubic metres, at an expense of about £200,000, and the terrace made is used for planting olive groves and grape vines, and lately *Eucalyptus globulus*.

ORE EXTRACTION.—The extraction of the ore of the upper stories is made by locomotives of 30 horse-power, and that of the lower ones is made by a stationary steam-engine of 90 horse-power placed at about 180 metres from the mouth of the tunnel that communicates with them.

A second stationary engine works the draining of the mine, transmitting the movement to a single-acting pump at a distance of 200 metres.

DRESSING.—Several systems were tried, and until now none has given a definite result that would secure the enterprise more advantages than the exportation of the ore. The lower part of the mass is withal very poor, not bearing the cost of exportation; in order to profit the copper out of this ore, the enterprise resolved to establish a system of natural lixiviation inside the mine, by which means the water saturated with sulphate of copper is pumped and afterwards placed in precipitating tanks in contact with metallic iron to obtain the cement copper. Besides this there is a part of the ore that it is necessary to extract in the course of the work in open air that on account of its low quality cannot be exported. This ore is ground and placed in heaps at a short distance from the mine, where they are sprinkled and the water, after going through the heaps and being saturated with copper, is gathered in precipitating tanks to cement.

The pyrites in the presence of air and water are decomposed by great elevation of the temperature which helps the lixiviation.

This process will take a long time, but the quantity of copper obtained is almost the same as if the ore was previously calcinated, which is the ordinary way of the peninsula when the standard of the ore is very inferior.

EXCAVATION.—The transportation of the ore to the landing place is done over a railroad three feet six inches wide by locomotives built in Leith, in Scotland, of an average of 55 horse-power. The distance is about 17 kilometers, but in part of the way, the trafic is automatic. The construction of this road has been very difficult, with grades of 1:19 and curves of 50 metres of radius. It was necessary to have locomotives of great strength and very short; the transport reaches from 150 to 200 thousand tons. In 1875 there were employed in this service eight locomotives and 300 to 400 cars; besides this, 15 locomotives were used in extracting the ore and earth digging.

SHIPPING.—On the shores of the Guadiana river a large wharf was built, where from 1,500 to 2,000 tons can be loaded daily. The Pomarao landing is thirty miles from the mouth of the river Guadiana, and there is an annual arrival of 400 to 500 vessels, with a tonnage of 250 to 1,500 English tons.

BUILDINGS.—The population of S. Domingos, founded by the enterpise, has at present 500 dwellings, a hospital and pharmacy where the wounded are cared for gratuitously, a church, a large building wherein are the offices and also a public hall and library, besides this large factories for the construction and repairing of cars and maintainauce of the locomotives, foundries, and blacksmiths shops, &c.

The personnel of the mine is from 1,500 to 2,500 hands, according to the activity of the labors.

For the water-works two reservoirs were built to gather rain water, the larger one being able to hold from 5 to 6 million cubic metres. The consumption of water is very large on account of the treatment of the ore, besides the feeding of the steam-engines and locomotives.

The capital invested in the mine and its dependencies is as follows:

Constructions, machines, railooads...............£282,000
Stock: Material in depot............................ 30,000
Rolling stock........ ................................. 58,000
Agriculture and other sundry undertaking.... 2,500

Total........................... .........................£372,500

The principal market for the ore is England and a little in Portugal for the manufacture of chemicals.

The commercial movement of the mine is as follows:

| Years. | Working expenses. | Production in kilograms. | Prices at the mouth of the mine. | Fixed Impost. | Proportional Impost. |
|---|---|---|---|---|---|
| | Reis. | | | | Reis. |
| 1859 | | 7,887,565 | | | |
| 1860 | | 36,892,109 | | | |
| 1861 | 95,722,514 | 45,372,528 | 162,555,120 | 1,320 | 3,231,758 |
| 1862 | 108,172,104 | 69,166,737 | 231,189,818 | 1,320 | 6,150,885 |
| 1863 | 129,353,385 | 109,301,280 | 443,552,340 | 1,320 | 15,709,947 |
| 1864 | 147,828,958 | 124,968,000 | 507,129,000 | 1,320 | 17,965,002 |
| 1865 | 169,963,656 | 142,478,760 | 578,188,905 | 1,320 | 20,411,262 |
| 1866 | 184,427,600 | 167,020,240 | 850,718,250 | 1,320 | 33,314,532 |
| 1867 | 170,281,128 | 108,870,490 | 441,804,188 | 1,320 | 13,576,153 |
| 1868 | 120,934,672 | 84,595,000 | 343,455,700 | 1,320 | 11,126,051 |
| 1869 | 146,541,612 | 138,646,000 | 444,221,784 | 1,320 | 14,884,008 |
| 1870 | 287,540,682 | 189,090,000 | 529,073,920 | 1,320 | 12,076,656 |
| 1871 | 197,203,237 | 114,836,000 | 382,633,552 | 1,320 | 9,271,515 |
| 1872 | 227,746,202 | 176,949,000 | 961,186,968 | 1,320 | 36,672,038 |
| 1873 | 258,174,821 | 211,355,000 | 1,184,298,650 | 1,320 | 46,306,191 |
| 1874 | 320,758,010 | 168,700,000 | 852,441,100 | 1,320 | 26,584,154 |
| Total.... | 2,474,648,581 | 1,896,123,709 | 7,912,449,177 | 18,480 | 267,280,152 |

If we were to add to these imposts other additional ones amounting to 14,129,358

it would result paid to the treasury, - - - 281,409,510

The director of the mine, representing the enterprise in Portugal, is Mr. James Mason, who, on account of services rendered to the Portuguese Industry, was made Baron de Pomarao, and afterwards Viscount Mason de S. Domingos, by His Majesty the King of Portugal.

The director of the commercial administration is M. F. T. Barry, whom the Government of Portugal decorated Commander of the Order of Christ.

Samples, Class 100:

1. Rock, contiguous to the surface of the mass.
2. " 10 m. to the N. and 10 m. on top the surface of the mass.
3. " 15 " " N. and 10 " " " " "
4, " 35 " " S. and 40 " " " " "
5. Outcrops, 20 " S. and 32 " " " " "
6. " 35 " S. and 40 " " " " "
7. Rock, 10 " N. and 4 " " " " "
8. " 6 " S. aud 8 " " " " "
9. " 12 " S. and 12 " " " " "
10. " 5 " N. and 10 " " " " "
11. " 20 " S. and 27 " " " " "
12. Outcrops, 60 " S. and 35 " " " " "
13. Rock, 5 " N. and 3 " " " " "
14. Rock, contiguous to the side of the mass.
15. Rock, 15 m. to the N. and 20 m. on top of the surface of the mass.
16. Rock, contiguous to the side of the mass.
17. Rock, contiguous to the surface of the mass.
18. Rock, con.iguous to the side of the mass.
19. Rock, 15 m. to the S. and 10 m. on top of the surface of the mass.
20. Rock, 7 m. to the N. and 2 m. on top of the surface of the mass.
21. Rock, 10 m. to the S. and 10 m. ou top of the surface of the mass.
22. Rock, 3 m. to the N. at the level of the surface of the mass.
23. Rock, 3 m. to the N. and 4 m. on top of the surface of the mass.
24. Rock, contiguous to the surface of the mass.
25. Rock, contiguous to the surface of the mass.
26. Rock, 7 m. to the N. and 9 m. on top of the surface of the mass.
27. Rock, from the valley at 100 m. to the N. of surface of the mass.
28. Rock, from the vallley at 150 m. to the S. of surface of the mass.
29. Rubbish of ancient labors.
30. ⎫
31. ⎪
32. ⎬ Cupreous pyrites from several parts of the deposit.
33. ⎪
34. ⎭
35. Silver ingot. See Class 110.
36. Gold ingot. See Class 110.
37. Model of a Roman wheel. See Class 120.
38. Plnas of the labors. See Class 120.
39. Photographic views of the mine. See Class 120.
30. Description of the mine.

### 33.—Mines of "Aljustrel."—Cupreous Pyrites,

Location—"Freguesia" and "Concelho" of Aljustrel, district of Beja.

**Legal Grantee**—"Companhia de Mineracao Transtagana," **Exhibitor.**
**Operator**—        "        "        "        "

Commencement of labors—In 1866.

Area—179 hect. 48 ar. 63 cent.

The Aljustrel mines are the object of two grants, known by the title of *Mine of Algares* and *S. Joao do Deserto*. The first of these deposits is situated at about 1300 metres to the south of the Castello de Aljustrel, and has the direction, N. 10° W. The second one, separated from the first by a distance of 2 kilometres, is also situated at about 1300 metres from the Castello de Aljustrel, and has an average direction, E.W.

These two deposits are exactly similar and belong to the same metalliferous formation as the mines of S. Domingos, Tharsis and Rio Tinto.

They are deposits in mass intercalated in the stratification of the schists.

A cross section of the former shows from east to west :

*First.* Several outcrops of ferruginous slates and quartzites brecciaform, constituting a strip of 10 meters wide.

To these outcrops correspond a mass of pyrites, which at some 40 meters deep were found with 3.70 m. wide, with the yield in copper of 4 to 5 per cent.

*Second.* A sterile zone of 100 meters wide.

*Third.* The outcrops of a second mass visibles in a longitudinal extension of a thousand meters and over, with a width of 25 to 30 meters.

*Fourth.* A zone of porphyric rocks.

*Fifth.* A strip of slates impregnated with carbonates and sulphates of copper, in contact with the porphyric rocks, having a width of 5 metres by 800 to 1000 metres long.

*Sixth.* A strip of quartzites and metamorphic slates of 10 to 15 metres at its largest width, situated at a little distance from the cupriferous slates, following also the direction of N. 10° W.

This section, taken at the point of Moinho dos Algares, occupies a width of 270 metres more or less.

In the mine of S. Joao do Dezerto there are found similar outcrops, but not so distinct as in the other one.

The labors executed in the second mass, of which we spoke, describing the section of the mine of Algares, show that this deposit is divided in two layers, separated by a sterile stripe of slates.

The thickness of the ore of the two layers together at the central part of the labors executed is 13.40m. at the level of 56 metres; 18.50m. at the level of 70 metres; 25m. at the level of 80 metres. The labors embrace a longitudinal extension of 280 metres.

At the mine of S. Joao de Dezerto the labors embrace a longitudinal extension of 470 metres, and this deposit shows thicknesses varying between 5 and 34 metres. In any of the two deposits the labors so far executed have not reached either to all the length or depth.

The quantity of ore already ascertained by these labors is about 1,500,000 tons. These mines are now prepared for a large production, which each year may increase. The cutting in open air, lately executed in the mine of S. Joao do Dezerto, will very much facilitate the operation. In the mine of Algares there is an Addit gallery serving for the drainage and transportation of the ore, which runs at a level of 70 metres. These mines communicate now with the Southeastern railroad by a private narrow-gauge railroad, thereby having direct communication with the important harbor of Lisbon.

Table of the assays of the ore of the Aljustrel mines from the years 1868 to 1872.

| Sampling Places. | YIELD IN COPPER. | | | | | | | | | | |
|---|---|---|---|---|---|---|---|---|---|---|---|
| | 0 to 1 p. c. | 1 to 2 p. c. | 2 to 3 p. c. | 3 to 4 p. c. | 4 to 5 p. c. | 5 to 6 p. c. | 6 to 7 p. c. | 7 to 8 p. c. | 9 to10 p. c. | 13to14 p. c. | Total |
| Mine Algares { Level of 56 m. | | | 39 | 62 | 35 | 89 | 129 | 36 | | 30 | 420 |
| Level of 70 m. | | | | | | 78 | | | | | 78 |
| Level of 80 m. | | | | | | 107 | | | | | 107 |
| Total No. of Assays. | | | 39 | 62 | 35 | 274 | 129 | 36 | | 30 | 605 |
| Mine of S. Joao do Deserto. { 1st Level | 17 | 15 | 25 | 20 | | | 6 | | | | 83 |
| 2nd " | 28 | 137 | 17 | 69 | | | 25 | 4 | | | 280 |
| 3rd " | | 174 | | 39 | 74 | | | | | | 287 |
| Total No. of Assays. | 45 | 326 | 42 | 128 | 74 | | 31 | 4 | | | 650 |

These assays are not sufficiently certain to determine the average yield of the ore of the Aljustrel masses. It seems, however, that the Algares deposit is richer than the one of S. Joao do Deserto, and that the ores of high yield are relatively more frequent than in other deposits of the same nature.

The vestiges of ancient labors found in this mine are very interesting. Besides large piles of ancient rubbish, there were found small crucibles, containing yet the assay, ropes, shoes lamps, etc.

Samples, Class 100.

Algares mine
{ 1. Cupreous pyrite (level 80).
2. Cupreous pyrite (level 100).
3. Cupreous pyrite (level 70).
4. Cupreous pyrite (level 70).
4 (a). Cupriferous slates (level 70).

S. Joao do De-zerto.
{ 5. Cupreous pyrite (level of Addit).
6. Cupreous pyrite (1st level).
7. Cupreous pyrite (cuttings).
8. Cupreous pyrite (2d level).

### 34.—Mine of "Serra da Caveira"—Cupreous Pyrite.

Location—" Concelho " of Graudola, District of Lisbon.
Legal Grantee.—Ernesto Deligny, Exhibitor.
Operator.— "        "
Commencement of labors—In 1863.

Area—150 hect. 00 ar. 00 cent.

Number of hands in 1875—15 to 40.

Enclosing rocks—Slates of the lower carboniferous age.

This mine is constituted by 3 masses of cupreous pyrite, entirely embedded in the stratification of the slates and exactly similar to the mines of Aljustrel and S. Domingos.

The labors in this mine have been always small and are reduced to the cognizance of the deposit.

There are found also in this mine the vestiges of ancient labors, manifested by large piles of rubbish.

Samples, Class 100.

1. Roman rubbish.
2. Outcrops of the deposit.
3. Timber from Roman labors.
4. Enclosing rocks, slates from hanging wall.
5. Enclosing rocks, slates from foot wall.
6. Cupreous pyrite from several levels.

### 35.—Mine of "Chanca."—Cupreous Pyrite.

Location—"Freguesia" of Corte de Pinto, "Concelho" of Mertola, District of Beja.

**Legal Grantee.—F. D. Feuerheerd, Exhibitor.**
**Operator.—** " " "

Commencement of labors—In 1874 (in searches).

Area—39 hect. 47 ar. 90 cent.

Number of hands in 1875—4 to 12. Wages, 340 to 1,200 reis.

Enclosing rocks—Porphyr, diorite, and silurian argillaceous slates.

Direction—N. 45° W.

Inclination—50° to the N. E.

This deposit is of the same nature as those of S. Domingos, Aljustrel and Serra da Caveira.

The labors are, so far, limited to pickings. By the outcrops it seems that this deposit is divided in three mineral layers, separated by layers of slates, having the general direction of N. 45° W.

Samples, Class 100.

1. Cupreous pyrite.

### 36.—Mine of "Logar d'Abolm."—Tin.

Location—"Freguesia" of Rebordosa, "Concelho" of Paredes, District of Oporto.

**Legal Grantee.—"Companhia Perseveranca," Exhibitor.**
**Operator.—** " " "

Area—50 hect. 00 ar. 00 cent.

This deposit occurs in stockwerk form in a mass of porphyric granite, having the maximum width of 30 metres by 65 long.

The labors in this mine are little active.

Samples, Class 100.
1. Cassiterite in chrystals.
2. Enclosing rocks and gangues, granite, wolfram and quartz.
3. Stanniferous sands.
4. Tin in bar.  See Class 113.


**37.—Mines of "Cabeco do Codeco" and Cabeco do Raposo"—Tin.**

Location  "Freguesia" of S. Martinho d'Angueira, "Concelho" of
   Miranda do Douro, District of Bragança.

**Legal Grantee.—Companhia Mineracao de estanho de Tras-os-Montes,
   Exhibitor.**
**Operator.—**          "          "     "      "      "         "

Commencement of labors—In 1864.
Area—234 hect. 00 ar. 00 cent.
There are a great number of veins ascertained, with directions
generally W.N.W.
The enclosing rocks are the metamorphic schists of the laurentian
age.
The gangues are the quartz, mica, wolfram.
In the Cabeço do Raposo mine there are many veins distributed
in a metalliferous region of 400 metres.
The veins have several directions between N. 30° W. and N. 55° E.
The thickness of the metallized part of these veins is always very
small, not exceeding 45 centimetres.
The labors have always been very small, and the veins have not
proved themselves very rich, whether in truth they are not very rich
or the system of the useful veins is not well known.
Until 1873 the work done is in the Cabeço do Codeço mine :

Galleries.............................................. 390 metres.
Wells .............................................. 120 metres.

In the Cabeço do Raposo mine is

Galleries.............................................. 580 metres.
Wells .............................................. 120 metres.

Since then the work done has been very little, and the deposits are
not known but to a small depth.
Samples, Class 100 :
1. Cassiterite (sample showing the nature of the lode.)
1. Cassiterite (sample showing the nature of the lode.)
2. Cassiterite.
3. Cassiterite in chrystals.
4. Cassiterite in chrystals.
5. Cassiterite with slate—enclosing rock.
6. Cassiterite with slate and tourmaline.
7. Cassiterite washed, product of mechanical dressing.
8. Tin in bar.  See Class 113.

### 38.—Mine of "Outeiro dos Hujos"—Tin.

Location—"Frequesia," of Serrazes, "Concelho," of S. Pedro do Sul, District of Vizeu.

**Legal Grantee.—Companhia da Mineracao de S. Pedro do Sul, Exhibitor**
**Operator.—** " " " "

Commencement of labors—In 1869.
Area—69 hect, 60 ar. 00 cent.
There are two veins ascertained, whose direction is N. 10° W.
with a thickness of 0.10 m. to 0.70 m.
Gangue—Quartz and tourmaline.
The enclosing rocks are the metamorphic slates of the laurentian age. The granites outcrop near by.
Samples, Class 100.
    1. Cassiterite and gangue.—quartz and mica.
    2. Tin in bars. See Classs 113.

### 39.—Mine of "Senhora do Castello."—Tin.

Location—"Concelho" of Vouzella, District of Vizeu.
**Exhibitor.—Joao Correa d'Oliveira.**
This mine is not yet granted: it is situated at a short distance from the mine of Outeiro dos Hujos.
Samples, Class 100.
    1. Cassiterite and gangues, quartz and mica.
    2. Tin in bars. See Class 113.

### 40.—Mine of "Serrinha da Cascalheira"—Tin.

Location—"Freguesia" of Fontes, "Concelho" of S. Martha de Penaguiao, District of Villa Real.

**Legal Grantee.—Carlos Goldbeck and Maximiliano Schreck, Exhibitor.**
**Operator.—** " " " "

Commencement of labors—In 1871.
Area—50 hect. 00 ar. 00 cent.
Number of hands in 1875 32.
    There are eight veins ascertained with the general direction N. 37° 20' E. with great inclination towards the N.W.
Maximum thickness—60 centimetres.
Gangue—quartz.
The enclosing rocks are the metamorphic slates of the cambrian system, next to the granite.
The labors of this mine are small.
Samples, Class 100.
    1. Cassiterite and gangue—quartz and mica.

### 41.—Mine of "S. Pedro da Cova."—Coal.

Location—"Freguesia" of S. Pedro da Cova," "Concelho" of Gondomar, District of Porto.
**Legal Grantee—Conde de Farrobo.**
**Operator—Bento Rodrigues de Oliveira, Exhibitor**

Commencement of labors—in 1801.
Area—123 hect. 03 ar. 70 cent.
Number of hands in 1875—180.  Wages, 100 to 800 reis.
Production in 1875:

| First quality..... 3,456 tons. | Price per ton at the mine...3,690 reis. |
| Second quality..17,459 tons. | Price per ton at the mine...2,100 reis. |
| Third quality... 1,050 tons. | Price per ton at the mine...1,080 reis. |
| Fourth quality.. 146 tons. | Price per ton at the mine... 490 reis. |

Samples, Class 101.
1. Anthracite.
2. Enclosing rock, argillaceous slate.

| Years. | Working expenses. Reis. | Production in metrical tons. | Value of coal at the mouth of the mine. | Total imposts paid. Reis. |
|---|---|---|---|---|
| 1803 to 1805 | ? | ? | ? | ? |
| 1806 to 1820 | 138,483$658 | 54,903,157 | 207,355$225 | 71,746$409 a |
| 1821 to 1824 | ? | ? | ? | |
| '25 to Dec. 10 '48 | ? | ? | ? | b |
| Dec. 11 to 31 '48 | 688$254 | } | 1,639$440 | |
| 1849 | 10,987$839 | } 11,009:439 | 20,064$530 | |
| 1850 | 9,209$720 | } | 17,150$260 | |
| 1851 | 11,314$150 | 5,241.276 | 17,372$480 | |
| 1852 | 11,406$345 | 5,342.877 | 18,121$220 | |
| 1853 | 11,739$100 | 5,681.696 | 20,422$800 | |
| 1854 | 12,385$993 | 6,123.600 | 20,085$700 | |
| 1855 | 14,628$660 | 6,108.858 | 20,952$580 | |
| 1856 | 16,132$375 | 6,199.578 | 21,197$620 | |
| 1857 | 15,742$225 | 5,800.410 | 19,371$000 | |
| 1858 | 9,621$370 | 6,193.446 | 20,699$240 | 582$614 |
| 1859 | 10,072$110 | 6,776.380 | 22,763$020 | 667$299 |
| 1860 | 11,084$400 | 7,046.693 | 26,749$500 | 823$444 |
| 1861 | 11,939$260 | 7,514.622 | 29,095$860 | 901$748 |
| 1862 | 13,295$959 | 7,410.953 | 29,137$380 | 832$700 |
| 1863 | 14,264$905 | 8,319.920 | 32,666$820 | 967$127 |
| 1864 | 16,838$440 | 8,371.170 | 32,751$420 | 836$458 |
| 1865 | 16,657$677 | 8,549.794 | 33,722$880 | 876$950 |
| 1866 | 16,350$395 | 9,115.860 | 36,144$720 | 1,040$228 |
| 1867 | 18,815$395 | 9,127.735 | 36,304$320 | 919$214 |
| 1868 | 18,256$120 | 8,852.902 | 36,066$750 | 937$089 |
| 1869 | 16,040$885 | 8,962.044 | 36,099$920 | 1,060$484 |
| 1870 | 20,260$095 | 9,067.227 | 36,615$000 | 882$983 |
| 1871 | 21,605$962 | 9,355.632 | 38,017$740 | 920$817 |
| 1872 | 21,048$317 | 9,943.752 | 40,103$890 | 937$307 |
| 1873 | 23,422$121 | 11,024.422 | 44,834$250 | 1,137$589 |
| 1874 | 27,315$577 | 11,170.700 | 48,733$560 | 1,133$560 |
| 1848 to 1852 | 43,606$308 | 27,275.288 | 74,347$930 | |
| 1853 to 1874 | 357,516$981 | 171,035.698 | 682,535$970 | 15,457$611 |

REMARKS.—a. Profit for the State.
    b. This Mine and that of Buarcos were rented during this period
        for 10,000$000 annually.

### 42.—Mine of "Barral."—Coal.

Location—"Freguesia" of Lomba, "Concelho" of Gondomar, District of Oporto.

**Legal Grantee.—Bento Rodrigues de Oliveira, Exhibitor.**
**Operator.—** " " " "

Commencement of labors—In 1872.
Area—117 hect. 92 ar. 75 cent.
Enclosing rocks—Slates and sanstone.
Direction of the coal bed—N. 15° W.
Thickness—0.33 metres to 0.80 metres.
   Samples, Class 100.
     1. Anthracite.
     2. Enclosing rock, argillaceous slate.

### 43.—Mine of " Pijao"—Coal.

Location—"Freguesia" of S. Pedro do Paraiso, "Concelho" of Castello de Paiva, District of Aveiro.

**Legal Grantee—F. A. de Vasconcellos Pereira Cabral, Exhibitor.**
**Operator—** " " " "

Commencement of labors—In 1865.
Area—136 hect. 50 ar. 00 cent.
The coal bed has the direction of N. 30° W., having in some places a thickness of 3 metres. It belongs to the carboniferous formation of S. Pedro da Cova, and Barral.
This basin furnishes a great quantity of coal dust, which is utilized by making bricks aglomerating the coal with calcareous cement.
   Samples, Class 101.
     1. Hard anthracite.
     2. Friable anthracite.
     3. Anthracite aglomerated in rolls with calcareous cement.
     4. Anthracite aglomerated in rolls with calcareous cement.

### 44.—Mine of "Povoa de Pedorido "—Coal.

Location—"Freguesia" of Pedorido, "Concelho" of Castello de Paiva, District of Aveiro.
Legal Grantee—F. S. da Costa Couraca.

**Operator.—Companhia Union Industrial, Exhibitor.**

Commencement of labors—In 1868.
Area—90 hect. 00 ar. 00 cent.
This basin is constituted by 3 anthracite beds belonging to the carboniferous age, whose thickness varies between 0.80 metres and 1,50 metres. Its general direction is N.N.W., with the inclination of 45° to the E.N.E.
It belongs to the same carboniferous formation as the mine of S. edro da Cova.

Samples, Class 101.
1. Compact anthracite.
2. Anthracite in fragments.
3. Enclosing rocks (argillaceous fossiliferous schist).
4. Sandstone of carboniferous formation.
5. Slate of the foot wall.
6. Psamites of the hanging wall.

---

**45.—Barreto, Antonio Tavares,**
**THOMAR.**

Quinta da Granja Quarry.

**Operator—Francisco Nunes da Costa,**

Yellow limestone.
Production in 1875—265 tons.
Price at the place of production—3,100 reis per ton.

**46.—Board of Sabicheira Parrish,**
(Junta de Parochia da Sabicheira).

Valle dos Ovos Quarry.
Yellowish limestone.

**47·—Bureau of Mines,**
**LISBON.**

Marbles.

|  | Locality. |
|---|---|
| 1. White, with yellowish veins | Extremoz. |
| 2. White | Extremoz. |
| 1. White | Borba. |
| 2. Dark blue | Borba. |
| 3. Blue with white veins | Borba. |
| 1. White, with green and rose-colored stains | Alvito. |
| 2. White, with blue veins | Alvito. |
| 1. White, with yellow veins | Vianna do Alemtejo. |
| 2. White | Vianna do Alemtejo. |
| 1 to 6. Breccia | Serra da Arrabida. |

**48,—Carvalho, Wenceslau Martins de,**
**CONDEIXA-A-VELHA.**

6 samples of marble from the District of Coimbra.

# CLASSES 102 to 106,

## 49.—Direction of the Mondego and Figueira Bar Works,

### COIMBRA.

| No. | Material. | Concelho. | Locality. | Price per c. m. | Weight per c. m. |
|---|---|---|---|---|---|
| 1. | Gypsum | Soure | Soure | 1$000 reis, | 1,300 to 1,600 |
| 2. | Quicklime | Cantanhede | Andorinha | 2$000 reis, | |
| 3. | Quicklime | Cantanhede | Ançan | 2$250 reis, | |
| 4. | Quicklime | Cantanhede | Ançan | 2$100 reis, | |
| 5. | Quicklime | Cantanhede | Covões | 2$000 reis, | |
| 6. | Quicklime | Cantanhede | Zambujal | 2$000 reis, | |
| 7. | Quicklime | Coimbra | Monte Arroio | 3$000 reis, | |
| 8. | Quicklime | Coimbra | Cuzelhas | 3$000 reis, | |
| 9. | Quicklime | Coimbra | Pampilhosa | 2$000 reis, | |
| 10. | Quicklime | Condeixa | Ega | 3$900 reis, | |
| 11. | Quicklime | Figueira da Foz | Cabo Mondego | 2$400 reis, | |
| 12. | Quicklime | Figueira da Foz | Brenha | 2$400 reis, | |
| 13. | Quicklime | Figueira da Foz | Salmanha | 2$400 reis, | |
| 14. | Quicklime | Penacova | Sazes | 3$000 reis, | |
| 15. | Quicklime | Poiares | S. Miguel de Poiares | 3$000 reis, | |
| 16. | Marble | Cantanhede | Andorinha | 8$000 reis, | 2,790 |
| 17. | Marble | Cantanhede | Andorinha | 8$000 reis, | 2,720 |
| 18. | Limestone | Cantanhede | Ançan | 5$000 reis, | 2,150 |
| 19. | Limestone | Cantanhede | Ançan | 320 reis, wallstone, | 2,150 |
| 20. | Limestone | Cantanhede | Zambujal | 5$000 reis, | 2,450 |
| 20. | Limestone | Cantanhede | Zambujal | 320 reis, wallstone, | 2,450 |
| 21. | Limestone | Cantanhede | Covões | 300 reis, wallstone, | 2,500 |
| 22. | Limestone | Cantanhede | Outil | 5$000 reis, | 2,430 |
| 23. | Limestone | Coimbra | Bordalo | 4$500 reis, | 2,400 |
| 24. | Limestone | Coimbra | Povoa de S. Martinho | 4$500 reis, | 2,555 |
| 25. | Limestone | Coimbra | Cuzelhas | 2$000 reis, | 2,290 |
| 25. | Limestone | Coimbra | Cuzelhas | 600 reis, wallstone, | 2,290 |
| 26. | Limestone | Coimbra | Monte Arroio | 2$000 reis, | 2,470 |
| 26. | Limestone | Coimbra | Monte Arroio | 600 reis, wallstone, | 2,470 |

| No. | Material | Locality | Place | Price | Value |
|---|---|---|---|---|---|
| 27. | Limestone | Coimbra | Ilhastro | 5$000 reis, | 2,560 |
| 28. | Limestone | Coimbra | Pampilhosa | 300 reis, wallstone, | 2,720 |
| 29. | Limestone | Cantanhede | Outil | 4$500 reis, | 2,210 |
| 30. | Marble | Condeira | Condeira a Velha | 8$000 reis, | 2,750 |
| 31. | Marble | Condeira | Condeira a Velha | 8$000 reis, | 2,810 |
| 32. | Marble | Condeira | Condeira a Velha | 8$000 reis, | 2,675 |
| 33. | Marble | Condeira | Condeira a Velha | 8$000 reis, | 2,735 |
| 34. | Marble | Condeira | Condeira a Velha | 8$000 reis, | 2,810 |
| 35. | Marble | Condeira | Ega | 8$000 reis, | 2,830 |
| 36. | Marble | Condeira | Alto do Sangradao | 8$000 reis, | 2,810 |
| 37. | Marble | Condeira | Loureira | 9$000 reis, | 2,065 |
| 38. | Marble | Condeira | Aneixoeira | 9$000 reis, | 2,695 |
| 39. | Lithographic stone | Condeira | Ega | 7$200 reis, | 2,740 |
| 40. | Lithographic stone | Condeira | Pedreiras do Coiço | 7$200 reis, | 2,858 |
| 41. | Limestone | Condeira | Ega | 5$000 reis, | 2,565 |
| 42. | Limestone | Condeira | Ega | 400 reis, | 2,690 |
| 43. | Sandstone | Condeira | Condeira a Velha | 15$000 reis, | 2,430 |
| 44. | Limestone | Figueira da Foz | Salmanha | 600 reis, | 2,630 |
| 45. | Marble | Figueira da Foz | Salmanha | 8$000 reis, | 2,800 |
| 46. | Marble | Figueira da Foz | Salmanha | 8$000 reis, | 2,770 |
| 47. | Limestone | Figueira da Foz | Salmanha | 600 reis, | 2,705 |
| 48. | Limestone | Figueira da Foz | Salmanha | 600 reis, | 2,690 |
| 49. | Sandstone | Figueira da Foz | Salmanha | 600 reis, | 2,290 |
| 50. | Sandstone | Figueira da Foz | Salmanha | 1$200 square metre. | 2,250 |
| 51. | Limestone | Figueira da Foz | Cabo Mondego | 15$00 square metre. | 2,650 |
| 52. | Limestone | Figueira da Foz | Cabo Mondego | 600 reis, | 6,655 |
| 53. | Limestone | Figueira da Foz | Serra da Boa Viagem | 5$000 reis, | 2,600 |
| 54. | Limestone | Figueira da Foz | Dta. de Sto. Amaro | 5$000 reis, | 2,765 |
| 55. | Marble | Figueira da Foz | Pincho | 10$000 reis, | 2,745 |
| 56. | Marble | Figueira da Foz | Esperança | 10$000 reis, | 2,650 |
| 57. | Limestone | Figueira da Foz | Alhadas | 5$000 reis, | 2,215 |
| 58. | Limestone | Figueira da Foz | Boiça | 5$000 reis, | 2,240 |
| 59. | Limestone | Figueira da Foz | Carvalhal | 4$500 reis, | 2,200 |
| 60. | Limestone | Figueira da Foz | Brenha | 500 reis, | 2,745 |
| 61. | Marble | Figueira da Foz | Brenha | 9$000 reis, | 2,760 |
| 62. | Marble | Figueira da Foz | Farrestello | 9$000 reis, | 2,655 |

**49.—Continued.**

| No. | Material | Concelho | Locality | Price per c. m. | Weight per c. m. |
|---|---|---|---|---|---|
| 63. | Limestone | Figueira da Foz | Frarestello | 7$200 reis, | 2,575 |
| 64. | Limestone | Figueira da Foz | Arroella | 8$000 reis, | |
| 65. | Limestone | Figueira da Foz | Arroella | 5$000 reis, | 2,525 |
| 66. | Marble | Figueira da Foz | Arneiro de fora | 7$000 reis, | 2,790 |
| 67. | Marble | Figueira da Foz | Zam eirao | 7$000 reis, | 2,470 |
| 68. | Limestone | Montemor o Velho | Porto Barrao | 4$500 reis, | 2,650 |
| 69. | Limestone | Verride | Verride | 4$500 reis, | 2,580 |
| 70. | Limestone | Penacova | Penacova | 300 reis, | 2,785 |
| 71. | Marble | Penacova | Sazes | 9$000 reis, | 2,870 |
| 72. | Marble | Penacova | Sazes | 9$000 reis, | 2,705 |
| 73. | Sandstone | Penacova | Penacova e Friumes | 6$600 reis, | 2,370 |
| 74. | Sandstone | Penacova | Penacova e Friumes | 6$600 reis, | 2,605 |
| 75. | Marble | Penella | | | 2,725 |
| 76. | Marble | Penella | | | 2,760 |
| 77. | Marble | Penella | | | 2,670 |
| 78. | Marble | Penella | Quarries denominated Ferrarias, Fabricas, Sedadura, and Sobral, situated in the "Freguesias" of S. Miguel and Sta. Eufemia. | From 6$000 to 9$000 reis, | 2,710 |
| 79. | Marble | Penella | | | 2,750 |
| 80. | Marble | Penella | | | 2,835 |
| 81. | Marble | Penella | | | 2,730 |
| 82. | Marble | Penella | | | 2,640 |
| 83. | Marble | Penella | | | 2,840 |
| 84. | Marble | Penella | | | 2,805 |
| 85. | Marble | Penella | | | 2,770 |
| 86. | Marble | Penella | | | 2,820 |
| 87. | Marble | Penella | | | 2,835 |
| 88. | Marble | Penella | | | 2,805 |
| 89. | Marble | Penella | | | 2,735 |
| 90. | Marble | Penella | | | 2,795 |
| 91. | Marble | Penella | | | 2,890 |
| 92. | Marble | Penella | | | 2,735 |
| 93. | Limestone | Penella | Janianes | 5$000 reis, | 2,255 |
| 94. | Limestone | Penella | Janianes | 3$000 reis, | 2,340 |
| 95. | Limestone | Penella | Ponte do Espinhal | 340 reis, | 2,280 |

| | Material | Locality | Location | Price | |
|---|---|---|---|---|---|
| 96. | Sandstone | Penella | In all the "concelho." | 1$000 reis, | 2,845 |
| 97. | Sandstone | Poiares | | | 2,360 |
| 98. | Sandstone | Poiares | Near S. Miguel in the mountain of Poiares. | From 2$000 to 4$000 reis, | 2,280 |
| 99. | Sandstone | Poiares | | | 2,465 |
| 30. | Limestone | Poiares | | | 2,780 |
| 101. | Granite | Oliveira do Hospital | Bobadella | From | 2,670 |
| 102. | Granite | Oliveira do Hospital | Gramaços | | 2,565 |
| 103. | Granite | Oliveira do Hospital | Santa Ovaia | 3$000 to 4$000 reis, | 2,460 |
| 104. | Granite | Oliveira do Hospital | Lagares | | 2,450 |
| 105. | Granite | Taboa | Pedreira da Sé | From | 2,750 |
| 106. | Slate | Taboa | Espariz | 3$000 to 4$000 reis, | 2,640 |
| 107. | Lithographic stone | Coimbra | Bordallo | 6$000 reis. | |

## CLASS No. 102.

### 50.—Direction of the Public Works of the District of Coimbra. COIMBRA.

| No. | Description | Concelho | Locality | Name of the Proprietor | Price per cubic metre at the Locality. | Production in cubic metres. |
|---|---|---|---|---|---|---|
| 1. | Limestone | Cantanhede | Pena | Joaquim Nobre | | 450 |
| 2. | Limestone | Cantanhede | Portunhos | Joaquim Goncalves | | 125 |
| 3. | Limestone | Cantanhede | Ontil | Manuel Pereira & Co | 1$500 reis | 912 |
| 4. | Limestone | Cantanhede | Boica | J. F. Carmazao | | 228 |
| 5. | Limestone | Cantanhede | Ancan | Jose Fernandes | | 200 |
| 6. | Limestone | Coimbra | Nalle de Lobo | A. Peixeiro | 580 reis | 1165 |
| 7. | Limestone | Coimbra | Bordallo | Joaquim Coelho | 570 reis | 1560 |
| 8. | Limestone | Coimbra | Ilhastro | Antonio Figueiredo | 2$400 reis | 100 |
| 9. | Limestone | Coimbra | Ilhastro | Joao Ferreira Maia | 3$000 reis | 140 |
| 10. | Limestone | Coimbra | Ilhastro | M. da C. Serra | 3$000 reis | 135 |
| 11. | Limestone | Coimbra | Ilhastro | Francisco Moura | 3$000 reis | 200 |
| 12. | Limestone | Condeixa | Ameixieira | Antonio P. do Rio | 1$100 reis | 908 |
| 13. | Limestone | Condeixa | Condeixa a Velha | Antonio P. do Rio | 700 reis | 1876 |
| 14. | Limestone | Condeixa | Barroca da Judia | J. P. dos Santos | 700 reis | 620 |
| 15. | Limestone | Condeixa | Jenianes | J. Christovam | | |
| 16. | Marble | Condeixa | Ega | | | |
| 17. | Marble | Condeixa | Ega | | | 58 |
| 18. | Limestone | Condeixa | Valle das Pias | | | |
| 19. | Marble | Figueira da Foz | Salmanha | | | |
| 20. | Sandstone | Goes | Musqueiro | | | |
| 21. | Limestone | Monte Mor-Velho | Verride | | | |
| 22. | Limestone | Monte Mor-Velho | Carvalhal | Julio Maia | 600 reis | |
| 23. | Granite | Oliveira do Hospital | Sta. Ovaia | Antonio Ferreira | | 2,750 |
| 24. | Marble | Penacova | Sazes | | | |
| 25. | Marble | Penacova | Alveite | B. D. Madeira | 5$000 reis | |
| 26. | Sandstone | Poiares | Murcella | | | |
| 27. | Sandstone | Poiares | Sabonga | | | |
| 28. | Sandstone | Poiares | Ceral | | | |
| 29. | Limestone | Soure | Ceral | | | |
| 30. | Limestone | Soure | Mucifas | | | |

## CLASS No. 102.

### 51.—Direction of the Public Works of the District of Leiria.

#### LEIRIA.

| No. | Description. | Concelho. | Locality. | Names of the proprietors of the Quarries. |
|---|---|---|---|---|
| 1. | Marble | Anciao | Lagarteira | Manoel Zuarte. |
| 2. | Marble | Anciao | Lagarteira | M. Dias da Cabeça Redonda. |
| 3. | Marble | Anciao | Serrada do Lagar.. | Joaquim Pires. |
| 4. | Marble | Anciao | Serrada do Lagar.. | Joaquim Pires. |
| 5. | Marble | Anciao | Serrada do Lagar.. | Joaquim Pires. |
| 6. | Marble | Anciao | Poleiro | Joaquim Duarte Manço. |
| 7. | Granite | Pombal | Pombal | Public grounds. |
| 8. | Marble | Leiria | Opeias | Public grounde· |
| 9. | Granite | Leiria | Almointas | Public grounds. |
| 10. | Granite | Leiria | Lapa | Public grounds. |
| 11. | Granite | Leiria | S. Miguel | Public grounds. |
| 12. | Limestone | Batalha | Reguengo | Public grounds. |
| 13. | Limestone | Batalha | Lombas | Public grounds. |
| 14. | Limestone | Porto de Moz | Corredoura | João Carlos and others. |
| 15. | Limestone | Porto de Moz | Carvalhos | Public grounds. |
| 16. | Marble | Porto de Moz | Juncal. | Public grounds. |
| 17. | Marble | Porto de Moz | Alqueidão. | Public grounds. |
| 18. | Marble | Alcobaça | Nazareth | Public grounds. |
| 19. | Marble | Alcobaça | Nazareth | Public grounds. |
| 20. | Marble | Alcobaça | Nazareth | Public grounds. |

Price, 4$000 to 4$800 per cubic metre.

### 52.—Direction of Public Works of the District of Aveiro.

#### AVEIRO.

| No. | Description. | Locality. | Concelho. | Density |
|---|---|---|---|---|
| 1. | Granite | Agoncida· | Feira | 2,578 |
| 2. | Granite | Agoncida | Feira | 2,577 |
| 3. | Granite | Bustello | Oliveira d'Azumeis | 2,531 |
| 4. | Granite | Varziella | Coimbra | 2,575 |
| 5. | Granite | Serra de Perrinho | Coimbra | 2,529 |
| 6. | Granite | Anta | Coimbra | 2,547 |
| 7. | Granite | Anta | Coimbra | 2,581 |
| 8. | Granite | Gallinheiro | Coimbra | 2,573 |
| 9. | Granite | Talhadas | Agueda | 2,425 |
| 10. | Granite | Baralhas | Oliveira d'Azemeis | 2,652 |
| 11. | Granite | Crasto | Oliveira d'Azemeis | 2,568 |
| 12. | Granite | Crasto | Oliveira d'Azemeis | 2,597 |
| 13. | Granite | Sebradello | Oliveira d'Azemeis | 2,592 |
| 14 | Granite | Aguincheira | Oliveira d'Azemeis | 2,587 |
| 15. | Granite | Aguincheria | Oliveira d'Azemeis | 2,546 |
| 16. | Granite | Sêrro | Oliveira d'Azemeis | 2,500 |
| 17. | Granite | Sêrro | Oliveira d'Azemeis | 2,558 |
| 18. | Granite | Gatiande | Oliveira d'Azemeis | 2,511 |
| 19. | Gneiss | Outeiro de Sapo | Oliveira d'Azemeis | 2,597 |
| 20. | Gneiss | Outeiro de Sapo | Oliveira d'Azemeis | 2,573 |
| 21. | Gneiss | Outeiro de Sapo | Oliveira d'Azemeis | 2,491 |
| 22. | Granites | Giestosa | Arouca | 2,511 |
| 23. | Granites | Giestosa | Arouca | 2,596 |
| 24. | Granites | Caracuste | Arouca | 2,508 |
| 25. | Granites | Caracuste | Arouca | 2,588 |
| 26. | Granites | Casinha | Arouca | 2,536 |
| 27. | Granites | Sta. Marinha | Arouca | 2,513 |

| 28. Granites | Pedras Medrozas | Arouca | 2,577 |
| 29. Limestone | Seixal | Aveiro | 2,387 |
| 30. Limestone | Diversos | Anadia | 2,598 |
| 31. Limestone | S. Mathens | Anadia | 2,613 |
| 32. Limestone | S. Lourenço | Anadia | 2,578 |
| 33. Limestone | Montouro | Anadia | 2,583 |
| 34. Limestone | Matta de Tamengos | Anadia | 2,608 |
| 35. Limestone | Ancas | Anadia | 2,523 |
| 36. Limestone | Ancas | Anadia | 2,635 |
| 37. Limestone | Tamengos | Anadia | 2,658 |
| 38. Limestone | Mogofores | Anadia | 2,655 |
| 39. Red Sandstone | Villa-Nova | Anadia | 2,332 |
| 40. Yellow Sandstone | Villa-Nova | Anadia | 2,368 |
| 41. Red Sandstone | Lamas | Agueda | 2,247 |
| 42. Red Sandstone | Eirol | Aveiro | 2,550 |
| 43. Red Sandstone | Ponte da Rata | Aveiro | 2,430 |
| 44. Red Sandstone | Taipa | Aveiro | 2,492 |
| 45. Red Sandstone | Recardaes | Agueda | 2,318 |
| 46. Slate | Diversos | Estarreja | 2,229 |
| 47. Slate | Diversos | Estarreja | 2,068 |
| 48. Slate | Carvoeiro | Albergaria | 2,836 |

**53.—Direction of Public Works of the District of Oporto.**

## OPORTO.

| No. | Description. | "Concelho." | No. | Description. | "Concelho." |
| --- | --- | --- | --- | --- | --- |
| 1. | Sawed pine | Gaya | 35. | Sawed oak | Marco de Canavezes |
| 2. | Planed pine | Gaya | 36. | Planed oak | Marco de Canavezes |
| 3. | Sawed pine | Sto. Thyrso | 37. | Sawed chestnut | Gaya |
| 4. | Planed pine | Sto. Thyrso | 38. | Planed chestnut | Gaya |
| 5. | Sawed pine | Villa do Conde | 39. | Sawed chestnut | Sto. Thyrso |
| 6. | Planed pine | Villa do Conde | 40. | Planed chestnut | Sto Thyrso |
| 7. | Sawed pine | Maia | 41. | Sawed chestnut | Villa do Conde |
| 8. | Planed pine | Maia | 42. | Planed chestnut | Villa do Conde |
| 9. | Sawed pine | Penafiel | 43. | Sawed chestnut | Maia |
| 10. | Planed pine | Penafiel | 44. | Planed chestnut | Maia |
| 11. | Sawed pine | Penafiel | 45. | Sawed chestnut | Penafiel |
| 12. | Planed pine | Penafiel | 46. | Planed chestnut | Penafiel |
| 13. | Sawed pine | Maia | 47. | Sawed chestnut | Penafiel |
| 14. | Planed pine | Maia | 48. | Planed chestnut | Penafiel |
| 15. | Sawed pine | Penafiel | 49. | Sawed chestnut | Penafiel |
| 16. | Planed pine | Penafiel | 50. | Planed chestnut | Penafiel |
| 17. | Sawed pine | Marco de Canazezes | 51. | Sawed chestnut | Maia |
| 18. | Planed pine | Marco de Canazezes | 52. | Planed chestnut | Maia |
| 19. | Sawed oak | Gaya | 53. | Sawed chestnut | Penafiel |
| 20. | Planed oak | Gaya | 54. | Planed platan | Penafiel |
| 21. | Sawed oak | Sto. Thyrso | 55. | Sawed platana | Povoa |
| 22. | Planed oak | Sto. Thyrso | 56. | Planed platan | Povoa |
| 23. | Sawed oak | Villa do Conde | 57. | Sawed poplar | Penafiel |
| 24. | Planed oak | Villa do Conde | 58. | Planed poplar | Penafiel |
| 25. | Sawed oak | Maia | 59. | Sawed poplar | Gaya |
| 26. | Planed oak | Maia | 60. | Planed poplar | Gaya |
| 27. | Sawed oak | Amarante | 61. | Sawed poplar | Sto. Thyrso |
| 28. | Planed oak | Amarante | 62. | Planed poplar | Sto. Thyrso |
| 29. | Sawed oak | Penafiel | 63. | Sawed poplar | Maia |
| 30. | Planed oak | Penafiel | 64. | Planed poplar | Maia |
| 31. | Sawed oak | Maia | 65. | Sawed poplar | Penafiel |
| 32. | Planed oak | Maia | 66. | Planed poplar | Penafiel |
| 33. | Sawed oak | Penafiel | 67. | Sawed poplar | Penafiel |
| 34. | Planed oak | Penafiel | 68. | Planed poplar | Penafiel |

| | | | |
|---|---|---|---|
| 69. Sawed poplar....................Maia | 102. Granite.............................Maia |
| 70. Planed poplar...................Maia | 103. Granite.......................Penafiel |
| 71. Sawed walnut................Penafiel | 104. Granite........Marco de Canareses |
| 72. Planed walnut................Penafiel | 105. Granite..........................Paredes |
| 73. Sawed walnut.....................Gaya | 106. Graniie...........................Maia |
| 74. Planed walnut.. ................Gaya | 107. Granite..........................Oporto |
| 75. Sawed walnut.............St. Thyrso | 108. Granite...........................Maia |
| 76. Planed walnut............St. Thyrso | 109. Granite.......................Penafiel |
| 77. Sawed walnut.......Villa do Conde | 110. Quartz.............................Maia |
| 78. Planed walnut......Villa do Conde | 111. Quartz.................St. Thyrso |
| 79. Sawed walnut.....................Maia | 112. Quartz.............................Gaya |
| 80. Planed walnut....................Maia | 113. Quartz..........Villa do Conde |
| 81. Sawed walnut.................Penafiel | 114. Quartz.....................Penafiel |
| 82. Planed walnut............ ...Penafiel | 115. Slate............................Vallongo |
| 83. Sawed walnut...............Maia | 116. Slate......... ...............Vallongo |
| 84. Planed walnut...................Maia | 117. Slate............................Povoa |
| 85. Sawed walnut...................Penafiel | 118. Sandstone........ .........Paredes |
| 86 Planed walnut..... .........Penaflel | 119. Quartzite....................Vallongo |
| 87. Sawed cork wood..............Maia | 120. Quartz..... ..............Vallongo |
| 88. Planed cork wood..............Maia | 121. Quartz..........................Vallongo |
| 89. Sawed cork wood..............Maia | 122. Sandstone....................Vallongo |
| 90. Planed cork wood.............Maia | 123. Sandstone.................St. Thyrso |
| 91. Granite..........................Boucas | 124. Quartzite..................Amarante |
| 92. Granite............................Oporto | 125. Quartzite.................Amarante |
| 93. Granite..........................Boucas | 126. Iron ore...........................Povoa |
| 94. Granite..............................Gaya | 127. Slate.............................Povoa |
| 95. Granite...........................Penafiel | 128. Slate...........................Povoa |
| 96. Granite................ ......St. Thyrso | 129. Granite..........................Gaya |
| 97. Granite..................................Gaya | 130. Slate..............................Gaya |
| 98. Granite.............................Gaya | 131. Paving brick.....................Gaya |
| 99. Granite..............................Gaya | 132. Brick.............................Gaya |
| 100. Granite...........................Penafiel | 133. Brick............................Gaya |
| 101. Granite................ ............Penafiel | 134. Tile..................................Gaya |

NOTE.—The woods are not separated from the stones on account of being a collective exhibit.

---

CLASS No. 102.

**54.—Direotion of Public Works of Vizeu.**

**VIZEU.**

| No. | Description. | Locality. | "Concelho." |
|---|---|---|---|
| 1. | Porphyritic granite..............Monte da Povoa.............................. | Lamego. |
| 2. | Fine granite.......................S. Domingos..................................... | Lamego. |
| 3. | Porphyritic granite.............Monte da Penuda.......................... | Lamego. |
| 4. | Fine granite.......................Monte da Penuda.......................... | Lamego. |
| 5. | Coarse granite...................Monte da Penuda.......................... | Lamego. |
| 6. | Fine granite.......................Monte de Lenhos........................ | Mangualde. |
| 7. | Coarse granite...................Santo Antonio de Cabaços........... | Mangualde. |
| 8. | Fine granite.......................Senhora de Castello...................... | Mangualde. |
| 9. | Fine granite......... ... .......Monte de Pamuigos...................... | Lamego. |
| 10. | Coarse granite...................Monte de Valle de Maias................ | Lamego. |
| 11. | Fine granite......................Senhora de Castello.................... | Mangualde. |
| 12. | Very fine granite...............Monte do Castello....................... | Mangualde. |

**54.—Continued.**

| No. | Woods. | Botanical Name. | Concelhos. |
|---|---|---|---|
| 1. | Walnut | Fuglans regia (Lin.) | Taboaço |
| 2. | Cherry | Prunus cerasus (Lin.) | Taboaço. |
| 3. | Pine | Pinus maritima (Lin.) | Sinfaes. |
| 4. | Chestnut | Castanea vulgaris (Lin.) | Sinfaes. |
| 5. | Oak | Quercus robur (Lin.) | Sinfaes |
| 6. | Chestnut | Castanea vulgaris (Lin.) | Rezende. |
| 7. | Cherry | Prunus cerasus (Lin.) | Rezende. |
| 8. | Walnut | Fuglans regia (Lin.) | Rezende. |
| 9. | Pine | Pinus maritima (Lin.) | Mortagoa. |
| 10. | Oak | Quercus robur (Lin.) | Mortagoa. |
| 11. | Chestnut | Castanea vulgaris (Lin.) | Mortagoa. |

NOTE.—The exhibits are not separated on account of being a collective exhibit of building materials.

---

## CLASSES Nos. 102, 206, 207, 208 AND 600.

**55.—Direction of the Public Works of the District of Braga.**

| No. | Description. | "Concelho." | Locality. | Price per c. m. |
|---|---|---|---|---|
| 1. | Granite | Braga | Monte Pedroso | 4$000 reis |
| 2. | Granite | Barcellos | Penedo do Ladrao | 4$000 reis |
| 3. | Granite | Guimaraes | Mte. de S. Eufemia | 3$600 reis |
| 4. | Granite | Braga | Mte. das Caldas | 4$000 reis |
| 5. | Granite | Barcellos | Mte. da Penida | 4$500 reis |
| 6. | Granite | Guimaraes | Mte. de S. Martinho | 3$600 reis |
| 7. | Granite | Braga | Mte. de Castro | 4$500 reis |
| 8. | Granite | Fafe | Mte. de S. Jorge | 4$000 reis |
| 9. | Granite | Guimaraes | Mte. de Sabroso | 4$000 reis |
| 10. | Porphyr granite | Guimaraes | Mte. de S. Jorge | 3$500 reis |
| 11. | Granite | Amares | Mte. de S. Martha | 3$800 reis |
| 12. | Granite | Famalicao | Mte. de Mogeiges | 4$000 reis |
| 13. | Granite | Povoa de Lanhoso | Mte. do Carvo d'Est.e. | 4$000 reis |
| 14. | Granite | Famalicao | Mte. de Mogeiges | 4$200 reis |
| 15. | Granite | Amares | Mte. de S. Martha | 4$000 reis |
| 16. | Granite | Esposende | Faro de Palmeira | 4$000 reis |
| 17. | Granite | Villa Verde | Pesa Folles | 3$500 reis |
| 18. | Granite | Arcos | Carqueijal | 3$800 reis |
| 19. | Granite | Barca | Mte. da Naia | 4$000 reis |
| 20. | Porphyr granite | Feigueiras | Mte. de S. Joao | 3$000 reis |

| No. | Description | Concelho | Locality | Price |
|---|---|---|---|---|
| 1. | Gravel | Barcellos | Barcello | 100 |
| 2. | Gravel | Povoa de Varzim | Povoa de Varzim | 300 |
| 3. | Black earth | Famalicao | Terra Negra | 15$000 |
| 4. | Ferruginous clay | Barcellos | Telheiras | 1$000 |
| 5. | Plastic clay | Barcellos | Telheiras | 600 |
| 6. | Sand | Braga | Rio d'Este | 430 |
| 7. | Plastic clay | Barcellos | Telheiras | 600 |
| 8. | Figuline clay | Villa Verde | Prado | 400 |
| 9. | Fragments of quartz and granite | Braga | Confeiteira | 800 |
| 10. | Gravel | Braga | Area | 400 |

| No. | Description | Concelho | Locality | Price |
|---|---|---|---|---|
| 1. | Straight Clay Tube | Villa Verde | Lugar de Penedo | 100 reis each tube |
| 2. | Curved Clay Tube | Villa Verde | Lugar de Penedo | 100 reis each tube |
| 3. | Brick for Vaults | Braga | S. Bras do Carmo | 750 reis per hundred |
| 4. | Brick for Vaults | Braga | S. Bras do Carmo | 750 reis per hundred |

```
 1. Straight clay tube......Barcellos .....Lugar de Sto. Amaro....    90 each tube
 2. Curved clay tube.......Barcellos ....Lugar de Sto. Amaro...    90 each tube'
 3. Brick for pavements...Braga .........S. Bras da Carmo.........2$500 per hundred
 4. Brick for vaults.........Barcellos ...Telheiras ..................5$000 per hundred
 5. Brick for pavement....Barcellos ...Telheiras ...................4$000 per hundred
 6. Brick for vaults.........Barcellos ...Telheiras ....................  500 per hundred
 7. Tile for gutter...........Braga .........S. Bras da Carmo.........4$000 per hundred
 8. Tile for gutter..........Barcellos ...Telheiras ...................4$000 per hundred
 9. First quality tile.......Braga .........S. Bras da Carmo........ · 900 per hundred
10. Ordinary tile............Braga .........S Bras da Carmo........   550 per hundred
11. Tile of "propianho"....Braga .........S. Bras da Carmo........   450 per hundred
12. Covering tile ...........Barcellos ...Telheiras ...................2$000 per hundred
13. Ridge tile...............Barcellos ...Telheiras ...................3$000 per hundred
14. Ordinary tile............Barcellos ...Telheiras.........  : .......   400 per hundred
15. Clay to make tiles.....Barcellos ...Telheiras....................   600 per cubic m.
16. Covering tile...........Barcellos ...Telheiras ...................1$500 per hundred
17. Guttering tile...........Barcellos ...Telheiras ...................1$200 per hundred
18. Ordinary tile............Barcellos ...Telheiras ..................   420 per hundred
```

```
 1. Chestnut, Castanea Vulgaris (Lin)......Famalicao...........Calendario .....30$000
 2. Pear.......Pyrus Comunnis (Lin)........Braga..............Barrio...........45$000
 3. Ash......Fraxinus Excelsior (Lin)....Terras do Bouro...Lugar da Cruz50$000
 4. Oak......Quercus robur (Lin) ..........Povoa de Lanhozo, Simaes...........25$000
 5. Pine......Pinus Maritina (Lin)..........Guimaraes ........Brito ............10$000
 6. Olive ....Olea Europoea (Lin).........Braga...............Cedafeito .... ...36$000
 7. Plantan Acer-pseudo-plantanus(Lin), Terras do Bouro...Penhalonga....36$000
 8. Cherry...Prunnus Cerasus (Lin).......Braga...............Esparoes........25$000
 9. Cork .....Quercus Suber (Lin).........Braga.............Sete Fontes.....35$000
10. Walnut..Juglans regia (Lin)..........Braga..............Lijo... .........35$000
```

NOTE.—The exhibits are not separated on account of being a collective exhibit of building materials.

## 56—Direction of the Public Works of the District of Vianna do Castello

### VIANNA DO CASTELLO.

| Nos. | Description. | Locality. | Concelho. | Price at the quarry Reis. | Price pr. c. m. where used. Reis. |
|---|---|---|---|---|---|
| 1. | Granite ..Quarry of Rego da Fonte....... | Vianna do Castello | .....3$440 | 6$440 |
| 2. | Granite ..Monte de Affife.................... | Vianna do Castello | .....3$440 | 6$440 |
| 3. | Granite ..Monte de Anha................... | Vianna do Castello | .....2$180 | 3$680 |
| 4. | Granite ..Quarry of Monte de Meadella.. | Vianna do Castello | .....2$100 | 3$300 |
| 5. | Granite ..Quarry of Monte de Meadella.. | Vianna do Castello | .....1$300 | 2$500 |
| 6. | Granite ..Quarry of Monte de Meadella.. | Vianna do Castello | .....  480 | 900 |
| 7. | Granite ..From the bottom of the dock under construction in Vianna do Castello. | | .............................. | 240 | 450 |
| 8. | Granite ..Monte das Pedras finas.......... | Ponte de Lima | ........3$300 | 5$000 |
| 9. | Granite ..Monte de S. Gançalo............ | Ponte de Lima | ........3$200 | 4$200 |
| 10. | Granite ..Monte da Snra. da Conceiçao ... | Ponte de Lima | ........3$100 | 4$000 |
| 11. | Granite ..Monte de Santo Ovidio .......... | Ponte de Lima | ........  720 | 1$620 |
| 12. | Granite ..Quarry of Sabadao ................ | Ponte de Lima | ........3$900 | 4$800 |
| 13. | Granite ..Quarry of Sabadao................ | Ponte de Lima | ........  800 | 1$520 |
| 14. | Granite ..Quarry of Santa Cruz ........... | Ponte de Lima | ........  .... | 400 |
| 15. | Granite ..Valle de Escadas ................. | Ponte da Barca | .....2$800 | 5$000 |
| 16. | Granite ..Quarry of Sobredo.............. | Ponte da Barca | ........3$200 | 4$800 |
| 17. | Granite ..Logar de Naia.................... | Ponte da Barca | ........2$000 | 5$000 |
| 18. | Granite .Quarry of Peralva................ | Ponte da Barca | ........3$200 | 5$000 |

19. Granite ..Quarry of Taveças.................Arcos de Val de Vez...1$500   2$300
20. Granite ..Quarry of Ramalheira............Arcos de Val de Vez..1$800   4$000
21. Granite ..Quarry of Tavarella...............Arcos de Val de Vez..3$200   3$200
22. Granite ..Quarry of Penoças.................Arcos de Val de Vez..3$200   5$000
23. Granite ..Monte da Snra. da Graça........Monsao...............3$200   5$000
24. Granite ..Monte da Galvao...................Monsao.................2$100   3$100
25. Granite ..Monte da Prado.....................Melgaço .................2$100   3$100
26. Granite ..Monte da Prado.....................Melgaço .................3$200   4$200
27. Granite ..Marco de Ganfey....................Valença.....................   1$500
28. Granite ..Marco de Ganfey....................Valença....................   9$000
29. Granite ..Quarry of Areal do Prado........V. N. da Cerveira......1$200   2$000
30. Granite ..Monte de Goios.....................Caminha..................3$000   5$440
31. Granite ..Quarry of Lanhelas...............Caminha..................1$900   3$100
32. Granite ..Monte do Facho.....................Caminha.................3$300   5$740
33. Slate......Costa do Oceano....................Vianna do Castello.....3$535   4$255
34. Slate......Costa do Oceano....................Vianna do Castello ...3$200   3$920
35. Slate......Sitio da Fonte........................Vianna do Castello.....   400   2$500
36. Slate.....Valle das Flores......................Vianna do Castello....   320   1$820
37. Slate.....Talhazeres ...........................Vianna do Castello.....   300   1$800
38. Slate.....S. Joao.................................Vianna do Castello.....   280   1$240
41 to 60. Tiles, large tiles, bricks, drain pipes.

Worked.
Per c.m.

61. Chestnut ......Fagus Castanea (Lin.).........Vianna do Castello...22 to 35$000
62. Oak............Quercus robur (Lin.)...........Vianna do Castello...15 to 24$000
63. Corkwood.....Quercus suber (Lin.)...........Vianna do Castello...18 to 26$000
64. Pine ...........Pinus pinea (Lin.).............Vianna do Castello...12 to 20$000
68. Chestnut ......Tagus Castanea (Lin.).........Vianna do Castello...20 to 24$000
69. Pine ...........Pinus sylvestris (Lin.).........................................12 to 20$000
70. Chestnut ......Fagus Castanea (Lin.).........Vianna do Castello...20 to 24$000
71. Pine ...........Pinus pinaster (Sol.)...........Vianna do Castello...12 to 20$000
72 to 79. 8 samples of mortar manufactured at Vianna do Castello, prices ranging 5$750, 5$330, 4$535, 4$520, 3$980, 4$220, 4$200.
80 and 81. 2 samples of Beton manufactured at Vianna do Castello.
82. Lime ...............Algarve ..................................................... 9$600
83. Lime ...............Algarve ...................In limestone before burning... 9$600
84. Lime ...............Lisbon ..................................................... 8$750
85. Lime ...............Coimbra..................................................... 8$865
86. Coarse sand..............Bar of Lima .....................Vianna.................... 113
87. Fine sand ..............Bar of Lima .....................Vianna.................... 124
88. Fine sand ..............Monte da Anha...................Vianna.................... 250
89. Sifted sand...............Bar of Minho'river .........Vianna.................... 213
90. Granite powder waste. ..........
91. Mina sand..............Darque....................Vianna.................... 1$080
92. Pozzuolana..............Meadella....................Vianna.................... 7$200
93. Pozzuolana..............S. Miguel Island..............Vianna.................... 5$566
94. Limestone...............Ancos quarry....................Aveiro.............. ... 4$750
95. Limestone...............Algarve quarry.................................. 4$100
96. Limestone...............Suburbs of Lisbon............................... 3$215
97. Limestone...............Coimbra........................................... 3$335
Broken stone for causeways from :
98. Gandra..............................................Arcos de Valde Ves.............. 400
99. Scroas.....................................Barca................................. 500
100. Frega. da Feitosa.......................Ponte do Lima.................... 500
101. ........................................................................... 360
102. Monte de Camena................................................. 960
103. Portella de S. Simao...................Bridge of Nerva... ................. 600
104. Quarry of Camande.....................Caminha......................'.......... 600
105. Quarry of Monte de Camande.........Vianna........................... 450
106. Monte de S. Ovidio.....................Ponte do Lenia.................... 600

107. Monte de Lages............................Ponte do Lenia...................... 840
108. Freguesia de Baiaes........................Barea............................ ............ 550
109. Freguesia de Oleiros.......................Barea............ .................... 550
110. Fregvesia de Covas........................Villa Verde........... ............. 600
111. S. Joao da Ribeira.........................Ponte do Lima.......... ........... 700
112. Monte do Prado............... .............Ponte do Lima... ... ............... 800
113. Alluvial deposits.................................................................. 560
114. Freguesia de Fornellos.............. .....Ponte do Lima.................... 550
115. Convento dos Cruzios..................Vianná do Castello................ 1$800
116. Monte dos Lagos............................Ponte do Lima...... ............... 1$700
117. Black locust...Robinia pseudo acacia ( Lin.).
118. Laurel ........Laurus nobilis (Lin.)..........Vianna do Castello...   12$740
119. Cherry........Prunus cerasus (Lin.).........Vianna do Castello...   16$360
120. Poplar .......Populus nigra (Lin.)..........Vianna do Castello...   10$920
121. Walnut ........Juglans regia (Lin.)..........Vianna do Castello...   34$600
122. Pear.............Pyrus communis (Lin.)........Vianna do Castello...   29$120
123. Ash.............Fraxinus excelsior (Lin)......Vianna do Castello...   38$220
124. Olive ..........Olea Europea (Lin.)............Vianna do Castello...18 to 20$000

Note.—The exhibits are not separated on account of being a collective exhibit of building materials.

CLASS No. 102.

**57.—Extremoz Marble Quarrying Company,**
EXTREMOZ.

Four samples of marble.

Paice on Board.

No. 1. White.............................22$000 ⎫
No. 2. Rose color......................22$000 ⎪ Price at the place of production per
No. 3. Yellow...........................24$000 ⎬ cubic metre from 12$000to 20$000reis.
No. 4. Blue .............................27$000 ⎭

Employs 19 workmen.
Wages from 280 to 420 reis.
Raw materials from Extremoz and Borba.
Annual production—4,000$000 reis.
Markets—Portugal and Spain.

**58.—Sales, Germano Jose de,**
LISBON.

Marbles.

1. 1 from Pero Pinheiro............22$500 reis per cubic metre.
2. 1 from Porto Salvo...............11$000 reis per cubic metre.
3. 1 from Cintra........................26$000 reis per cubic metre.
4. 1 from S. Pedro.....................28$000 reis per cubic metre.
5. 1 from Negraes.......................24$000 reis per cubic metre.
6. 1 from Maceira.....................25$000 reis per cubic metre.
7. 1 from Carrasqueira..............25$000 reis per cubic metre.
8. 1 from S. Pedro....................28$000 reis per cubic metre.
9. 1 from Arrabida......................36$000 reis per cubic metre.
10. 1 from Arrabida...................36$000 reis per cubic metre.
11. 1 from Monte de Luiz............40$000 reis per cubic metre.

12. 1 from Montes Claros...............40$000 reis per cubic metre.
13. 1 from Moura........................40$000 reis per cubic metre.
14. 1 from Montes Claros............40$000 reis per cubic metre.
15. 1 from Montes Claros............40$000 reis per cubic metre.
16. 1 from Montes Claros............40$000 reis per cubic metre.
17. 1 from Montes Claros............40$000 reis per cubic metre.
18. 1 from S. Cruz do Tojal.........28$000 reis per cubic metre.
19. 1 granite from Oporto.............30$000 reis per cubic metre.
20. 1 granite from Lameira........... 1$100 reis per cubic metre.
21. 1 granite from Mattos d'Alvíde    550 reis per cubic metre.
22. 1 granite from Passo d'Arcos... 1$900 reis per cubic metre.
23. 1 granite from S. Domingos de
        Rana...............................    650 reis per cubic metre.
24. 1 granite from S. Domingos.de
        Rana.......................... 1$100 reis per cubic metre.

5 mortars from Péro Pinheiro, thus :

No. 1.....................    900 reis.
No. 2.....................1$000 reis.
No. 3.....................1$200 reis.
No. 4.....................1$700 reis.
No. 5.....................2$500 reis.

A freestone measuring 1.20m. × 0.37m. × 0.42m.

**59.—Manilha, Francisco dos Santos Lopes,**
                                           **VALLONGO.**
School Slates and Slate Pencils.

------

CLASSES Nos. 102, 103, and 104.

**60. Administrative Board of Ponta Delgada Artificial Harbor Works.**

1. Trachyte.—Hewn and rubble stone, in the localities where there
    is no other building stone; very easy to cut in blocks of any
    size.
2. Basalt.—Hewn stone of inferior quality to remain in sight in
    buildings of a superior construction, but very proper to be ap-
    plied in them as an imitation of hewn stone, when covered with
    cement, which adheres very well to the asperities of the stone ;
    hewn and rubble stone in inferior constructions.
3. Basalt.—Very hard and difficult to hew; on that account not
    employed as hewn stone, but only as rubble and loose stone ;
    the best loose stone in the breakwater.
4. Basalt—Second-class hewn stone, usually employed, being the
    most vulgar,
5. Basalt.—First-class hewn stone, for buildings of a superior con-
    struction, rare enough.
6. Small Volcanic Scoriæ (red).—Used as ballasting for rail and
    macadamized roads, and for garden and park alleys.
7. Small Volcanic Scoriæ (black).— Analogous, except in colour,
    to those of No 1, but not so much used in park and garden al-
    leys on account of the colour.

8. Volcanic Scoriæ in Broken Stone.—Broken stone proceeding directly and naturally from the mining and fall of basalt quarries, and serving with economy for all the applications of artificial broken stone, as for ballasting of macadamized roads and fabrication of concretes, as those of No. 6 and No. 8.
9. Volcanic Scoriæ.—Same nature and application, after broken. as No. 3.
10. Volcanic Tuff.—Analogous to No. 1 in employments.
11. Pozzuolana.—Volcanic argil, employed with great success to give when mixed with lime not hydraulic or slightly hydraulic the properties which the latter requires for composing hydraulic mortars : very abundant in St. Michaels, and explored in great scale in the suburbs of Ponta Delgada for the buildings of the locality and for exportation to the continent of Portugal. It is generally employed in all the public works of the country.

The analysis made at the " École des Ponts et Chaussées," of Paris, prove it to be the best of pozzuolanas.

In constructions out of water, or in hydraulic works by tides, or in fresh water, the masonry is made with mortar composed of 1 part of lime to 3 parts of pozzuolana, using lime (not hydraulic) for the first kind of works, and slightly hydraulic lime for the second. For works constantly exposed to the sea, slightly hydraulic lime, pozzuolana and coarse sand must be mixed together in equal columns.
12. Tetin.—Volcanic argil, only profitable as ochre, coloring substance.
13. Coarse Sea Sand.—Used in hydraulic mortars for works constantly exposed to the sea, as specimen No. 8.
14. Specimen of Mortar.—Three parts of pozzuolana to one of slightly hydraulic lime of Portugal, for the uses explained at No. 4.
15. Double T of Hydraulic Mortar.—Composition of Specimen No. 6 ; intended to prove its resistance in being pulled up.
16. Artificial Stone-Concrete.

Hydraulic mortar : 1 (volume) of pozzuolana, No. 4.
        1 (volume) of sand, No. 7.
        1 (volume) of lime (slightly hydraulic) of Portugal,
      Broken stone (natural), No. 3.
17. Plastic Clay.—For making tiles, pipes, &c.
18. Tiles.—For covering roofs ; before baking and when baked.

**61.—Bureau of Districtal Public Works of Ponta Delgada.**

| No. | Description. | Observations. |
|---|---|---|
| 1. | Basalt | Employed for unhewn stones and to build breakwaters. |
| 2. | Frachyte | Employed for unhewn stones and free stone. |
| 3. | Basalt | Employed for second-class free stone. |

4. Basalt..............................Employed for lower quality free stone.
5. Volcanic soft gravel stone......Employed for unhewn stone.
6. Artificial stone........................This stone is formed with broken stone and plaster, whose composition in volumes is three of pozzuolana to one of coarse lime.
7. Pozzuolana............................This clay is combined with coarse lime in the following proportions:

Three parts of pozzuolana to one of lime makes a mortar imminently hydraulic and adapted for building in sweet water, but when it has to be used in buildings exposed to sea water there ought then to be used lime moderately hydraulic, pozzuolana and coarse sand in equal quantities.

8. Tetim............................Used as ochre.
9. Sundry objects........................A cube of 0.1 $\times$ 0.1 of second-class basalt for free stones, another of 0.24 $\times$ 0.10 of first quality for the same: small pieces of stone, volcanic rubbish, employed as broken stones in roads: a brick for the purpose of testing the resistance of the pozzuolana at the pulling out.
10. Volcanic rubbish....................Employed as gravel on the roads.
11. Clay........................................Employed for the manufacture of tiles, drains,&c.

---

CLASS No. 102.

**62.—Rato, Antonio Moreira,**

**LISBON.**

Bas relief in " lioz " stone, with marble moulding, representing commerce, industry and arts. Price, 450$000 reis.

Samples of marbles:

| No. | Shade. | Place of production. | Price pr.c.m. |
|---|---|---|---|
| 1. | Rose coloured | Pero Pinheiro | 22$500 reis |
| 2. | Flesh coloured | Pero Pinheiro | 22$500 reis |
| 3. | Red | Pero Pinheiro | 22$500 reis |
| 4. | Red | Pero Pinheiro | 22$500 reis |
| 5. | Lioz | Pero Pinheiro | 22$500 reis |
| 6. | Vidraço | Pero Pinheiro | 22$500 reis |
| 7. | Yellow | Pedra Furada | 22$500 reis |
| 8. | Flesh coloured | Pedra Furada | 22$500 reis |
| 9. | Blue | Cintra | 22$500 reis |
| 10. | Black | Cintra | 22$500 reis |
| 11. | Breccia | Arrabida | 28$200 reis |
| 12. | Hypuritic | Tojal | 22$500 reis |
| 13. | Purple | Largateira | 28$200 reis |
| 14. | White | Extremoz | 28$200 reis |
| 15. | Yellow | Extremoz | 28$200 reis |
| 16. | Vidraço | Oeiras | 15$000 reis |

Four flower-stands and six " consolas " of marble.
A slab from Pero Pinheiro, 1 square metre, 3$300 reis.
A slab from Paço d'Arcos, " " 1$000 reis.
Granite from Oporto, " " 28$000 reis.

Granite from Cascaes,  1 square  metre,  20$000 reis.
Basalt from Oeiras,            "        "     1$300 reis.
Building stone from Pero Pinheiro.
    Worked—One metre, 24$000 reis.
    Rough state—One metre, 20$000 reis.
    Seps for gardens—Pero Pinheiro, one metre, 24$000 reis.
Worked stone for building from Paço d'Arcos.
    Worked—One metre, 14$000 reis.
    Rough state—One metre, 8$000 reis.
Stones for walling purposes from Oeiras.
    Worked—One metre, 9$000 reis.
    Rough state—One metre, 7$000 reis.
Main office—Lisbon.
Employs at the office—50 men.        Wages, 700 to 1,300 reis.
             10 children.      "      100 to   300   "
Employs at the working of the stones at Pero Pinheiro and Paço
  d'Arcos—150 men.      Wages, 600 to 700 reis.
             20 children.     "      100 to 300  "
Employs also a hydraulic wheel of 10 horse-power.
  Origin of the material—Pero Pinheiro, Montalvar Pedra Furada,
Carrasqueira, Lameiras, S. Pedro de Cintra, Mem Martins, Villa
Verde.

### 63.—Santos, Joaquim Antunes dos, LISBON.

A frame with 12 samples of Portuguese marbles.
A blue marble bath tub from Cintra, price 200 dollars.

### 64.—The Vallongo Slate and Marble Quarries Co., limited.

1. Slate slab, sawn and faced.   Price, 13$500 reis.
2. Slate tank, composed of 5 slabs and 4 bolts.   Price, 7$200 reis.
3. 4 pieces of ridge roll.
4. 2 pieces of Imperials, 5 cent. wide. } Per metres 500 reis.
5. 4 pieces of Imperials 6 cent. wide.
6. 1 round garden table.   Price, 3$375 reis.
7. 1 round garden table.   Price, 2$800 reis.
8. Tripod stand (slate).   Price, 4$500 reis.
9. Tripod stand (wrought iron).   Price, 3$000 reis.
10. Enamelled round table.   Price 22$500 reis.
11. Enamelled oval table.   Price, 13$500 reis,
12. Tripod stand (cast iron).   Price, 3$000 reis.
13. Tripod stand (cast iron).   Price, 3$000 reis.
14. 2 slabs for 13 table. } Each, 54$000 reis.
15. 3 slabs for 13 table.

16. Roofing slates, composed of 3 patterns—round, square and oval.

66 cent. x 41 cent......60$000 reis per 1000.
61 cent. x 35 cent......50$000 reis per 1000.
61 cent. x 30 cent......45$000 reis per 1000.
56 cent. x 20 cent......35$000 reis per 1000.
50 cent. x 25 cent......31$000 reis per 1000.
46 cent. x 25 cent......25$000 reis per 1000.
41 cent. x 25 cent......21$000 reis per 1000.
4J cent. x 20 cent......16$000 reis per 1000.

17. 1 jam and cross piece. 
18. 1 jam and ornamental pieces. 62$000 reis.
19. 1 shelf for same. 
20. 1 enamelled table.  Price 6$500 reis.
21. 1 enamelled table.  Price, 6$500 reis.
22. 1 enamelled table.  Price, 8$100 reis.
23. 1 enamelled table.  Price, 8$100 reis.

---

CLASSES Nos. 102 AND 103.

**65.—Visconde de Bessone.**

### Penha Longa Quarries—CINTRA.

1. Dark ashy marble........................Nuncio quarry, Cintra.
2. Dark marble with white veins.........Nuncio quarry, Cintra.
3. White rubbed marble....................Cruz dos quatro Caminhos.
4. White rubbed marble....................Cruz dos quatro Caminhos.
5. White rubbed marble....................S, Jeronimo.
6. White rubbed marble....................Cruz dos quatro Caminhos.
7. Ashy marble...............................S. Gonçalo.
8. Ashy marble...............................S Gonçalo.
9. Ashy maible with white veins..........S. Gonçalvo.
10. Reticular yellow marble................Terra do Tanque.
11. White rose-colored marble. ............Terra do Tanque.
12. White rose-colored marble..............Terra do Tanque.
13. Polished granite...........................Mina quarry.
14. Powder from stones 11 and 12.  Used in making stucco.
15. Powdered lime............................Fornos de Penha Longa.
    Price 2$000 to 2$500 reis per cubic metre.

---

CLASS No. 102.

**66.—Brites, Antonio Pereira,**

### Torres Novas.

Hard stone edgings.
Soft stone edgings.
Hard stone edgings.
Soft stone edgings.

CLASS No. 103.

**67.—Lisbon Dyeing and Cotton Printing Company,**
**LISBON.**

Quicklime—15 kilogrames, 110 reis.
Pulverized lime—1 cubic metre, 1,850 reis.
Established in 1873.
Employs—22 men. Wages, 300 to 400 reis.
Work, manual—Material from the country.
Markets—Portugal, Brazil, and Africa.

**68.—Rasca Cement Exploring Company,**
**LISBON.**

Hydraulic cement.
Employs a steam-engine of 10 horse-power and 10 men. Wages, 300
to 700 reis.
Annual production—5,000$000 reis.
Price—6,000 reis per 1,000 kilogrames.

CLASS No. 104.

**69.—Neuville, Luiz,**
**LISBON.**

Kaolin. See Class 207.

CLASS No. 106.

**70.—Administration of the Mint and Stamped Paper,**
**LISBON.**

A lithographic stone. See Class 344.

**71.—Manilha, Francisco dos Santos Lopes.**
**VALLONGO.**

Whetstone.

CLASS No. 107.

**72.—Civil Governor of Portalegre.**
**MARVAO.**

Phosphorite of Marvao.

**73.—Administrative Board of the Sulphurous Baths of Cabeco de Vide.**
**CABECO DE VIDE.**

Mineral Waters.

**74.—Fialho & Irmao,**
**LISBON.**

Mineral waters from Cabeço de Vide.

**75.—Freitas, Albino Jose de,**
**EGA.**

One bottle with mineral water.

**76.—Pedras Salgadas Mineral Water Company,**
**OPORTO.**

Mineral waters.

The *Springs of Pedras Salgadas* are situated at a few kilometres to the north of Villa Pouca de Aguiar, on the left side of the old road from Villa Real to Chaves, being about from the present high-road 400 metres. Various springs have appeared within the space of two hundred metres, of which four have already been explored and analyzed, two of them, Penedo and Rebordechao, being utilized for drinking and bathing, the other two as yet are only used for bathing.

These waters, on account of their principal ingredients, belong to the class of alkaline-gaseous waters, or rather to the bicarbonated and to the species of the bicarbonate of soda ; but together with these ingredients others of such an importance are found as to render them quite characteristic. The action of these waters is quite incontestable for diseases in the organs of digestion ; and even if given in smaller doses than as usual with similar national and foreign waters, they produce more advantageous and even more rapid result, at least at their source, their medicinal virtues are indubitable in curing diseases of the skin, have long been celebrated in the neighboring villages. It has moreover been remarked that when given in doses equal to those of strong mineral waters the digestive organs cannot support them, a fact observed by the medical men of the place in many patients who have used the waters at their source.

The chemical composition of these waters, more complex and richer in mineral principles of the first order, than the best known at home and abroad, their therapeutic effects in various diseases certified by enlightened and conscientious physicians, the unsuspected testimony of the jury of the universal exhibition of Vienna which conferred on these waters the *diploma of merit*, the highest prize that can be granted to mineral waters, assure to the mineral *waters of Pedras Salgadas* the first rank among all those of the peninsula.

If we add to the excellent qualities of these waters, considered in themselves and compared with others, the superiority of the hygienic conditions in which they are found, the abundance of their springs, the differences in their composition, which render them applicable to different diseases and even to different patients with the same disease, the pure state in which they are obtained, the unchangeableness in their composition in every season, it will not be difficult to admit that the *Springs of Pedras Salgadas* have a right to be well considered.

The *Waters of Pedras Salgadas* on account of their low temperature and richness in free carbonic acid, can be transported to the most distant places without losing their medicinal properties, and without any alteration when kept out of the light in cool dry places.

The analysis of the springs of the alkaline gazeous waters of Pedras Salgadas, was made by the professor of chemistry in the Polytechnic School of Lisbon, Dr. Joseph Julius Rodrigues.

| Composition of the waters. | Peneda. — By 1,000 | Rebordechão — By 1000 | Rio. | Estrada. |
|---|---|---|---|---|
| Bicarbonate of soda..................... | 1.8386 | 1.791587 | | |
| " of lithia.................... | 0.0154 | 0.008434 | | |
| " of magnesia.............. | 0.1573 | 0.449562 | | |
| " of lime................ | 0.6197 | 0.570050 | | |
| " of strontiana.... ......... | 0.0012 | 0.001545 | | |
| " of baryta ................. | 0.0004 | 0.000470 | | |
| " of iron..................... | 0.0212 | 0.022862 | | |
| " of manganese ............ | 0.0023 | 0.002923 | | |
| Free carbonic acid...................... | 1.1851 | 1.865914 | | |
| Sulphate of potassa.................... | 0.0448 | 0.003680 | The same composition as Rebordechão, but with a larger quantity of free carbonic acid. | Identical to the Penedo distant only 17 metres. |
| Chlorate of potassa..................... | 0.0377 | 0.056779 | | |
| " of soda................. | 0.0434 | 0.013481 | | |
| Azotate of soda........................... | 0.0385 | 0.008788 | | |
| Arseniate of soda ..................... | 0.0019 | Vestiges. | | |
| " of alumina.................. | 0.0004 | Vestiges. | | |
| Phosphate of alumina ................. | 0.0003 | 0.000590 | | |
| Alumine.................................. | 0.0008 | 0.001812 | | |
| Silica..................................... | 0.0833 | 0.071907 | | |
| | 4.0953 | 4.570414 | | |
| Density............. ..................... | 1.002130 | 1.002226 | | |
| Temperature...... ..................... | 19°.4c | 12° 6c | | |
| N. B. Organic matters................. | Vestiges. | Vestiges. | | |

For further particulars concerning these mineral waters address (post prepaid) the manager of the company, A. R. Ferreira Vianna, Porto.

*Awards—At Vienna, 1873. Examined and approved by the Society of Medical Sciences of Lisbon.*

**77.—Vidago Mineral Waters Company.**

LISBON.

Mineral Waters.

ANALYSIS OF MINERAL WATERS OF VIDAGO.—The waters have been analyzed by Dr. Agostinho Vicente Lourenço, Professor of Chemistry at the Polytechnic School of Lisbon, and member to the Academy of Sciences. He says in his relation:

Those excellent gaseous alkaline waters may be compared, for their mineralization and good effects, to the best mineral waters of Europe. In order to prove the relative value of the mineral waters, which composition I have justly shown, I have the honor of sending you a map containing the fourteen mineral springs, alkaline and gaseous.

Those waters are ordered according to their value in carbonate and soda, principal agent of their mineralization. When we read that relation, we can see that the water from the commune of Chaves, called Vidago, is the best of the gaseous waters of Europe.

I must note that the waters of Vidago are much preferable to those of Vichy, because they contain more iron-carbon, and that is very important in many cases when gaseous and alkaline waters are employed.

In a meeting held on the 2d of December, 1874, by the Society of Medical Sciences of Lisbon, it was proved by the last analysis, made by Dr. A. V. L., that the water of Vidago contains not only double quantity of *bicarbon* of soda, but yet more carbonic acid than that of Pedras Salgadas. It contains, too, lithic-acid in double quantity, and soda-arsenite, but less than those of Villa Pouca.

We read in the journal, *Medical Post of Lisbon*, of June 15, 1873: "A new analysis has been made by Dr. A. V. Lourenço, showing the true value of the chemical composition of the waters of Vidago, and he says that we can do without those of Vichy, since the first are better, on account of their composition, for the use of the Therapeutics."

As to the effects of the Therapeutics obtained by the waters of Vidago, they are so well known by Portuguese and foreign physicians, especially the Spanish and Brazilian, that it is useless to remember them. The sick people recovered, and those who feel better continually praise the efficacy of those waters.

GRAND HOTEL OF VIDAGO.—Every year, from the 15th of May, the hotel receives travellers till the 15th of October. Those who will use the waters of Vidago, find in that establishment all the comfort required by their health.

There are other houses near the hotel prepared for the travellers that wish to take baths of alkaline thermal waters. The sick people can be treated, if they chose, by the physicians of the establishment.

The number of sick people going to Vidago augments every year.

The King of Portugal has been, in 1875, at the Grand Hotel, in order to make internal and external use of the waters.

The grantees are always improving their establishments, for the sick persons to find there all the comforts required.

We go to Vidago by the railway of Oporto to Paredes, and from there in a stage-coach to Vidago, in the rich and magnificent Valle d'Oura (Valley of Oura) commune of Chaves.

. Every complaint and correspondence must be directed to the Undertaking of the waters of Vidago, Lisbon, Abegoaria Square, No. 28, third floor.

### Alkaline Vidago.

Analysis of Dr. A. V. Lourenço, Professor of Chemistry at the Polytechnic School of Lisbon, and member of the Sciences Academy, Lisbon, by 1000 kil.:

| | |
|---|---:|
| Bicarbonate of soda | 4,629017 |
| Bicarbonate of potassa | 0,048396 |
| Bicarbonate of lithia | 0,037331 |
| Bicarbonate of strontiana | 0,000963 |
| Bicarbonate of lime | 0,971350 |
| Bicarbonate of magnesia | 0,255404 |
| Bicarbonate of protoxyde of iron | 0,013131 |
| Bicarbonate of manganese | 0,001053 |
| Sulphate of baryta | 0,008939 |
| Sulphate of potassa | 0,001002 |
| Chloride of potassium | 0,179530 |
| Phosphate of alumina | 0,000724 |
| Silicious acid | 0,061170 |
| Free carbonic acide | 1,449408 |

7,647418

Vestiges of arsenical acid, ammoniac, phosphate sodium, acid organic substances.

## ALKALINE–GASEOUS WATERS, LASTLY DISCOVERED.

Analysis of the alkaline mineral waters of Villa Verde, de Oura and Sabroso, by Dr. A. V. L., Professor of Chemistry at the Polytechnic School of Lisbon, and member of the Sciences Academy, Lisbon.

| EVERY THOUSAND KILOS. | SPRINGS NEAR VIDAGO. | | |
|---|---|---|---|
| | Va. Verde. | Oura. | Sabroso. |
| Bicarbonate of soda............................ | 2,193032 | 1,722131 | 1,955895 |
| Bicarbonate of potassa....................... | 0,006805 | 0,031247 | |
| Bicarbonate of lithia.......................... | 0,018014 | 0,008048 | 0,009612 |
| Bicarbonate of strontiana .................. | 0,000641 | 0,001031 | 0,001020 |
| Bicarbonate o lime....... ................. | 0,385750 | 0,532722 | 0,541987 |
| Bicarbonate of magnesia..................... | 0,098386 | 0,163544 | 0,169014 |
| Bicarbonate of protoxide of iron........ | 0,008338 | 0,020742 | 0,001957 |
| Bicarbonate of manganese.................. | 0,001044 | 0,001463 | 0,001824 |
| Sulphate of baryta.. ......................... | 0,000125 | 0,000294 | 0,000626 |
| Sulphate of potassa.... ...................... | 0,008241 | 0,001053 | 0,000723 |
| Chloride of potassium........................ | 0,063225 | 0,058943 | 0,068223 |
| Arseniate of potassa.......................... | 0,000158 | 0,000286 | |
| Phosphate of potassa......................... | | 0,001170 | |
| Chloride of sodium............................ | | 0,059918 | 0,001949 |
| Arsenate of sodium....... ............. ... | | | 0,000255 |
| Phosphate of alumina........................ | | 0,000724 | 0,001811 |
| Alumina....................................... | 0,000761 | | |
| Silicious acid................................. | 0,057899 | | 0,055005 |
| Total ............................. | 2,842419 | 2,603316 | 2,809444 |
| Free carbonic acid........................... | 1,609427 | 1,518410 | 1,276720 |
| Total. .............................. | 4,451845 | 4,121726 | 4,086164 |

Besides above-mentioned substances the waters of Villa Verde contain :

Vestiges.—Phosphate of sodium—Phosphate ammonium—Nitrogen —Organic substances.

### The waters of Oura.

Vestiges.—Ammonium—Nitrogen—Organic substances.

### The waters of Sabroso.

Vestiges.—Phosphate of iron protoxyde—Phosphate ammonium— Nitrogen—Organic substances.

### Use of the Therapeutics.

The same as those of Vidago.

*Awards.—Diploma of Merit at Vienna,* 1873.

**78.—Official Commission of Ponta Delgada.**

## PONTA DELGADA.

Mineral waters from S. Miguel Island. Memorandum about the said waters.

This memorandum is made up of two reports; one from the distinguished chemist of Paris, Mr. F. Fouqué, the other from Dr. Philomeno da Camara Mello Cabral, physician of the University of Coimbra, who has under his charge the hospital and the clinics of the "Valle das Furnas."

The labors of Mr. Fouqué were undertaken by order of the General Board of Ponta Delgada district.

The thermal waters of the island of S. Miguel may be divided in respect to their topographical positions in four principal groups. The first, the most important, is formed by the Valle das Furnas; the second by the waters surrounding Ribeira Grande; the third comprises only the spring of Ladeira Velha; and the fourth is constituted by the waters of Morteiros and of Ponta Ferraria.

---

CALDEIRA-GRANDE SPRINGS (Furnas).—From the observations made, it results that the temperature of the water flowing is of $98°.5$; from which may be deducted that the temperature of the spring ought to be $100°$ and some decimals.

The analysis made on the composition of the gaseous mixture of the spring is as follows:

| | |
|---|---:|
| Carbonic acid | 988.90 |
| Sulphidric acid | 9.50 |
| Azote | 1.46 |
| Oxygen | 0.14 |
| | 1,000.00 |

A litre of water from Caldeira-Grande evaporated gives a dry residue weighing 1.818 grammes.

Attending the super-oxidation of the sulphate of soda, the weight of the dry residue not modified would be equal to 1.767 grammes, which is composed in the following manner:

| Immediate data of the Analysis: | | Interpretative table. | |
|---|---:|---|---:|
| Carbonic acid | 293 | Carbonate of soda | 707 |
| Sulphuric " | 19 | Sulphate of soda | 25 |
| Chlorhydric acid | 401 | Sulphate of potassa | 16 |
| Sulphydric " | 26 | Chloride of sodium | 646 |
| Silica | 299 | Sulphuret of sodium | 64 |
| Soda | 829 | Silica | 285 |
| Potassa | 8 | Silicate of soda | 24 |
| | 1.875 | | 1.767 |

This water contains besides this, vestiges of an arotated organic matter not volatile, colloidal, and of ammoniacal salt.

CALDEIRA D'ASMODEO SPRINGS (Furnas.)--The water of this spring gushes with such violence that it is not possible to precisely determine which is its temperature; withal some trials arrive to the conclusion that it may be about 100°.

The violence, high temperature, and the position of the main spout of this spring do not allow the collection of gases that are emitted abundantly.

A litre of water evaporated gives a dry residue of 1.2669.

| Immediate data of the Analysis: | | Interpretative table. | |
|---|---|---|---|
| Carbonic acid | 298 | Carbonate of soda | 719 |
| Sulphuric " | 118 | Sulphate of soda | 190 |
| Chlorhydric acid | 260 | Sulphate of potassa | 22 |
| Sulphydric " | 25 | Chloride of sodium | 420 |
| Silica | 222 | Sulphuret of sodium | 60 |
| Soda | 779 | Silica | 220 |
| Potassa | 11 | Silicate of soda | 5 |
| | 1.713 | | 1.636 |

AGUA SANTA.—This spring is of a small flow, possesses at the outflow a temperature of 88°, and it is not sensibly gaseous.

A litre of this water evaporated slowly by the air gives a residue weighing 0.726 grammes.

Attending the transformation of the sulphuret in sulphate during the evaporation, the weight of the dry residue not acidified would be equal to 0.706 grammes, decomposing itself as follows:

| Immediate data of the Analysis: | | Interpretative table. | |
|---|---|---|---|
| Carbonic acid | 49 | Carbonate of soda | 120 |
| Sulphuric " | 20 | Sulphate of soda | 36 |
| Chlorhydric acid | 111 | Sulphate of potassa | traces |
| Sulphydric " | 10 | Chloride of sodium | 180 |
| Silica | 220 | Silica | 134 |
| Soda | 328 | Silicate of soda | 212 |
| Potassa | traces | Bicarbonate of lime | traces |
| Lime | " | Sulphuret of sodium | 24 |

PADRE JOSÈ SPRING.—This spring is not abundant; the water possesses at the outflow a temperature of 57°. The gaseous development is insignificant.

A litre of this water submitted to ebullition loses 102 cubic centimetres of gas, composed in the following manner:

| | |
|---|---|
| Carbonic acid | 86.3 |
| Azote | 12.0 |
| Oxygen | 1.7 |
| | 100.0 |

A litre of this water evaporated leaves a dry residue weighing 0.612 gramme, as follows :

| Immediate data of the Analysis: | | Interpretative table. | |
|---|---|---|---|
| Carbonic acid | 73 | Bicarbonate of soda | 214 |
| Sulphuric " | 64 | Bicarbonate of lime | 31 |
| Chlorhydric acid | 70 | Bicarbonate of iron | 20 |
| Sulphydric " | traces | Sulphate of soda | 114 |
| Silica | 201 | Chloride of sodium | 113 |
| Soda | 199 | Silica | 201 |
| Lime | 12 | Sulphydric acid | traces |
| Peroxide of iron | 10 | | |
| | 629 | | 693 |

PEDRO BOTELHO SPRING.—The water of this spring is enclosed in a small basin, its temperature being approximately 100°.

A litre of this water evaporated gives a dry residue weighing 1.003 grammes.

| Immediate data of the Analysis: | | Interpretative table. | |
|---|---|---|---|
| Sulphuric acid | 447 | Sulphate of soda (weight of salt) | 651 |
| Chlorhydric " | 12 | Sodic alum (supposed anhydrous) | 87 |
| Soda | 296 | Sulphate of lime | 34 |
| Alum | 18 | Sulphate of iron | traces |
| Lime | 14 | Silica | 300 |
| Oxide of iron | traces | Chlorhydric acid | 12 |
| Silica | 300 | Sulphuric acid | 3 |
| | 1.087 | | 1.087 |

QUENTURAS SPRING.—This spring in its opening has a temperature of 48°. The analysis of the gaseous mixture coming out of the spring is as follows :

| | |
|---|---|
| Carbonic acid | 995.5 |
| Azote | 4.1 |
| Oxygen | 0.4 |
| | 1000.0 |

A litre of water of this spring submitted to ebullition loses 200 cubic centimetres of gas composed in the following manner :

| | |
|---|---|
| Carbonic acid | 192.5 |
| Azote | 6.0 |
| Oxygen | 1.5 |
| | 200.0 |

From a litre of water of the Quenturas spring the evaporation leaves a dry residue which weighs 1.014 grammes, viz :

| Immediate data of the Analysis: | | Interpretative table. | |
|---|---|---|---|
| Carbonic acid | 984 | Bicarbonate of soda | 956 |
| Sulphuric " | 15 | Bicarbonate of lime | 8 |
| Chlorhydric acid | 69 | Bicarbonate of iron | 8 |
| Silica | 192 | Sulphate of soda | 26 |
| Soda | 469 | Silica | 192 |
| Lime | 3 | Chloride of sodium | 111 |
| Peroxide of iron | 4 | | |
| | 1736 | | 1301 |

AGUA AZEDA SPRING.—This spring furnishes an acidulated water, of 16² of temperature, excessively gaseous, without of sensible.

A litre of this water submitted to ebullition loses 930 cubic centimetres of a gas composed thus:

$$
\begin{array}{lr}
\text{Carbonic acid} & 890 \\
\text{Azote} & 35 \\
\text{Oxygen} & 5 \\
\hline
& 930
\end{array}
$$

A litre of water evaporated leaves a residue which weighs 0.334 gramme, thus:

| Immediate data of the Analysis: | | Interpretative table. | |
|---|---|---|---|
| Carbonic acid | 57 | Bicarbonate of soda | 170 |
| Sulphuric " | 24 | Bicarbonate of lime | 10 |
| Chlorhydric acid | 41 | Bicarbonate of iron | 8 |
| Silica | 91 | Sulphate of soda | 40 |
| Soda | 124 | Sulphate of potassa | 4 |
| Potassa | 2 | Chloride of sodium | 67 |
| Lime | 4 | Silica | 91 |
| Peroxide of iron | 4 | | |
| | 347 | | 390 |

AGUA FRIA SPRINGS.—This spring furnishes a considerable quantity of water of a temperature of 16° and slightly acidulated.

A litre of this water submitted to an evaporation, leaves a residue which weighs 1.068 grammes, as follows:

| Immediate data of Analysis: | | Interpretative table. | |
|---|---|---|---|
| Carbonic acid | 371 | Bicarbonate of soda | 1219 |
| Sulphuric " | traces | Bicarbonate of lime | 36 |
| Chlorhydric acid | 49 | Bicarbonate of iron | 20 |
| Silica | 90 | Chloride of sodium | 80 |
| Soda | 549 | Sulphates | traces |
| Lime | 14 | Silica | 90 |
| Oxide of iron | 10 | | |
| | 1083 | | 1445 |

SANGUINHAL SPRINGS (Furnas).—The abundance of heat in these springs is so remarkable that it gives a high temperature to the water of a creek which traverses the town of Furnas and runs near it.

A litre of water submitted to evaporation gives a residue whose weight is of 0.543 gramme, and whose analysis gives the following result:

| Immediate data of Analysis: | | Interpretative table. | |
|---|---|---|---|
| Carbonic acid | 135 | Bicarbonate of soda | 412 |
| Sulphuric " | traces | Bicarbonate of lime | 41 |
| Chlorhydric acid | 37 | Bicarbonate of iron | 44 |
| Silica | 140 | Chloride of sodium | 60 |
| Soda | 204 | Silica | 140 |
| Lime | 16 | Sulphates | traces |
| Pyroxide of iron | 22 | | |
| | 554 | | 697 |

AGUA DOCE DO HOSPITAL (Hospital sweet water.)—This water is the one in common use of the hospital, and for this reason its composition is important.

A litre of this water submitted to evaporation leaves 22 cubic centimetres of gas of a gaseous matter composed of:

| | |
|---|---:|
| Carbonic acid | 54.5 |
| Azote | 31.9 |
| Oxygen | 13.6 |
| | 100.0 |

A litre of water evaporated gives a residue weighing 0.137 gramme, thus:

| Immediate data of the Analysis: | | Interpretative table. | |
|---|---:|---|---:|
| Carbonic acid | 17 | Carbonate of soda | 40 |
| Sulphuric " | 1 | Sulphate of soda | 2 |
| Chlorhydric acid | 45 | Chloride of sodium | 75 |
| Silica | 20 | Silica | 20 |
| Soda | 63 | | |
| | 146 | | 137 |

CALDEIRAS DO LAGO DAS FURNAS SPRINGS.—These springs gush at the northern extremity of Lago das Furnas; they are not very abundant.

A litre of this water evaporated leaves a residue which weighs 0.278 gramme, as follows:

| Immediate data of the Analysis. | | Interpretative table. | |
|---|---:|---|---:|
| Sulphuric acid | 56 | Sulphate of soda | 85 |
| Chlorhydric " | 59 | Sulphate of potassa | 6 |
| Silica | 95 | Chloride of sodium | 79 |
| Soda | 79 | Sulphate of lime | 9 |
| Potassa | 3 | Oxide of iron | 4 |
| Lime | 4 | Chlorhydric acid | 10 |
| Peroxide of iron | 4 | Silica | 95 |
| | 300 | | 288 |

CALDEIRA VELHA SPRING (Ribeira Grande.)—There exists in this place two localities where there is outflow of hot gas and vapors coming from the middle of natural or artificial basins.

The waters in small quantity which gush from the springs mix themselves with common water to feed the baths.

The temperature in one of the localities is 87°.5 and 95° in two springs, one north and the other east; in the other one it is of 97°.

A litre of water submitted to evaporation leaves a residue that weighs 1.115 grammes, thus:

| Immediate data of the Analysis. | | Interpretative table. | |
|---|---|---|---|
| Sulphuric acid (S. O.²)............... | 976 | Sulphate of soda......................... | 155 |
| Chlorhydric acid........................ | 10 | Sulphate of peroxide of iron........ | 610 |
| Soda...................................... | 67 | Silica..................................... | 350 |
| Peroxide of iron........................ | 321 | Sulphuric acid (S. O⁴ H.)............ | 680 |
| Sulphydric acid........................ | 3 | Chlorhydric acid........................ | 10 |
| | | Su phydric acid ....................... | 3 |
| | 1.377 | | |
| | | | 1.808 |

LADEIRA DA VELHA SPRING. —The temperature is nearly 3 J°.
A litre of water evaporated gives a residue weighing 0.141 gramme, thus:

| Immediate data of the Analysis. | | Interpretative table. | |
|---|---|---|---|
| Chlorhydric acid........................ | 74 | Chloride of sodium.................... | 120 |
| Soda........................................ | 63 | Chlorhydric acid........................ | 2 |
| Silica...................................... | 21 | Sulphuric acid........................traces | |
| Sulphydric acid......................traces | | Silica:.................................... | 21 |
| | 158 | | 143 |

MOSTEIROS E DE PONTA FERRARIA SPRINGS.—These springs are daily covered by the sea-water, and that of *Mosteiros* is only uncovered in large tides and the wind not blowing from the West.

It is not possible to analyse these waters, because they are mixed with sea-water.

These data on the mineral waters of the Isles are taken from the excellent report presented by Mr. F. Fouqué during the intelligent and zealous administration of the Governor of Ponta Delegada district, His Excellency the Count of Praia da Victoria.

## METALLURGICAL PRODUCTS.

CLASS 110.—Precious metals.

CLASS 111.—Iron and steel in the pig, ingot, and bar, plates and sheets, with specimens of slags, fluxes, residues, and products of working.

CLASS 112.—Copper in ingots, bars, and rolled, with specimens illustrating its various stages of production.

CLASS 113.—Lead, zinc, antimony, and other metals, the result of extractive processes.

CLASS 114.—Alloys used as materials, brass, nickel, silver, solder, etc.

## CLASS No. 110.

**79.—Visconde de Mason de S. Domingos,**
### MERTOLA.

#### Mine of "S. Domingos." (See page 67.)

Ingot of gold—Weight, 3 English ounces, value £13.
Ingot of silver—Weight, 204 English ounces, value £49.

These ingots were produced from 500 tons of Mason's pyrites, by Frederick Claudet's Patent Process for the recovery of silver and gold from copper pyrites treated by wet extraction.

**80.—Ferreira & Souza,**
### OPORTO.

Gold-leaf, gold dust, and gold fillings for dentists.

**81.—Cardozo Junior, Jose Pereira.**
### OPORTO.

Gold leaf of different qualities; silver, alluminum and platina leaf. gold for gilding metals; gold, silver and tin for dentists' use; Annual production—36,000$000 to 40,000$000 reis.

Markets—Portugal, Spain and Brazil.

*Awards: Medal at Paris, 1855 and 1857; Oporto, 1857, 1861 and 1865; Braga, 1865, and Vienna, 1873.*

---

## CLASS No. 113.

**82.—Diedrick Mathias Feuerheerd & Co.**
### SEVER DO VOUGA.

#### Mines of "Malhada" and "Coval da Mo." (See page 55.)

Lead.

**83.—Companhia Minercao de Estanho de Traz-os-Montes,**
### MIRANDA DO DOURO.

#### Mines of "Cabeco do Codeco" and "Cabeco do Ráposo."

Tin. (See page 77.)

**84.—Companhia de Mineracao de S. Pedro do Sul,**
### S. PEDRO DO SUL.

#### Mine of "Outeiro dos Hujos"—See Page 78.

Tin.

85.—Joao Correa de Oliveira,

**S. PEDRO DO SUL.**

Tin.

**Mine of "Senhora do Castello."** (See page 78.)

86.—Companhia Perseveranca,

**OPORTO.**

**Mine of "Logar de Aboim."** (See page 76.)

Tin.

---

## MINING ENGINEERING.—MODELS, MAPS AND SECTIONS.

CLASS 120.—Surface and underground surveying and plotting. Projection of underground work, location of shafts, tunnels, etc. Surveys for aqueducts and for drainage.

Boring and drilling rocks, shafts and tunnels, etc. Surveys for aqueducts, and for ascertaining the nature and extent of mineral deposits.

Construction. Sinking and lining shafts by various methods, driving and timbering tunnels, and the general operations of opening, stopping and breaking down ore, timbering, lagging, and masonry.

Hoisting and delivering at the surface, rock, ore or miners.

Pumping and draining by engines, buckets or by adits.

Ventilation and lighting.

Subaqueous mining, blasting, etc.

Hydraulic mining, and the various processes and methods of sluicing and washing auriferous gravel, and other superficial deposits.

Quarrying.

CLASS 121.—Models of mines, of veins, etc.

---

87.—Bureau of Mines,

**LISBON.**

Surveys whose execution the Government orders to ascertain the existence of the mineral deposits and determine the area of the grants of mines.

1. Plan of the Moncorvo Iron Mines (See page 7), surveyed by Lourenco Malheiro and P. V. da Costa Sequeira, Mining Engineers. Scale, $\frac{1}{10000}$.

This map shows the shape of the deposit of the iron mine of Moncorvo, the distribution of the ore on the surface outlined in blue ink; the extension of the legal grants of mines, embracing 33, which are outlined in red ink, as likewise the mineralogical nature of the soil.

---

Plans of mining labors that the grantees are obliged to send annually to the Ministry of Public Works.

2. Horizontal plan of the works of the iron mine of Monges in 1873 Scale, $\frac{1}{500}$.

3. Longitudinal and transversal sections of the deposit of Monges in 1873. Scale, $\frac{1}{500}$.
4. Horizontal and vertical projection of the works of the lead mine of Malhada in 1873. Scale, $\frac{1}{500}$.
5. Horizontal and vertical projection of the works of the antimony mine of Monte Alto in 1874. Scale, $\frac{1}{200}$.
6. Horizontal and vertical projection of the works of the coal mine of S. Pedro do Cova in 1874. Scale, $\frac{1}{1000}$.

### 88. –Lourenco Malheiro, Mining Engineer.
#### LISBON.

1. The Pentagonal System in Spain and Portugal.
2. The Pentagonal System in Portugal.
These two maps comprise the graphical determination of the Great Circles of the Pentagonal System (Réseau Pentagonal) which pass through Spain and Portugal (See page 38.)

### 89.–Visconde de Mason de S. Domingos,
#### MERTOLA.

1. Plan of the works in open air of the cupreous pyrites mine of S· Domingos in 1874. Scale, $\frac{1}{400}$.
2. Plan of the works in the story 12 metres under the surface of the deposit in 1874. Scale, $\frac{1}{400}$.
3. Plan of the works in the stories 28 and 52 metres under the surface of the deposit in 1874. Scale, $\frac{1}{400}$.
4. Longitudinal section of the deposit in 1874. Scale, $\frac{1}{400}$.
5. Transversal sections of the deposit in 1874. Scale, $\frac{1}{400}$.
6. Model of a Roman wheel found in the ancient labors.
7. Several photographic views of the labors, buildings and grounds attached to the mine.

### 90.–Companahia de Minracao Transtagana.
#### LISBON.

1. Horizontal projection of the works of cupreous pyrites of. mine "Algares" in 1875. Scale, $\frac{1}{500}$.
2. Longitudinal section, and transversal profiles of the same deposit in 1875. Scale, $\frac{1}{500}$.
3. Horizontal projection of the works of the cupreous pyrites mine of S. Joao do Deserto in 1875. Scale, $\frac{1}{500}$.
4. Horizontal and vertical projection of the works of the Copper Mine of Sobral in 1875. Scale, $\frac{1}{500}$.

### 91.–Silva, S. A. P. da, & E. A. Marques,
#### AVEIRO·

Plan of a salt pit with description of the same.

# ERRATA.

Page 40, Note (*), Latitude 11° 25′ 56″.925, should read Longitude 11° 25′ 56″.925 E.

Page 44, Note (*), Longitude should read Latitude.

> Latitude 10° 56′ 18″.79 should read Longitude 10° 56′ 18″.79 W.
>
> Latitude 0° 29′ 38″.135 should read Longitude 0° 29′ 38″.135 E.

The word "rubbish," which occurs in pages 15, 73, 75 and 76 should read "slag."

Page 61, "Perseverança Company" should read Companhia Perseverança.

Page 67, "Forrg Merendas" should read Forra Merendas.

# DEPARTMENT II.

# MANUFACTURES.

# INTRODUCTION.

## INDUSTRY.

There is not a complete statistic of the Portuguese Industrial Establishments; we will give, however, some informations that are based upon an statistic of 1867, above all the informations given by Gerardo A. Pery in his excellent work "Geographia e Estatistica Geral de Portugal e Colonias," and upon special informations collected for the Philadelphia Exposition.

In a statistic made in 1867, of the professions and industrial establishments, with a view to the distributing of the industrial taxes, there were in the census 199,174 taxables. This number was made up of the following :

| | |
|---|---:|
| Large industries, | 9,402 |
| Small industries | 106,157 |
| Commerce | 73,368 |
| Professions | 10,247 |
| The industries and professions counted were | 421 |

In the large industry this statistic is made up of 55 spinning factories; 178 of cording; 12 of stamping; 488 of weaving; 39 dyeing; 24 of soap; 45 of paper; 28 foundries; 255 fulling mills; 13 of earthen-ware; 1 of porcelain-ware; 6 of glass-ware; 288 of leather tanning; 3 of Dutch bricks; 2 of ice; 22 of macaroni; 4 of oil-cloth; 10 of chemical products; 1 of manure; 15 cork factories; 81 typographical establishments; 484 gold and silversmiths; 3,500 olive-oil factories; 601 of rum.

In the small industry is comprised the following establishments : 10,984 mills; 2,773 bakeries; 1,383 baking establishments; 4,162 weaving factories; 646 tailors; 2,360 shoemakers; 1,255 clog-shoemakers; 195 hatters; 122 seamstresses; 2,299 barbers; 571 joiners; 3,570 locksmiths; 1,086 blacksmiths; 155 tubmakers; 25 sculptors in wood; 377 tinsmiths.

This statistic is very deficient, and it has been acknowledged that there are a great many more than what are stated here.

### I.

### Ceramical Arts and Glass Factories.

The official statistics of 1867 furnishes the following numbers relative to several industries, which employ plastic clay and the manufacture of glassware :

| | | | |
|---|---|---|---:|
| Manufactories of | tiles or bricks | | 620 |
| " | " | earthenware | 1,406 |
| " | " | faïence ware | 13 |
| " | " | porcelain ware | 1 |
| " | " | glassware | 6 |

The personnel of these establishments is of 4,700 hands.

In all the districts there is manufactured earthenware; the localities that distinguish themselves the most are: in the district of Leiria, Caldas da Rainha; in that of Evora, Extremoz and Vianna; in that of Lisbon, Lisbon and Abrigada, where there is a manufactory of drain pipes and fire-clay bricks; in that of Vizeu, Mollelos, black earthenware; in that of Portalegre, Flor da Rosa.

The factories of stoneware and faïence are situated at Lisbon, Sacavem, Oporto, Coimbra, Olháo, and Caminha.

The porcelain-ware factory belongs to the Aveiro district, at Vista Alegre.

The glassware factories are in the following districts: Leiria, Marinha Grande factory; Lisbon; Aveiro, in Vista Alegre, and in Oliveira de Azemeis.

The manufactory of faïence and stoneware in Portugal dates from 1767. In that year the factory established by the Marquis of Pombal commenced work, in Lisbon in the place of Rato, adjoining the Mae de Aguá, for which he sent for an able instructor from Italy.

There was not manufactured in this factory of the State but earthenware and ordinary stoneware; it served, however, as a starting point for the establishment of other factories at the Capital, at Coimbra, and Oporto.

## II.

## Textile Materials.

**Linen.**—The manufacture of linen is very much disseminated throughout the Kingdom, and constitutes one of the most important elements of the domestic industry of the country.

The large industry is hardly represented in this specialty by the spinning and weaving factory of Torres Novas and by some small factories of drills, &c., in Oporto and Lisbon.

The small industry is found in great quantities in all the districts of the Kingdom, but some specially in the districts of Vianna, Braga, Oporto, Villa-Real, Aveiro, Vizeu, Coimbra, Guarda, Castello-Branco, Leiria, Lisbon, and Portalegre.

This domestic industry produces large quantities of linen and linen goods, of which we cannot give the value.

It is unknown the number of hand-looms that this industry employs throughout the Kingdom.

**Cotton.**—The cotton industry has been greatly developed in the last few years. The importation of raw cotton that in 1856 was of 354,-000 $ 000 reis, increased in 1872 to 568,000 $ 000 reis, the value of 1,968,549 kilograms.

The maunfacture of spinning and weaving cotton is carried on at Oporto, Lisbon, Penafiel and Vizella.

There is, in the district of Oporto, 277 small weaving factories and three spinning ones. In Lisbon there are five large spinning and weaving factories, five stamping and one of weaving nets.

Lately several new factories have been established for manufacturing cotton woven goods, for dyeing and printing the same.

This industry has lately attained in Portugal a great progress, not only as regards to the quality of the articles manufactured, but in relation to the production which increases yearly.

**Wool.**—The woollen industry is at present the most important of the country, mainly on account of the perfection in the mechanical processes and the machines employed in its manufacture.

Besides the industry carried on at factories there exists throughout the Kingdom the same at home, which for a long time backwards has produced textures more or less coarse, that have been worn by the people in the provinces.

The development of factories is indebted to the powerful initiation of the Marquis of Pombal.

There were established during his administration the Royal establishments of Covilhâ e Fundao in 1764, and the one of Portalegre in 1772. In 1788 these factories were sold by the State to two private associations.

During the French invasion these factories came to a great degree of decadence.

In 1821–22 these properties passed into the hands of other owners.

In 1867 there were in the district of Lisbon 3 woollen factories; in Oporto, 39; Castello Branco, 71; Guarda, 42, and Portalegre, 4.

The most important industrial centre is Covilhâ, in the Castello Branco district. There are there 27 carding and spinning factories; 8 spinning and weaving; 47 mechanical and 17 manual spinning; 35 fulling mills; 20 dyeing; 13 finishing establishments.

It has 557 looms, of which 37 are Jacquard's. Employs 900 men, 314 boys, 290 women and 26 girls: total, 1,596.

Capital invested........................ about 900,000 $ 000 reis.
Annual consumption of wool...............1,400,000 kilograms.
Annual production, 2,540 pieces, with...   133,350 ·    "

**Silk.**—The silk industry, which is very ancient in Portugal, received from the Marquis of Pombal a great impulse, promulgating laws and granting privileges tending to make the development of the raising of the worm and the manufacture of its texture.

In the Royal factory the number of looms footed up in 1784 to 236, and 72 galoon looms.

The production of silk footed up 36,720 kilograms.

This industry was successively decading until 1850.

In 1856 the exportation of cocoons was of 862 kilograms, and 1,080 of raw silk.

In 1872 the exportation increased to 33,707 kilograms of cocoons and to 2,833 of raw silk.

The production of silk in 1872 was of about 210,000 kilograms.

The most productive district is Bragança, which produced 98,000 kilograms.

Guarda............................................58,200 kilograms.
Vizeu.............................................41,000    "
Villa Real.......................................10,500    "

The following table of the commercial movement of silk gives an idea of the production and consumption of this article:

| Years. | Importation. | Exportation. |
|--------|-------------|--------------|
| 1842 | 215,628 $ 000 | 47,327 $ 000 |
| 1848 | 222,656 $ 000 | 40,458 $ 000 |
| 1851 | 260,747 $ 000 | 60,379 $ 000 |
| 1856 | 535,793 $ 000 | 83,481 $ 000 |
| 1868 | 626,564 $ 000 | 149,441 $ 000 |
| 1870 | 560,930 $ 000 | 117,123 $ 000 |
| 1872 | 694,681 $ 000 | 148,642 $ 000 |

The average price of the kilogram of cocoon is 700 reis.
Great quantity of the eggs are exported to France and Italy.

## III.

## Dressing Industry.

The census of 1867 gave 5,714 establishments for furnishing wearing apparel.
The exportation corresponding to these industries was in 1872 as follows:

Ready-made Clothing.................................. 65,280 $ 000 reis
Hats ................................................ 40,830 $ 000  "
Caps................................................. 3,219 $ 000  "
Boots and Shoes...................................... 198,277 $ 000  "
Gloves............................................... 11,694 $ 000  "
Umbrellas............................................ 4,407 $ 000  "

Total .............................................323.707 $ 000  "

**Ready-made Clothing.**—In 1867 there were 166 establishments of ready-made clothing; 58 peddlers; 646 tailors, and 122 dressmakers and seamstresses.

**Hat Industry.**—It is a very ancient industry in Portugal. Braga was the productive centre of felt and coarse wool hats, and, even now, in the district of Aveiro this manufacture exists in great quantity. The Marquis of Pombal animated this industry very much, establishing in 1759 a hat factory at Pombal—at the same time others were started—the national industry producing sufficient hats, not only for consumption throughout the Kingdom, but also to supply the markets of Brazil and the colonies in Africa and Asia.

In 1826 there were in the Kingdom 50 felt hat factories, and three of silk hats, besides a great number of woolen hat factories in Minho.

The average export of hats in the years previous to 1826 were from 208,000 to 210,000, with a value of 280,000 $ 000 reis.

This manufacture commenced to fall off under the influence of different causes, among which takes the lead, the destitution to which fashion condemned the felt hats, substituting them by the silk ones, whose manufacture only later was introduced in Portugal.

The protective duties that were established afterwards in the custom tariffs made this industry revive to the point of manufacturing products equal to the imported, and be ready to compete with the first foreign industries of its kind.

By the census of 1867 there were in that time 195 hat factories. In 1868 Lisbon had 76 hat stores, with 116 hatters. At present there are nearly 90, whose production is calculated at 900,000 $ 000 reis, footing up the production of the Kingdom to about 2,000,000 $ 000 reis.

The importation of raw materials for this industry in 1872 was the following :—Silk shag, 575 kilograms, to the value of 8,000 $ 000 reis ; hair, 25,435 kilograms, 40,000 $ 000 reis; felt, 35,366 kilograms, 10,000 $ 000 reis.

**Boots and Shoes.**—The census statistics in 1867 gives 2,360 shoemakers and 1,255 clog-shoemakers. In Lisbon the statistics of 1868 counted 328 shoe stores, with 920 shoemakers. The number of shoemakers in all the Kingdom is calculated at 6,000.

This is one of the industries that have been perfected the most.

The considerable increase of the exportation, which from 1856 to 1872 footed up from 32,000 $ 000 to 198,000 $ 000 reis, proves the importance of this industry, which furnishes completely the consumers of all the Kingdom. The importation of boots and shoes is relatively insignificant.

**Gloves.**—The same statistics gives 23 glovemakess in all the Kingdom, employing 100 seamstresses and 30 tradesmen.

## IV.

## Paper—Printing.

There are 45 writing and printing-paper mills and 25 of wrapping-paper and paste-board.

They employ 1,921 hands, being 748 men, 937 women, and 236 children. The wages are, for the men, 240 to 600 reis ; for women, 80 to 120; for children, 40 to 100 reis.

These mills consume annually about 4,000,000 kilogroms of rags.

The production of paper is at present calculated at 2,000,000 kilograms.

In 1862 there were 52 paper mills, which produced 1,500,000 kilograms and consumed three million kilograms of rags.

By the statistics of 1867 there were 89 rag establishments. These establishments collected larger quantities of rags than what was necessary for the consumption of the mills. In 1861 there was imported 2,302 kilograms of rags, and there was exported 32,148 kilograms.

In 1872 the importation of rags was of 625 kilograms, and the exportation of 989 kilograms.

The paper mills are established in the districts of Aveiro, Lisbon, Santarem, Braga, Coimbra, Oporto, Leiria, and Vizeu.

The district of Aveiro is the one which possesses the greater number of mills. The best belong to the districts of Lisbon (Abelheira and Alemquer), Santarem (Thomar) and Coimbra (Louza).

The statistics of 1867 gives 81 typographies. At present there are over 90.

Besides these, there are the following establishments of the state; Lisbon National Printing Office, printing office of the Coimbra University, and printing office of the Academy of Sciences.

The introduction of the typographical art in Portugal commenced, according to some authors, by the establishment of a typography in the city of Leiria, about the years 1470 and 1474. But what is certain is, that the most ancient publication that is known is printed at Lisbon, and has a date of 1489,

This great invention propagated itself rapidly through the principal cities of the Kingdom. It flourished under the protection of the Kings and of the public as a private industry till the middle of the eighteenth century. Having suffered some decadence, principally after the earthquake of 1755, the Marquis of Pombal, wishing to restore and perfect the typographical art, established in December, 1768, the Royal Printing Office, annexing to it the Royal Type Foundry, which, by proposal of the board of commerce, had been established in 1758, adding to it an engraving school.

In the following year, 1769, there was annexed to it a playing-card factory, which during many years furnished the principal income of that establishment.

In the first twenty years, that is, till 1789, the Royal Printing Office rendered more than 78,000 $ 000 reis. The playing-card factory rendered from 1790 to 1795 18,000 $ 000 reis.

In 1801 the income of the printing office amounted to 38,000 $ 000 reis, and continued gradually to increase, footing up an average of 51,000 $ 000 reis from 1811 to 1821, decreasing afterwards to 40,000-$ 000 reis.

With the change of government in 1833, the Royal Printing Office came to be called, National Printing Office. After this period, it has continued in progressive development, as indicated very well by the following table of its income and personnel :

| Economical Years. | Personnel. | Receipts. |
| --- | --- | --- |
| 1848—49 | 129 | 46,778 $ 000 |
| 1856—57 | 211 | 73,890 $ 000 |
| 1865—66 | 290 | 116,202 $ 000 |
| 1873—74 | 295 | 143,602 $ 000 |

As a state establishment, the Lisbon National Printing Office is administered by a functionary of royal appointment; but, as any other industrial establishment, its outlay is made by the receeipts produced by the printing for the State and private parties, by the sale of types and playing-cards.

The personnel of the administration is composed, besides the general administrator, of five accounting employees and four janitors.

This great establishment consists of four principal offices: the typography, the type foundry, the lithographic and the playing-card factory.

In the execution of its various labors, the National Printing Office has attained so great a degree of perfection, that in the great concourses of the London, Paris and Vienna Universal Expositions, it received the highest distinctions, and deserved to be qualified as one of the most notable typographical establishments of Europe.

V.

## Metals.

The census of 1867 gives 3,566 iron and locksmith factories; 40 cutlery; 65 iron furniture; 20 gunsmiths; 11 wire and iron band; 28 foundries; 10 of bronze, 63 of copper; 11 pewterers; 3 factories of scales and weights; 2 of lead shot; 169 brass smiths, and 484 gold and silversmiths.

The importation of raw materials for these industries was as follows:

| Metals. | 1872. | | 1873. | |
|---|---|---|---|---|
| | Kilograms. | Value. | Kilograms. | Value. |
| Steel, | 606,640 | 53,000 $ 000 | 937,696 | 244,645 $ 000 |
| Antimony, | ............... | ............... | 11,478 | 3,307 $ 000 |
| Mercury, | ............... | ............... | ·15,592 | 27,249 $ 000 |
| Bismuth, | ............... | ............... | 14 | 128 $ 000 |
| Britannia, - | ............... | ............... | 13,201 | 23,166 $ 000 |
| ·Bronze, | ............... | ............... | 739 | 754 $ 000 |
| Lead, | 328,263 | 23,000 $ 000 | 361,946 | 34,010 $ 000 |
| Copper, | 197,507 | 63,000 $ 000 | 240,479 | 96,434 $ 000 |
| Tin, | 59,735 | 26,000 $ 000 | 75,940 | 43,201 $ 000 |
| Iron, - | 14,916,715 | 960,000 $ 000 | 24,932,899 | 1,360,276 $ 000 |
| Tin plates, | 918,679 | 112,000 $ 000 | 1,138,928 | 152,366 $ 000 |
| Brass, | 135,791 | 51,000 $ 090 | 323,867 | 211,721 $ 000 |
| | | | Grammes. | |
| Gold, | ............... | ............... | 73,597 | 30,346 $ 000 |
| Platinum, | ............... | ............... | 4,789 | 847 $ 000 |
| Silver, | 12 | 163 $ 000 | 223,877 | 16,070 $ 000 |
| | | | Kilograms. | |
| Zinc, | 5,050 | 546 $ 000 | 164,779 | 28,181 $ 000 |

The exportation of raw material and the products of the domestic industry were as follows:

| Raw and manufactured metals. | 1872. | | 1873. | |
|---|---|---|---|---|
| | Kilograms. | Value. | Kilograms. | Value. |
| Steel, | 23,165 | 5,100 $ 000 | 92,381 | 8,622 $ 000 |
| Britannia, | ................ | ............... | 114 | 1,070 $ 000 |
| Rronze, | 3,101 | 1,800 $ 000 | 1,493 | 1,003 $ 000 |
| Lead, | 62,359 | 6,200 $ 000 | 54,417 | 7,072 $ 000 |
| Copper, | 47,510 | 13,800 $ 000 | 50,621 | 34,513 $ 000 |
| Tin, | 798 | 600 $ 000 | 730 | 260 $ 000 |
| Iron, | 685,497 | 100,400 $ 000 | 1,665,063 | 117,323 $ 000 |
| Tin plates, | 5,360 | 800 $ 000 | 3,442 | 981 $ 000 |
| Brass, | 28,133 | 9,000 $ 000 | 96,121 | 23,971 $ 000 |
| Mercury, | ................ | ............... | 80 | 130 $ 000 |
| | | | Grammes. | |
| Gold, | 43 | 20,000 $ 000 | 145,910 | 31,776 $ 000 |
| Silver, | 1,892 | 73,000 $ 000 | 2,552,808 | 57,943 $ 000 |
| | | | Kilograms. | |
| Zinc, | 195 | 100 $ 000 | 140 | 10 $ 000 |

In this statistic is not comprehended the importation and exportation of coin, which was in 1873.

Importation.—Gold Coin ..............................7,439,962 grammes
Value.............. .................3,907,193 $ 000 reis
Silver Coin......... .....................556,440 grammes
Value....................................21,137 $ 000 reis
Exportation.—Gold Coin......................4,515 grammes
Value ...............................2,528 $ 000 reis
Silver Coin............. .....................7,745 grammes
Value...................................25,300 $ 000 reis

The State possesses two important manufacturing establishments, the Army Arsenal and the Navy Yard.

In the first one there is a foundry shop for cannons and an arms shop.

The value of the articles manufactured at the Army Arsenal from October, 1871, to October, 1873, reaches 207,576 $ 000 reis.

The several shops of the Navy Yard produced :

1870—71.................................................. 265,707 $ 942 reis
1871—72.................................................. 224,789 $ 248 "
1872—73.................................................. 272,979 $ 028 "

The National Rope Works is a branch of the Navy Yard. It is composed of two shops, one of cording and another of spinning and weaving.

The Cording shop produced :

1870—71.................................................. 17,830 $ 454 reis
1871—72.................................................. 23,205 $ 747 "
1872—73.................................................. 27,534 $ 319 "

The Spinning and Weaving shop produced :

1870—71.............................................................. 16,854 $ 739 reis
1871—72............................................................. 13,790 $ 479  "
1872—73............................................................. 18,706 $ 855  "

————:o:————

# FOREIGN COMMERCE.

The importance of the foreign commerce and the movement of the imports and exports can be valued by the following table :

| Merchandise. | 1872. |
|---|---|
| **IMPORTS.** | |
| Live stock | 1,441,000 $ 000 |
| Animal refuse | 1,859,000 $ 000 |
| Fisheries | 1,756,000 $ 000 |
| Wool and hair | 3,193,000 $ 000 |
| Silk | 694,000 $ 000 |
| Cotton | 5,075,000 $ 000 |
| Linen | 783,000 $ 000 |
| Woods | 689,000 $ 000 |
| Farinaceous food | 1,953,000 $ 000 |
| Colonial goods | 3,348,000 $ 000 |
| Metals | 3,650,000 $ 000 |
| Wines and liquors | 250,000 $ 000 |
| Glass and stone ware | 248,000 $ 000 |
| Paper and its applications | 294,000 $ 000 |
| Sundry manufactures | 1,038,000 $ 000 |
| Mixed textures | 114,000 $ 000 |
| **EXPORTS.** | |
| Live stock | 1,615,000 $ 000 |
| Animal refuse | 1,521,000 $ 000 |
| Fisheries | 269,000 $ 000 |
| Wool and hair | 400,000 $ 000 |
| Silk | 102,000 $ 000 |
| Cotton | 504,000 $ 000 |
| Linen | 62,000 $ 000 |
| Woods | 1,351,000 $ 000 |
| Farinaceous food | 375,000 $ 000 |
| Colonial goods | 585,000 $ 000 |
| Metals | 419,000 $ 000 |
| Wines and liquors | 9,317,000 $ 000 |
| Glass and stoneware | 44,000 $ 000 |
| Paper and its applications | 44,000 $ 000 |
| Sundry manufactures | 375,000 $ 000 |

The importance of the commercial relations with the principal nations is indicated by the following table:

| Nations. | Importation, 1872. | Exportation, 1872. |
|---|---|---|
| Great Britain and, Possessions | 15,321,000 $ 000 | 13,196,000 $ 000 |
| France and Possessions | 2,920,000 $ 000 | 827,000 $ 000 |
| Brazil | 2,903,000 $ 000 | 3,524,000 $ 000 |
| Spain and Possessions | 1,575,000 $ 000 | 1,750,000 $ 000 |
| United States | 900,000 $ 000 | 211,000 $ 000 |
| Russia | 2,247,000 $ 000 | 755,000 $ 000 |
| North Germany | 398,000 $ 000 | 692,000 $ 000 |
| Holland and Possessions | 382,000 $ 000 | 473,000 $ 000 |
| Sweden and Norway | 478,000 $ 000 | 210,000 $ 000 |
| Italy | 135,000 $ 000 | 223,000 $ 000 |
| Portuguese Possessions } Africa | 742,000 $ 000 | 600,000 $ 000 |
| Asia | 85,000 $ 000 | 23,000 $ 000 |
| Belgium | 2,000 $ 000 | 182,000 $ 000 |
| Morocco | 41,000 $ 000 | 4,000 $ 000 |
| Argentine Republic | 5,000 $ 000 | 123,000 $ 000 |

# NAVIGATION.

The steam vessels arriving and departing from Portugese ports during the year 1872 were as follows: .

| NATIONALITIES. | ARRIVING. | | | DEPARTING. | | |
|---|---|---|---|---|---|---|
| | No. of vessels | Tonnage | Crews | No. of vessels | Tonnage | Crews |
| English | 1,003 | 769,381 | 32,675 | 1,008 | 869,727 | 32593 |
| Spanish | 135 | 49,117 | 3,125 | 133 | 69,791 | 3,063 |
| French | 127 | 74,277 | 5,784 | 126 | 125,523 | 5,511 |
| German | 27 | 22,080 | 759 | 26 | 25,500 | 744 |
| United States | ...... | ...... | ...... | ...... | ...... | ...... |
| Dutch | 26 | 17,796 | 669 | 25 | 18,929 | 642 |
| Sweedish and Norwegian | 10 | 3,573 | 136 | 10 | 3,374 | 138 |
| Brazilian | 2 | 557 | 34 | 3 | 1,717 | 45 |
| Danish | 1 | 977 | 22 | ...... | ...... | ...... |
| Portuguese { To and from foreign ports | ...... | ...... | ...... | 24 | 15,256 | 714 |
| To and from Portuguese ports | 8 | 8,273 | 353 | 12 | 13,092 | 491 |
| | 1,356 | 957,261 | 44,080 | 1,367 | 1142909 | 43941 |

The sailing vessels arriving and departing from Portuguese ports during the year 1872 were as follows :

| NATIONALITIES. | ARRIVING. | | | DEPARTING. | | |
|---|---|---|---|---|---|---|
| | No. of vessels | Tonnage | Crews. | No of vessels. | Tonnage | Crews. |
| English - | 895 | 174,104 | 6,699 | 904 | 185,966 | 6,739 |
| Spanish - | 846 | 16,623 | 768 | 916 | 18,699 | 6,409 |
| Swedish and Norwegian | 249 | 63,853 | 2,276 | 253 | 67,657 | 2,313 |
| Dutch | 114 | 16,623 | 768 | 109 | 16,522 | 726 |
| French - | 102 | 17,765 | 825 | 98 | 14,877 | 796 |
| United States | 11 | 4,335 | 101 | 11 | 4,595 | 102 |
| German | 69 | 11,767 | 502 | 64 | 11,499 | 481 |
| Austrian | 5 | 1,927 | 62 | 2 | 975 | 25 |
| Belgium | 5 | 1,098 | 37 | 5 | 1,157 | 37 |
| Brazilian | 5 | 1,451 | 68 | 5 | 1,448 | 70 |
| Danish | 55 | 7,531 | 350 | 57 | 7,402 | 396 |
| Italians. | 14 | 2,726 | 131 | 13 | 2,671 | 123 |
| Russians - | 72 | 20,917 | 735 | 70 | 21,167 | 710 |
| Portuguese { To and from foreign ports | 624 | 104,515 | 5,741 | 941 | 115,799 | 7,212 |
| { To and from Portuguese possessions | 55 | 13,429 | 642 | 54 | 12,877 | 628 |
| | 3,121 | 458,288 | 24,182 | 3,502 | 483,311 | 26767 |

————:0:————

# MEANS OF COMMUNICATIONS.

**Highways.**—The length of the highways constructed up the end of 1874 is as follows :

| | |
|---|---|
| Royal causeways, . . . | 3,136,419 metres. |
| District causeways, . | 701,322 " |
| Municipal causeways, . | 130,122 " |
| Total, . . . | 3,967,862 " |

Under way in the above year :

| | |
|---|---|
| Royal causeways, | 206,636 metres. |
| District causeways, . | 104,432 " |
| Municipal causeways, . | 1,972 " |
| Total, | 313,040 " |

The total amount of outlays up to the end of 1873 was 20,679,000-$ 000 reis. This total is made up the following items :

| | |
|---|---:|
| Work of construction, | 16,268,000 $ 000 |
| Technical and administrative personnel, | 1,246,000 $ 000 |
| Surveying, | 430,000 $ 000 |
| Ordinary repairing, | 2,001,000 $ 000 |
| Extraordinary repairing, | 715,000 $ 000 |
| Donations, | 19,000 $ 000 |
| Total, | 20,679,000 $ 000 |

The average outlay per kilometre is :

| | |
|---|---:|
| Construction, | 4,171 $ 000 |
| Personnel, | 319 $ 000 |
| Surveying, | 110 $ 000 |
| Ordinary repairing, | 513 $ 000 |
| Extraordinary repairing, | 183 $ 000 |

**Railroads.**—The following table shows the number and length of roads operated, under construction and planned up to the end of July, 1875, as well as the date of the commencement of work :

| RAILROADS. | Commencement of Labor. | Number of Kilometres. | | |
|---|---|---|---|---|
| | | Working. | Under Construction. | Surveyed. |
| Eastern Line—Lisbon to Badajoz | 1853 | 278 | .... | ... |
| Northern Line—Junction to Oporto | 1860 | 229 | .... | ... |
| Southeastern Line—Barreiro to Beja | 1856 | 154 | ... | ... |
| Algarve Line—Beja to Casevel | 1864 | 47 | 30 | 95 |
| Line from Evora to Extremoz | 1870 | 78 | ... | ... |
| Setubal Branch | ...... | 12 | ... | ... |
| Southeastern Line—Beja to frontier | 1864 | 20 | ... | 42 |
| Minho Line | 1873 | 55 | 34 | 46 |
| Douro Line | 1873 | 38 | 20 | 40 |
| Beira Alta Line | ...... | ...... | ... | 196 |
| Beira Baixa Line | ...... | ...... | ... | 140 |
| | | 911 | 84 | 559 |

Besides these main lines there are the following railroads employed in industrial establishments :

| | |
|---|---|
| S. Domingos Mine (private) | 17 Kilometres |
| Braçal Mine " | 8 " |
| Leiria to S. Martinho government pine forests | 37 " |
| Aljustrel Mine (private) | 17 " |

The total receipts and gross income per Kilometre was in the North and Eastern R. R.:

| Years. | Number of Kilometres Worked. | Total Receipts. | RECEIPTS PER KILOMETRE. | | |
|---|---|---|---|---|---|
| | | | Fast Trains. | Slow Trains. | Total. |
| 1868 | | 1,019,508 $ 000 | 1,133 $ 000 | 874 $ 000 | 2,007 $ 000 |
| 1869 | 508 | 1,119,466 $ 000 | 1,149 $ 000 | 1,055 $ 000 | 2,204 $ 000 |
| 1870 | | 1,160,831 $ 000 | 1,160 $ 000 | 1,125 $ 000 | 2,285 $ 000 |
| 1871 | | 1,218,743 $ 000 | 1,243 $ 000 | 1,185 $ 000 | 2,428 $ 000 |
| 1872 | | 1,372,551 $ 000 | 1,373 $ 000 | 1,361 $ 000 | 2,734 $ 000 |
| 1873 | 502 | 1,713,131 $ 000 | 1,518 $ 000 | 1,895 $ 000 | 3,413 $ 000 |
| 1874 | | 1,667,778 $ 000 | 1,643 $ 000 | 1,679 $ 000 | 3,322 $ 000 |

The income of the South and Southeastern R. R.:

| Years. | Number of Kilometres Worked. | INCOME. | | | Gross income per Kilometre. | Expenses per Kilometre. | Net income per Kilometre. | Relations of expenses to Receipts. |
|---|---|---|---|---|---|---|---|---|
| | | From Passengers. | Merchandise Cattle. | Total. | | | | |
| 1870 | 212 | 75,746 $ 000 | 151,014 $ 000 | 226,760 $ 000 | 1,070 $ 000 | 617 $ 000 | 453 $ 000 | 57.6 |
| 1871 | 259 | 89,279 $ 000 | 190,511 $ 000 | 279,790 $ 000 | 1,080 $ 000 | 575 $ 000 | 505 $ 000 | 53.2 |
| 1872 | 284 | 99,753 $ 000 | 217,140 $ 000 | 316,893 $ 000 | 1,116 $ 000 | 573 $ 000 | 543 $ 000 | 51.3 |
| 1873 | 312 | 110,532 $ 000 | 241,211 $ 000 | 351,743 $ 000 | 1,127 $ 000 | 542 $ 000 | 585 $ 000 | 48.1 |

————:o:————

# PUBLIC INSTRUCTION.

The administration of affairs relative to public instruction is in charge of a general direction in the Ministry of the Interior. A consulting board of public instruction acts together with this Ministry, giving its vote on the works that are submitted to its examination and consulting on questions of public education. The special military education is under the direction of the Ministry of War, and the naval education under that of the Ministry of Marine.

The public instruction is divided into three branches: higher, secondary and primary, having besides the special instruction of the fine arts.

The expenses, in charge of the Ministry of the Interior, of the public instruction was the following:

| | |
|---|---|
| 1874—1875, | 777,611 $ 000 |
| Estimate for 1875—76 | 798,614 $ 000 |

This estimate of expenses is distributed in the following manner.

| | |
|---|---:|
| Consulting Board, | 1,200 $ 000 |
| Coimbra University, | 87,285 $ 000 |
| Lisbon Polytechnic School, | 55,247 $ 000 |
| Oporto Polytechnic Academy, | 17,874 $ 000 |
| Lisbon Medico-Surgical School, | 13,573 $ 000 |
| Oporto Medico-Surgical School, | 12,840 $ 000 |
| Funchal Medico-Surgical School, | 1,027 $ 000 |
| Higher Course of Letters (Curso superior de letras) | 3,400 $ 000 |
| Extraordinary Gratifications | 4,000 $ 000 |
| Lisbon Academy of Fine Arts, | 9,050 $ 000 |
| Oporto Academy of Fine Arts, | 4,556 $ 000 |
| Subsidies to Pensionists, | 3,600 $ 000 |
| Lisbon Royal Conservatory, | 6,432 $ 000 |
| Subsidies to Theatres, | 33,552 $ 000 |
| Lyceums, | 67,418 $ 000 |
| Secondary Instruction outside of Lyceume, | 13,410 $ 000 |
| Extraordinary Gratifications, | 6,000 $ 000 |
| Primary Normal Schools, | 7,637 $ 000 |
| Primary Teachings, | 244,734 $ 000 |
| Other Expenses, | 35,400 $ 000 |
| Royal Academy of Sciences, | 12,609 $ 000 |
| Archives of Torre do Tombo, | 7,080 $ 000 |
| Public Libraries, | 11,730 $ 000 |
| State Printing Offices, | 138,830 $ 000 |
| | 798,614 $ 000 |

Added to the expenses in charge of other Ministries, as follows :

| | |
|---|---:|
| Military school, | 31,143 $ 000 |
| Military college, | 19,056 $ 000 |
| Naval school, | 7,470 $ 000 |
| Elementary agricultural teaching, | 3,500 $ 000 |
| General Institute of Agriculture, | 17,857 $ 000 |
| Lisbon Industrial Institute, | 14,320 $ 000 |
| Oporto Industrial Institute, | 10,770 $ 000 |
| Grand total, | 902,730 $ 000 |

The sum spent by the private parties can be estimated at 300,000-$ 000, being the total outlay of the country with the instruction estimated at 1,200,000 $ 000.

————:o:————

# HIGHER INSTRUCTION.

The higher teaching is furnished by the following establishments : Coimbra University, Lisbon Polytechnic School, Military School, Oporto Polytechnic Academy, Lisbon, Oporto and Funchal medico-surgical schools and Higher Course of Letters (Curso superior de letras).

**The Coimbra University** was established at Lisbon in the year 1290 by King D. Diniz, belonging to a friar of Santa Cruz the glory of promoting its creation. In 1307 it was transferred to Coimbra, returning to the capital seventy years afterwards; but, in 1537, D. Joao III had it moved anew to that city, where it has remained till to-day.

Until 1772 there were taught there only theology, law and medicine; but a great reform, effected by the Marquis of Pombal, created in that year the faculties of mathematics and philosophy. Afterwards, some chairs in the faculty of philosophy and an administrative course were established.

The teachings in the university embrace the following subjects:

| | |
|---|---|
| Theology, . . | 8 chairs. |
| Law, . . . | 15 " |
| Administrative course, | 9 " |
| Medicine, . . . | 12 " |
| Mathematics, | 8 " |
| Philosophy, . . | 8 " |

The statistical movement of the Alumni:

| FACULTIES. | 1870—1871. | | | | | 1871—1872. | | | | | 1872—1873. | | | | |
|---|---|---|---|---|---|---|---|---|---|---|---|---|---|---|---|
| | Matriculated | Examined. | Approved. | Rejected. | Awarded. | Matriculated | Examined. | Approved. | Rejected. | Awarded. | Matriculated | Examined. | Approved. | Rejected. | Awarded. |
| Theology . | 39 | 38 | 38 | ... | 3 | 63 | 45 | 45 | ... | 4 | 83 | 51 | 51 | ... | 3 |
| Law . . . | 343 | 338 | 330 | 8 | 16 | 368 | 353 | 346 | 7 | 15 | 398 | 383 | 378 | 5 | 15 |
| Administrative Course . } | 6 | 5 | 5 | ... | ... | 1 | 2 | 2 | ... | ... | 3 | 3 | 3 | ... | ... |
| Medicine . | 56 | 55 | 55 | ... | ... | 63 | 63 | 62 | 1 | 11 | 81 | 81 | 81 | ... | 17 |
| Mathematics | 104 | 76 | 71 | 5 | 15 | 128 | 65 | 60 | 5 | 16 | 129 | 80 | 72 | 8 | 9 |
| Philosophy . | 262 | 237 | 225 | 12 | 20 | 298 | 281 | 265 | 16 | 21 | 265 | 248 | 222 | 26 | 18 |
| Total . . | 810 | 749 | 724 | 25 | 61 | 921 | 809 | 780 | 20 | 67 | 959 | 846 | 807 | 39 | 62 |
| Design . . | 103 | 89 | 89 | ... | ... | 114 | 84 | 81 | 3 | ... | 125 | 101 | 98 | 3 | ... |
| Total | 913 | 838 | 813 | 25 | 61 | 1035 | 893 | 861 | 32 | 67 | 1084 | 947 | 905 | 42 | 62 |

**The Polytechnic School** embraces the teachings of higher mathematics, of natural history, and of political economy, taught by 13 chairs.

Statistical movement of the alumi in the Polytechnic School:

| ELECTIVE YEARS. | Number of Students. | Matriculations. | Approbations. | Rejections. | Did not come up for examination. | Prizes. |
|---|---|---|---|---|---|---|
| 1856—57 | 213 | 548 | 173 | 87 | 305 | 7 |
| 1857—58 | 181 | 487 | 154 | 41 | 307 | 3 |
| 1858—59 | 172 | 489 | 167 | 47 | 280 | 5 |
| 1859—60 | 161 | 485 | 161 | 44 | 282 | 10 |
| 1860—61 | 150 | 358 | 186 | 45 | 127 | 8 |
| 1861—62 | 161 | 387 | 205 | 52 | 130 | 10 |
| 1862—63 | 170 | 428 | 249 | 41 | 138 | 9 |
| 1863—64 | 183 | 437 | 257 | 46 | 134 | 8 |
| 1864—65 | 160 | 394 | 206 | 54 | 134 | 6 |
| 1865—66 | 115 | 337 | 198 | 25 | 114 | 3 |
| 1866—67 | 126 | 353 | 190 | 35 | 128 | 7 |
| 1867—68 | 156 | 449 | 295 | 20 | 134 | 13 |
| 1868—69 | 167· | 490 | 324 | 31 | 139 | 16 |
| 1869—70 | 198 | 574 | 356 | 38 | 180 | 16 |
| 1870—71 | 174 | 531 | 295 | 32 | 204 | 16 |
| 1871—72 | 174 | 480 | 303 | 40 | 137 | 14 |

**The Military School** is a school of application where the alumni finish their several courses in different branches of the military service and likewise civil engineering.

Statistical changes of the alumni of the Military School ;

| Elective years. | COURSES. | Finished their course. | Passed their year. | Did not pass, | Total of matriculated. | Awarded. | |
|---|---|---|---|---|---|---|---|
| | | | | | | Pecuniary prizes. | Honorific Prizes. |
| 1873 to 1874 | Military engineering, . | 5 | 23 | 1 | 29 | 3 | .... |
| | Artillery, | 10 | 16 | 3 | 29 | 2 | .... |
| | Staff, | 1 | 1 | ... | 2 | 2 | .... |
| | Civil engineering, . | 2 | 4 | 1 | 7 | 2 | 2 |
| | Cavalry and Infantry, . | 62 | 62 | 69 | 193 | 2 | 4 |
| | | | | | 260 | | |

**Naval School.**—In 1796 an academy of marine guards was established, and abolished in 1845, establishing in May of that year the Naval School. The marine-guards company had, however, been established in 1792.

. In the **Oporto Polytechnic Academy** there are taught mathematics, natural history, political economy, and the chairs of application to finish the course of civil engineering in 13 chairs.

The statistical changes in the alumni are as follows:

| ELECTIVE YEARS. | Number of the Alumni | Matricula-tions. | Approvals. | Rejections. | Did not get Examined. |
|---|---|---|---|---|---|
| 1870—71 | 90 | 205 | 190 | ... | 15 |
| 1871—72 | 98 | 221 | 196 | ... | 25 |
| 1872—73 | 109 | 226 | 208 | 2 | 16 |

**Lisbon and Oporto Medico-Surgical Schools** have 11 professors and 4 substitutes; 1 surgical demonstrator, 1 professor and preserver of the Museum of Anatomy, and 1 professor of the pharmaceutical dispensary.

The changes in the Alumni were as follows:

## LISBON MEDICO-SURGICAL SCHOOL.

| ELECTIVE YEARS. | Number of the Alumni | Matricula-tions. | Approba-tions. | Rejections. | Did not get Examined. |
|---|---|---|---|---|---|
| 1870—71 | 57 | 130 | 126 | 2 | 2 |
| 1871—72 | 69 | 141 | 130 | 2 | 9 |
| 1872—73 | 90 | 199 | 191 | 2 | 6 |

## OPORTO MEDICO-SURGICAL SCHOOL.

| | | | | | |
|---|---|---|---|---|---|
| 1870—71 | 84 | 203 | 188 | 2 | 13 |
| 1871—72 | 89 | 219 | 201 | 2 | 16 |
| 1872—73 | 98 | 247 | 235 | 1 | 11 |

In those two schools there are taught anatomy, physiology, and hygiene, natural history of the medicaments, external pathology, &c., surgical apparatuses and operations, obstetrics, internal pathology, medical clinics, surgical clinics, legal medicine, public hygiene, and pathological anatomy.

**The Funchal Medico-Surgical Schools** has 2 professors, 1 of anatomy and physiology and 1 of pathology and materia-medica, and 1 of pharmacy.

The changes in the Alumni were:

| ELECTIVE YEARS. | Matriculations. | Approbations. | Rejections. | Did not get Examined. |
|---|---|---|---|---|
| 1870—71 | 18 | 14 | 1 | 3 |
| 1871—72 | 11 | 10 | ... | 1 |
| 1872—73 | 4 | 4 | ... | ... |

In the **Higher Course of Letters** there are 5 chairs, in which are taught: 1st chair—Universal History; 2nd—Latin and Greek Literature; 3rd—Modern Literature of Europe, and specially of Portugal; 4th—Philosophy; 5th—Philosophical Universal History.

It has five professors.

This Course was founded by King D. Pedro V., donating it with a capital of 30,000 $ 000 reis in public funds.

The changes in the Alumni were as follows:

| YEARS. | Number of the Alumni | Matricula-tions. | Approba-tions. | Rejections. | Did not get Examined. |
|---|---|---|---|---|---|
| 1870—71 | 17 | 36 | 18 | 5 | 13 |
| 1871—72 | 18 | 38 | 10 | 1 | 27 |
| 1872—73 | 14 | 32 | 22 | 4 | 6 |

# SECONDARY INSTRUCTION.

For the official secondary teaching there are in the Kingdom 18 lyceums, 17 being at the capitals of the administrative districts and 1 in Lamego.

In the adjacent islands there are four lyceums at the capitals of the districts.

In order to be able to compare the changes in the Alumni among the several districts, as well of the continent as at the adjacent islands, we give the following table of the movements of the national lyceums in the elective year of 1873—74:

| LYCEUMS. | Number of the Alumni. | Matriculations. | Approbations. | Rejections. | Did not get Examined. | Approbations. | Rejections. | Approbations. | Rejections. |
|---|---|---|---|---|---|---|---|---|---|
| | Alumni of the Lyceums. | | | | | Outside of the Lyceums. MALES. | | FEMALES. | |
| Aveiro | 100 | 232 | 27 | 12 | 193 | 88 | 50 | 3 | ......... |
| Beja | 52 | 179 | 15 | 7 | 157 | 3 | 7 | ......... | ......... |
| Braga | 304 | 560 | 84 | 37 | 439 | 521 | 209 | ......... | ......... |
| Bragança | 93 | 275 | 24 | 9 | 242 | 3 | 11 | ......... | ......... |
| Castello Branco | 54 | 172 | 5 | 12 | 155 | 30 | 11 | ......... | ......... |
| Coimbra | 147 | 250 | 50 | 24 | 176 | 716 | 323 | ......... | ......... |
| Evora | 64 | 167 | 13 | 6 | 148 | 27 | 37 | 1 | ......... |
| Faro | 128 | 387 | 10 | 6 | 371 | 22 | 18 | ......... | ......... |
| Guarda | 165 | 465 | 35 | 30 | 400 | 57 | 28 | ......... | ......... |
| Leiria | 51 | 133 | 6 | 13 | 114 | 8 | 11 | 7 | ......... |
| Lisbon | 235 | 676 | 60 | 16 | 600 | 678 | 448 | 21 | ......... |
| Portalegre | 54 | 117 | 3 | 6 | 108 | 22 | 29 | ......... | ......... |
| Oporto | 257 | 551 | 63 | 48 | 440 | 378 | 299 | ......... | ......... |
| Santarem | 148 | 413 | 26 | 12 | 375 | 75 | 57 | ......... | ......... |
| Vianna | 112 | 284 | 15 | 13 | 256 | 55 | 42 | ......... | ......... |
| Villa Real | 74 | 197 | 5 | 3 | 189 | 40 | 13 | ......... | ......... |
| Viseu | 258 | 629 | 61 | 41 | 527 | 147 | 97 | ......... | ......... |
| Lamego | 89 | 231 | 3 | ... | 228 | 87 | 47 | ......... | ......... |
| | 2385 | 5918 | 505 | 295 | 5118 | 2957 | 1737 | 32 | ......... |
| Angra | 48 | 172 | 20 | ... | 152 | 27 | 12 | ......... | ......... |
| Horta | 46 | 180 | 18 | ... | 162 | ... | ......... | ......... | ......... |
| Ponta Delgada | 45 | 153 | 18 | 1 | 134 | 25 | 3 | ......... | ......... |
| Funchal | 118 | 460 | 60 | 8 | 392 | 22 | 3 | ......... | ......... |
| | 257 | 965 | 116 | 9 | 840 | 74 | 18 | | ......... |
| General Total | 2642 | 6883 | 621 | 304 | 5958 | 3031 | 1755 | 32 | ......... |

The lyceums are divided in two classes. The first class lyceums are those of the districts of Lisbon, Oporto, Coimbra, Braga, Evora, Santarem, Viseu, and Funchal.

The Lisbon Lyceum has 10 professors and 3 substitutes; that of Oporto 10 professors and 3 substitutes; that of Coimbra 12 professors and 3 substitutes; the lyceums of Braga, Evora, and Santarem have each one 10 professors and 3 substitutes; the Funchal Lyceum has 7 professors.

The second class lyceums have each 5 professors.

The total number of professors in the lyceumns is 157.

Outside of the lyceums there are in several towns of the Kingdom 57 professors of Secoudary Instructton and 5 in the adjacent islands.

**Royal Military College.**—This establishment was founded in 1803, and is destined to two principal purposes : to remunerate the services of the Army and Navy officers, giving free instruction to their sons and give these a military education.

At present the number of alumni, pensioners, and portionists is of 196. For the maintenance and expenses of the College it has in the estimate of the Ministry of War an appropriation of 18,000 $ 000 reis.

The personnel consists of 1 director, brigadier general, 1 subdirector, 1 adjutant, 1 secretary, 1 quartermaster, 4 staff officers, 1 surgeon, 1 chaplain, and 7 professors.

———:o;———

# PRIMARY INSTRUCTION.

There are in Lisbon two normal primary schools, one for males and the other for females; established by the decrec of the 14th of December, 1869, whose object is to prepare professors for the primary instruction.

The first one has two professors, who governs the primary school annexed to the normal.

The second one has a regent and three female teachers.

Each one of the normal schools may receive 20 students, for each one of which the State gives a pension of 6 $ 000 reis monthly.

There were in 1862 in the Kingdom 1,336 public schools for males and 127 for females. In 1874 there were already 1,987 of the former and 458 of the latter.

At the adjacent islands there were in 1862 ninety-three professors aud twenty-six female teachers, and in 1874 one hundred aud twenty-seven of the first and forty-scven of the second.

Besides this there were eight more municipal schools for males and four for females.

The total number of public schools in 1874 was therefore 2,631.

There were in 1862 four hundred and eighty professors and four hundred and sixty-four female teachers of free schools in the Kingdom and forty of the first and one hundred and thirty-four of the second in the adjacent islands.

In 1874 there were in the Kingdom 1,987 professors and 458 ruling female teachers and 8 professors and 4 municipal female teachers; at the adjacent islands 127 professors and 47 female teachers, the whole being 2,212 of the one and 509 of the other.

The following table shows, at different periods, the total number of schools, the number of alumni of both sexes, and the relation between the number of inhabitants and the number of alumni in the Kingdom and adjacent islands :

## IN THE CONTINENT.

| YEARS. | Number of Schools. | | Number of Alumni. | | Ready at the end of the Year. | | Relation between the population and the Alumni. | |
|---|---|---|---|---|---|---|---|---|
| | Males. | Females. | Males. | Females. | Males. | Females. | Males. | Females. |
| 1869–70 | 1733 | 274 | 88301 | 18108 | 7394 | 1160 | 39,6 | 203,3 |
| 1870–71 | 1777 | 286 | 85904 | 16741 | 6569 | 987 | 38,3 | 213,1 |
| 1871–72 | 1802 | 297 | 87359 | 17809 | 5708 | 1049 | 50,7 | 229,7 |

## IN THE ADJACENT ISLANDS.

| YEARS. | Males. | Females. | Males. | Females. | Males. | Females. | Males. | Females. |
|---|---|---|---|---|---|---|---|---|
| 1869–70 | 107 | 35 | 5842 | 2686 | 302 | 107 | 46,7 | 116,3 |
| 1870–71 | 108 | 37 | 5093 | 2328 | 256 | 129 | 59.8 | 152,6 |
| 1871–72 | 108 | 37 | 5475 | 2454 | 211 | 139 | 51,2 | 132,9 |

We join in the following table the statistic of the primary instruction examinations in order to obtain admission at the National Lyceums, and of the preparing examinations for the primary teachings, in the five years from 1870 to 1872, in the continent of the Kingdom and in the adjacent islands .

| YEARS. | Examinations for admission to the Lyceums | | | | | | Prepared for Teaching. | | | |
|---|---|---|---|---|---|---|---|---|---|---|
| | Examined. | | Approved. | | Rejected. | | Examined. | | Prepared. | |
| | Males. | Females. | Males. | Females. | Males. | Females. | Males. | Females. | Males. | Females. |
| 1870 | 2097 | 113 | 1617 | 102 | 480 | 11 | 324 | 107 | 123 | 64 |
| 1871 | 1802 | 118 | 1437 | 89 | 365 | 29 | 488 | 120 | 157 | 60 |
| 1872 | 1815 | 103 | 1486 | 91 | 329 | 12 | 341 | 93 | 129 | 63 |

# SPECIAL INSTRUCTION.

There is understood under this designation the teaching of the fine arts, for which there are the following establishments: Lisbon Royal Academy of Fine Arts, Oporto Academy of Fine Arts, and Lisbon Royal Conservatory.

**The Lisbon Royal Academy of Fine Arts** had an origin in the school of design established in 1781. It teaches historical design, ornamental and civil architectural, historic and landscape painting, sculpture, historic engraving, wood engraving, and from life. It has 6 professors.

In 1873-74 the change was the following: Attendance, 224—56 being in day and 148 in night schools, and 20 in both. There were 54 approbations and 28 rejections.

**The Oporto Academy of Fine Arts** had an origin in a drawing and designing school established in 1779. It has four schools—historical design, historical painting, civil architecture, sculpture, perspective and anatomy, with four professors.

The attendance in 1873-74 was of 33, having 40 approbations.

The government subsidizes 4 to 5 artists to study Fine Arts in foreign countries.

**The Lisbon Royal Conservatory** comprises a school of dramatic art and a music school. In the first there are 3 professors, 1 of the art of representation, 1 of recitation, and 1 of grammar and pronunciation. In the second there are 10 professors.

The following table shows the changes in the Alumni:

| ELECTIVE YEARS. | MALES. | | | | FEMALES. | | | |
|---|---|---|---|---|---|---|---|---|
| | Number of Alumni. | Matriculations. | Examinations. | Approbations. | Number of Alumni. | Matriculations. | Examinations. | Approbations. |
| 1871—72 | 127 | 167 | 132 | 121 | 149 | 213 | 256 | 206 |
| 1872—73 | 107 | 139 | 121 | 114 | 139 | 197 | 232 | 202 |
| 1873—74 | 95 | 120 | 111 | 105 | 118 | 157 | 235 | 204 |

# INDUSTRIAL AND COMMERCIAL TEACHING.

In 1852–53 there were established in Lisbon an **Industrial Institute** and an **Industrial School** in Oporto. The ancient Commercial School, established by the Marquis of Pombal, was annexed afterwards to the Lisbon Institute.

By the primitive organization this establishment was limited to the purely industrial and commercial teaching, but at present comprises the following courses: of general instruction for workmen, of factory directors, of industrial shops, superintendents and assistants, assistant civil engineers, of engineers and firemen, of telegraph operators, of masters of works, of constructors of instruments of precision, and of commercial course.

The following table shows the movement of the Alumni in this institute:

| YEARS. | Matriculated. | Approved. | Rejected. | Approved with Distinction. |
|--------|---------------|-----------|-----------|----------------------------|
| 1870—71 | 427 | 107 | 13 | 16 |
| 1871—72 | 576 | 109 | 27 | 7 |

In 1872–73 three hundred and eighty-eight alumni frequented the institute, and there were 705 matriculations.

The professors are 10 and 1 French and English professor.

The personnel of the administration consists of 1 director, 1 library secretary, 1 clerk, 1 janitor, and 1 preparator.

It forms part of the institute a shop of instruments of precision, with a special director.

The expenses for 1875–76 are estimated at 14,320 $ 000 reis.

The number of alumni matriculated in 1854 was 402.

**The Oporto Industrial Institute** has the same organization and has 10 professors.

The expenses are of 10,770 $ 000 reis.

The number of alumni matriculated in 1854 was of 328.

# AGRICULTURAL TEACHING.

The agricultual teaching, decreed in 1852, is divided into elementary and higher. For the elementary teaching there were established in 1852 model farms, and in 1869 there was decreed the establishment of experimental stations in the districts, and elementary courses of agriculture in the lyceums. For the higher agricultural teaching there exists the General Institute of Agriculture, which was established in 1852, incorporating to it in 1855 the veterinary teaching, which, up to that time, was in charge of a veterinary school.

There is at present for the elementary teaching only the Cintra model farm, which has an expense of 3,500 $ 000 reis, voted in the estimate of the State.

In some districts there were established experimental stations, and the agricultural and zootechnic courses were commenced. These courses are not obligatory; its purpose is only to disperse and divulge agricultural knowledge.

**The General Agricultural Institute** comprises the agricultural and veterinary courses, and it has 10 professors and 1 professor of design.

The administrative personnel consists of a director and 5 subaltern employees. It has 5 chiefs of the service.

————:o:————

# SCIENTIFIC ESTABLISHMENTS.

**The Royal Academy of Sciences** was established in 1779 by the initiative of the duke of Lafoes and the abbott José Correia da Serra. By its primitive statutes it was divided into three classes: 1st—Natural Sciences; 2nd—Mathematical Sciences; 3rd—Literature.

Each class had to have 8 effective members. Afterwards the number of supernumerary members was fixed at 12, the honorary ones at 12, and the corresponding ones at 100.

————:o:————

# ASTRONOMICAL ESTABLISHMENTS.

Portugal possesses 3 astronomical establishments: The Lisbon Royal Observatory, the Astronomical Observatory of Coimbra University, and that of the Lisbon Polytechnic School (in construction.)

In 1874 the ancient Marine Astronomical Observatory, in Lisbon, was abolished and annexed to the Naval School, for the practical study of astronomy and navigation in the course of the same school. It has under its charge the regulation of the chronometers and determination of error of the instruments destined for the men of war.

The principal instruments that this observatory possessed were :— 1 Repsold meridian circle, with a focal distance of 1.36 metres and the objective of 0.10 metre of diameter ; 1 instrument of passages ; 1 parallatic refractor, with a focal distance of 2.61 metres and objective of 0.165 metres, and 1 Repsold universal. The observatory possessed several other instruments, noting among them 1 zygometre, constructed by the able artist Mr. José Mauricio Vieira, at the shop of instruments of precision of the industrial institute of Lisbon.

**The Lisbon Royal Astronomical Observatory** es indebted to the love of science and liberality of the King D. Pedro V., and to the initiative of Dr. Filippe Folque. The plan of the observatory is similar to the one of Pulkowa. Height of the place 93 metres.

The collection of instruments of the observatory consists of 1 large equatorial of a focal distance of 7 metres and 0.38 metres of objective aperture ; 1 instrument of passages by the first vertical, Struve's system, with 2.31 metres of focal distance and 0.16 metres of aperture ; 1 meridian circle with 0.15 metres of aperture and 2 metres of focal distance ; 1 instrument of passages of the system of Oom, with 0.07 metres of aperture and 0.78 metres of focal distance ; 1 parallatic refractor of 1.95 metres. focal distance and 0.117 of aperture ; an explorator of 0.64 metres of focal distance and 0.077 metres of aperture ; a normal pendulum of Krille, regulator of electro-chronometric apparatuses ; several chronometres and pendulums ; 1 chronograph ; electric apparatuses ; 1 zigometre ; collimators, barometers, thermometers, and telegraphic apparatuses.

**The Coimbra Observatory**, whose establishment is indebted to the Marquis of Pombal, is built alongside of the University building, and is destined principally to the practical teaching of astronomy in the faculty of mathematics.

The principal instruments that it possesses are : equatorial, meridian circle, instrument of passage by the first vertical and sideral pendulum of Berthoud.

The technical personnel consists of a director, two astronomers, and two calculators.

# GEODETICAL LABORS.*

The geodetical labors in Portugal were commenced at the end of last century. In 1788, Dr. Francisco Antonio Ciera, professor of the naval academy, took charge of these labors, and commenced them in 1790, surveying a base between Buarcos and Monte Redondo, and another of verification between Montijo and Batel, and selecting 32 points for its triangulation of first order.

In 1796 these labors were suspended, and were only resumed in 1835, repeating the survey of the base of Montijo. The geodetical labors were then entrusted to General Pedro Folque, who had assisted Dr. Ciera in the first labors, and to his son Dr. Filippe Folque, who after the death of his father, was appointed to superintend these labors which in 1839 were again interrupted; they were recommenced in 1843 and kept on slowly till 1852, epoch, in which, with the establishment of the Ministry of Public Works, geodesy received a powerful impulse, creating in said Ministry a general direction of geodetical, topographical, and hydrographical labors, adding to it afterwards the Geological Survey.

It belongs to Dr. Ciera the honor of having initiated geodesy in Portugal; but to General Filippe Folque, who is deceased, certainly belongs the glory of having definitely established and organized the geodetical and topographical labors.

Until the end of 1874 the following labors were executed: Having newly surveyed the ancient base of Montijo and Batel, the general triangulation of the Kingdom was proceeded with, having selected 129 points as vertex of the large first order triangles, whose angles were being observed successively in order to proceed forthwith with the subdivision of the first triangles for commencing the survey of the general map of the Kingdom, and prosecute this work simultaneously with that of the triangulation. By this method, when the triangulation of first order was finished, already the secondary triangulation embraced all of Extremadura and almost the whole of the provinces of Alemtejo and Beira Alta, Beira Baixa and Minho, and a small part of Algarve along the Guadiana, and of the coast up to Tavira.

The survey of the general map of the Kingdom was commenced in the scale of 1 to 10,000, but the urgent necessity of maps that would serve as a basis for sundry services of the public administration, brought the government to order that the chorographical survey should be proceeded with in the scale of 1 to 100,000.

A few years afterwards the wants of the service called on the geodetical commission to prepare in the shortest possible period a geographical map of the whole Kingdom, which was carried out, executing in four years a rapid survey of the whole country, and tracing the geographical map in the scale of 1 to 500,000, which is published.

---

*Geographia e Estatistica de Portugal e Colonias by Gerardo Pery.

The atlas of the chorographical map of Portugal has to be made of 37 sheets, of which 22 are finished, 3 commenced, and 14 published. In the topographical scale of 1 to 2,500 and 1 to 5,000 several surveys were made, being the most important, the plan of the grounds of Mondego and the one of the suburbs of Lisbon.

The hydrographic labors had commenced in 1842, under the direction of the Ministry of Marine, executing the hydrographical plan of the bar of Lisbon and that of the river Tejo up to the tower of Belem, carrying the plan up to the meridian of the observatory of the castle of Lisbon. There was also made at this time the hydrographical plan of Berlengas islands and the soundings between them and Carvoeiro cape. But it was in 1852 that hydrography acquired greater developments. Up to to-day the hydrographical plans surveyed, and the respective studies made are in the following ports and rivers: Figueira da Foz and Mondego river; bar of Oporto and Douro up to the suspension bridge; bar and river of Aveiro; Vianna do Castello and Lima river; Caminha and Minho river; finally, the bar of Faro and Olhao, and Faro inlet, and the hydrographical labors in the river Guadiana and bar of Villa Real de Santo Antonio. Besides these labors the soundings of the Tejo were finished from the tower of Belem up to the eastern extremity of the capital. Of these labors there are already published the charts of the bars of Lisbon and Oporto, and the ones of the Berlengas.

As the geodetical observations of the first order had been made provisionally, and only with the necessary rigor to furnish the precise elements for the subdivision of the triangles, and for the geographical surveys, it was necessary for the solution of several cases of high geodesy to proceed to observations of an entirely exact and definite nature. It is what has been done in the last years, and is under way, having employed a new system of observations and calculations in harmony with the progress of science and the marvelous acuteness of the instruments.

The universals of Repsold and the altazimuths of Throughton, are used, employing at the stations Gauss' heliotropes. In the observations the reiterating method is used.

The observations of the chain of triangles of the parallel of Lisbon are finished, which unites with that of Spanish triangulation which passes by the Ciudad Real and the Balearic Islands, (thus facilitating the survey of a parallel of 13°), and the observations of the chain of the average meridian of the country are very much advanced.

The care and exactness in the observations and the perfection of the instruments are such that the greatest error probable of the medium directions does not exceed $\pm$ 0".3 in the horizontal directions and of $\pm$ 0".6 in the zenith distances.

For the definitive determination of altitudes it was commenced by determining the exact altitude of a point of first order (S. Felix, near Villa de Conde) by means of a geometrical leveling of precision between said point and a tides rule established next to that place.

Starting from that point the exact altitudes of several others in the province of Minho were determined.

The principal labors executed by the Geological Section up to the end of 1874 were the geological survey for the execution of the general geological map of the Kingdom in the scale of $\frac{1}{500,000}$, which is finished; the classification of the numberless collection of rocks and fossils gathered throughout the country, and the publication of several geological memoirs.

The drawing of all the works above mentioned have been executed at the Engraving Section of the same direction, to which is annexed a lithographic shop. The engraving is on stone and has attained a remarkable perfection.

In 1872 a Photographic Section was established with the object of substituting the stone engraving by the photo-lithography or by photo-engraving processes far more expeditious and economical than the first.

In Austria, France, Belgium, and Germany these processes are used after the sanction of some years' practice. Portugal, having made at intervals some trials and attempts, either at the national printing office or at the ministry of war, or at the same geodetical commission, that service was definitely put in operation in 1873, the chief of the section introducing such important modifications in some of the processes already known, that it came to get superior results to those that had been obtained in foreign countries. "In the short space of two years that section produced more than 14,000 photographs, nearly 500 photo-engravings, and more than 70 photrgraphic copies with salts of silver." With the exception of a chemical engraver, a Swiss, employed in December 1874, all of the personnel, composed of 9 employees, are Portuguese. Besides the labors above mentioned, this section has executed some reproductions employing phototypy and helio-engraving processes, and prosecutes assiduously in the perfection of photo-lithography and photo-engraving applied to the reproduction of geographical maps.

In regard to the photo-lithographic process the chief of the section says that "it is essentially Portuguese, belonging to us the honor of establishing ourselves on sure bases the use of very thin metallic sheets, that work excellently in several methods of photo-chemical impression."

The personnel of the direction of the geodetical labors is composed of 1 director, 7 chiefs of sections, and 29 assistants: officers of engineering, of the staff, of artillery, of hydrographic engineers, of cavalry and infantry; 12 engravers; 2 designers; 1 stamper, and 2 apprentices; 1 paying accountant; 2 clerks; 1 janitor; 1 porter; 2 collectors, and 3 servants; 1 sargeant; 2 corporals, and 27 soldiers of the battalion of engineers.

In the budget for 1875–76 the expenses of this general direction are of 62,466$300 reis.

# CATALOGUE.

# DEPARTMENT II.---MANUFACTURES.

*Location:*—MAIN BUILDING.

## CHEMICALS.

CLASS 200.—Chemicals, pharmaceutical preparations.
Mineral acids, and the methods of manufacture. Sulphuric, nitric, and hydrochloric acids.
The common commercial alkalies, potash, soda, and ammonia, with their carbonates.
Salt and its production. Salts from deposits—native salt. Salt by solar evaporation from sea water. Salt, by evaporation from water of saline sprinus or wells. Rock salt. Ground and table salt.
Bleaching powders and chloride of lime.
Yeast powders, baking powders.
CLASS 201.—Oils, soaps, candles, illuminating and other gases.
Oils from mineral, animal, and vegetable sources. Refined petroleum, benzine, naptha, and other products of the manufacture. Oils from various seeds, refined, and of various degrees of purity. Olive oil, cotton seed oil, palm oil. Animal oils, of various kinds, in their refined state. Oils prepared for special purposes besides lighting and for food. Lubricating oils.
Soaps and detergent preparations.
Candles, stearine, glycerine, paraffine, etc., spermaceti.
Illuminating gas and its manufacture.
Oxygen gas, and its application for heating, lighting, metallurgy, and as a remedial agent.
Chlorine and carbonic acid.
CLASS 202.—Paints, pigments, dyes, colours, turpentine, varnishes, printing inks, writing inks, blacking.
CLASS 203.—Flavoring extracts, essences, perfumery, pomades, cosmetics.
CLASS 204.—Explosive and fulminating compounds; in small quantities only, and under special regulations, shown in the building only by empty cases and cartridges. Black powder of various grades and sizes. Nitro-glycerine and the methods of using and exploding. Giant powder, dynamite, dualin, tri-nitro-glycerine.
CLASS 205.—Pyrotechnics for display, signalling, missiles.

---

## CLASS No. 200.

### 1.—Deligny Freres.

#### LISBON.

Sulphuric Acid of 66°.
Muriatic Acid.
Nitric Acid of 40°.
Nitric Acid of 54°.
Common sulphate of soda.
Sulphate of iron.
Carbonate of soda.

Carbonate of soda, chrystallized.
Sulphate of soda.
Epsom Salts.
Chloride of Lime.
Super-phosphate of Lime.
Sulphate of Lead.

Re-established in 1867 by Deligny Frères. Employs two rooms, of 3,500 cubic feet, for lead; a department for sulphate of soda, carbonate of soda, nitric acid, sulphate of iron, chloride of lime, and super-phosphate of lime.
Materials used are all domestic, and the employees are all Portuguese.
Market—Portugal.

## 2.—Serzedello & Co.

### LISBON.

| | Price per bottle | | | 500 | reis. |
|---|---|---|---|---|---|
| Acetic acid, - | | | | | |
| Boric acid - | " | " | " | 1,600 | " |
| Hydrochloric acid for medicinal purposes | " | " | " | 400 | " |
| " " " the arts, | " | " | " | 030 | " |
| Nitric acid (pure of 32°) - | " | " | " | 600 | " |
| " " of 36° made in iron | " | " | " | 160 | " |
| " " " 37° made in glass - | " | " | " | 300 | " |
| " " " 40° made in glass - | " | " | " | 400 | " |
| Tartaric acid - | " | " | " | 960 | " |
| Acetate of Potash, | " | " | " | 2,000 | " |
| Nitric Alcohol, - | " | " | " | 900 | " |
| White lime of Mercury, | " | " | " | 2,500 | " |
| Calomel prepared by steam, - | " | " | " | 5,500 | " |
| Carbonate of Potash, - | " | " | " | 300 | " |
| " " ammoniacal copper, | " | " | " | 700 | " |
| Citrate of Potash, - - | " | " | " | 2,000 | " |
| White cream of Tartar, | " | " | " | 600 | " |
| Brown " " " - | " | " | " | 400 | " |
| Collodium, | " | " | " | 4,000 | " |
| Essence of Lavender, - | " | " | " | 8,000 | " |
| " " Garden Rosemary, | " | " | " | 4,000 | " |
| " " Juniper, | " | " | " | 8,000 | " |
| " " Thyme, - | " | " | " | 4,000 | " |
| " " Rosemary, | " | " | " | 4,000 | " |
| Acetic ether, - | " | " | " | 1,000 | " |
| Hydrochloric ether, | " | " | " | 1,000 | " |
| Citric ether, | " | " | " | 9,000 | " |
| Sulphuric ether, - - | " | " | " | 1,000 | " |
| White glycerine, | " | " | " | 600 | " |
| Hoffman's liquor mineral anodine, | " | " | " | 600 | " |
| Nitrate of Baryta, - | " | " | " | 300 | " |
| " " Lead, - - | " | " | " | 400 | " |
| " " white silver in cylinder, - | " | " | " | 45,000 | " |
| " " strontia, - | " | " | " | 300 | " |
| Joannes' powders, - | " | " | " | 3,600 | " |
| Salt of Tin, - | " | " | " | 650 | " |
| " " " | " | " | " | 240 | " |
| White refined nitre, - | " | " | " | 160 | " |
| Sulphate of soda, - - | " | " | " | 050 | " |
| " " zinc, - | " | " | " | 160 | " |
| Tanio, - | " | " | " | 2,000 | " |
| Vermillion for painting, - | " | " | " | 3,600 | " |
| White varnish for wall-paper, - | " | " | " | 960 | " |

These products are prepared at the Laboratory of Marguelra—South of the Tagus.

| Essence of Absinthe, | - | Price per bottle 9,000 reis. |
|---|---|---|
| "  " Lavender, - | | price per bottle 1,250 to 2,5000 " |
| "  " Rosemary, A. T., | | Price per bottle 1,200 " |
| "  "      "   R. A., | - | "    "    "   900 " |
| "  " Celery | | |
| "  " Rue | | |
| "  " Blue Camomile, | | "   "   "  36,000 " |
| "  " Roman Camomile, | | "   "   "  36,000 " |
| "  " Geranium (red) | | "   "   "  18,000 " |
| "  " Guaphala, | | "   "   "   3,500 " |
| "  " Hyssop, | | "   "   "  14,000 " |
| "  " Myrtle, | - | "   "   "   4,500 " |
| "  " Common Origan, | | "   "   "   1,700 " |
| "  " Wild Mint, - | | "   "   "   4,500 " |
| "  " Garden Rosemary, | | "   "   "   3,900 " |
| "  " Grain, . | | "   "   "  15,000 " |
| "  " Parsley, | | "   "   "  15,000 " |
| "  " Thyme. | | "   "   "   '2,000 " |
| "  "  "   white, | . | "   "   "   2,500 " |
| "  " Juniper, | | price per bottle, 4,000 to 8,000 " |

These products are manufactured at the Laboratory of Paderne—Algarve.
Besides the chemicals already mentioned this firm will prepare in both their well-mounted Laboratories all other chemical compounds that chemistry is able to produce.'
In the Laboratory at Paderne the essences of plants and flowers are prepared and expressly cultivated for the purpose in the grounds adjoining the same.
The exportation to Foreign Countries is very important and extensive.

**3.—Bandeira, Antonio Souza Britto e Maldonado.**

**SETUBAL.**

Samples of Salt.

**4.—Baroneza de Samora Correa.**

**LISBON.**

Samples of Salt.

**5.—Bivar, Jeronimo d'Almeida Coelho de.**

**PORTIMAO.**

Samples of Salt.

Annual production, 96,000 Litros. Price per litre, 2 reis.

**6.—Branco, Anna Delfina.**

**ALCACER DO SAL.**

Samples of Salt.

Price per Kilolitre, at the pit, - -      900 reis
"   "   "   on board at Setubal,      1,130 reis

**7.—Castello Branco, Joao da Silva Ferrao.**

**SANTA IRIA.**

Samples of Salt.

**8.—Cooke & Co.**

### FIGUEIRA DA FOZ.

Samples of Salt.

| | |
|---|---|
| Annual production, | 500,000 litres |
| Price per Kilogram, | 10 reis |

**9.—Cresswell & Co.**

### LISBON.

Samples of Salt.

Salt-pit at "Furado."

| | |
|---|---|
| Annual production, | 3,300,000 litres |

Price per Kilolitre.

| | |
|---|---|
| First quality, | 2,820 reis |
| Second quality, | 2,020 reis |

**10.—Direction of Public Works of the Mondego River and Figueira Bar.**

### COIMBRA.

Samples of Salt and Implements used in working salt-pits.

This salt-pit is situated in Lavos.

| | |
|---|---|
| Annual production, - - | 500,000 litres |
| Price per kilolitre, | 1,000 reis |

**11.—Judice, A. J.**

### MEXILHOEIRO.

Samples of Salt.

**12.—Leite, Francisco de Paula.**

### ALCACER DO SAL.

Samples of Salt.

**13.—Meirelles, Antonio Moreira de Souza.**

### FARO.

Samples of Salt.

| | |
|---|---|
| Annual production, | 1,500 Tons |
| Price per ton at pit, | 1,300 reis |
| Price per ton on board, | 1,800 reis |

**14.—Miranda & Filhos.**

### LISBON.

Samples of Salt.

The salt-pit is situated in Alcochete.

**15.—Pedroza, D. Maria Jose Lopes.**

### LAVOS.

Samples of Salt.

**16.—Pires, Joao Luiz.**

### LISBON.

Samples of Salt.

Annual production, 500 Kilolitres

**17.—Silva, Silverio Augusto Pereira da, and Antonio Marques Moura.**

### AVEIRO.

Samples of Salt.

**18.—Tagus & Sado Low-lands Company.**

### LISBON.

Samples of Salt.

**19.—Torlades O'Neill.**

### SETUBAL.

Samples of Salt.

**20.—Viscount of Alcacer do Sal.**

### ALCACER DO SAL.

Samples of Salt.

**. 21.—Santos, Narciso Jose.**

### EVORA.

Animal Charcoal.

---

### CLASS No. 201.

**22.—Costá, Joaquim Soares da.**

### OPORTO.

| | | |
|---|---|---|
| Sweet Almond Oil, | Price per Kilogram, | 700 reis |
| Castor Oil, | " " " | 540 reis |
| Ginguba Oil, | " " " | 360 reis |
| Established in 1848. | | |
| Employs hand-presses and 4 men. | Wages, 380 to 520 reis | |
| 1 child. | " 120 to 160 reis | |

Raw materials are Portuguese almonds, ginguba from Africa, and Brazilian castor-oil beans, having a yearly value of 3.000 $ 000.

Annual production. 8,000 $ 000

Markets—Portugal and Brazil.

*Awards.—Silver medals at Oporto, 1861 and 1865; Braga 1863, and Paris 1867.*

**23.—Queiroz, Jose Sequeira Pinto.**

### VIANNA.

Essential Oil of Orange Skins.

Price per litre,                                                                2,000 reis

**24.—Viuva Burnay.**

### LISBON.

A box with samples of several kinds of Oils.

Established in 1840.
Employs a steam engine of 40 horse-power, and 60 men.  Wages,       860 to 1,000 reis
Raw materials from Africa.
Markets—Portugal, France, and England.
*Awards.—First-class medals at London and Paris.*

**25.—Navarro & Co.**

### BEJA.

Common Washing Soap.

Established in 1867.
Raw materials imported, palm and cocoanut oil and rosin.

**26.—Esmoriz, Manuel Ferreira de.**

### OPORTO.

Mixed Soaps, Soap Fat.

Established in 1868.
Employs a boiler of 8 horse-power, and 5 men.  Wages, 260 to 380 reis.
Raw material used — Domestic oil, tallow, and rosin, English soda, North America
     rosin, and North and South America tallow.
Market—Portugal.

**27.—Peres, Joaquim Manuel de Mattos.**

### EVORA.

Yellow, Dark, Mixed, and White Soaps.

**28.—Silva, Agostinho Freire da & Co.**

### Poco do Bispo.  LISBON.

Washing and Toilet Soaps.

Established in 1871.
Employs 2 steam engines, one of 20 and the other of 8 horse-power, and 30 men,
     whose wages range from 360 to 1,200 reis.
Raw materials used are from Portugal and the colonies England and France to the
     value of 57.000 $ 000.
Annual production,              -              -              -       70,000 $ 000
Markets—Portugal and the Colonies.

**29.—Tenorio, Francisco Domingues.**

### ELVAS.

Soap.

**30.—Vieira, Agostinho Jose.**

### Santo Ovidio, VILLA NOVA DE GAIA.

Colored Soaps.

Established in 1876.
Employs eight men.

**31.—Department of Public Works.**

### LISBON.

Wax Candles. .

**32.—Mello, Antonio Jose Teixeira.**

### LISBON.

Candles, Tape Candles, Torches, Carved and Colored, Samples of Wax.

Established in 1807.
Employs 16 men.   Wages. 500 to 1,000 reis.
Annual production,   -   -                                60,000 $ 000
Markets—Brazil and Portugal.
*Awards.—Second-class medal, Paris,* 1867.

**33.—Silva, Diogo Monteiro Da.**

### LISBON.

Wax Candles (Colored and Fancy.)

Established io 1872.
Annual production,   . -   -   -             2,000 $ 000
Markets—Portugal and Brazil.

---

### CLASS No. 202.

**34.—Braga, Joao Jose de Souza.** .

### OPORTO.

Several Samples of Writing Ink.

**35.—Costa, Rodrigo de Campos.**

### SOURE.

Writing Ink.

Price per Litre,                                      220 reis

**36.—Neuville, Luiz.**

### LISBON.

Ultramarine Blue. See class 206 and 207.

Established in 1857.
Employs 40 men; wages 400 reis; 20 children, and a hydraulic motor, 12 horse-power.
Raw materials from different parts of the country.
Annual production, - - - - - 120,000 $ 000 reis
Markets—Portugal, Brazil, and African possessions.

**37.—Torres, Feliciano Luis,**

### LISBON,

Three bottles containing *" Grinaldas,"* an article used to imitate blood in painting statues.
A bottle of *" Purpurinas,"* an article used in giving shine to artificial flowers and other objects. Price, 1250 each, 50 grammes.

---

### CLASS No. 204.

**38.—Juan Domingo.**

### LISBON.

Wax-Tape Matches.

Raw materials used—Domestic and Foreign.
Annual production, - 10,000 $ 000
Market—Portugal.

---

## CERAMICS—POTTERY, PORCELAIN, ETC.

---

CLASS 206.—Bricks, drain-tiles, terra-cotta, and architectural pottery,
CLASS 207.—Fire-clay goods, crucibles, pots, furnaces. Chemical stoneware.
CLASS 208.—Tiles, plain, enamelled, encaustic; geometric tiles and mosaics. Tiles for pavements and for roofing, etc.
CLASS 209.—Porcelain for purposes of construction. Hardware trimmings, etc.
CLASS 210.—Stone china, for chemists, druggists, etc., earthenware, stoneware, faïence, etc.
CLASS 211.—Maiolica and Palissy ware.
CLASS 212.—Biscuit-ware, parian, etc.
CLASS 213.—Porcelain for table and toilet use, and for decoration.

---

### CLASS No. 206.

**39.—Boim & Co.,**

### PONTA DELGADA.

Pottery for architectural purposes.

**40.—Coelho, Francisco,**
#### Meia Via, SANTAREM,

Bricks.

Established in 1866.
Markets—Lisbon and Torres Novas.


**41.—Cuco, Jose Maria,**
#### BEJA.

Paving, flooring, and building bricks.


**42.—Costa, Antonio d'Almeida da & Co.,**
#### OPORTO.

Bricks, Pedestals, Columns, Balustrades, &c.


**43.—Lamego, Antonio da Costa,**
#### LISBON.

Paving bricks.


**44.—Marcal, Joao Lopes,**
#### EVORA.

Paving, flooring, and building bricks.


**45.—Martins, Alberto Cypriano,**
#### LISBON.

Bricks, Terra-cotta mouldings, vases, and other architectural crnaments.

Established in 1820.
Employs 20 men. Wages from 100 to 1,000 rels.
Raw materials—Domestic.
Market—Portugal.


**46.—Mira, Jose Paulo de,**
#### EVORA.

Paving, flooring, and building bricks.


**47.—Moedas, Jose,**
#### MOURA.

Paving, flooring, and building bricks.


**48.—Soares, M. E. d'Oliveira,**
#### EVORA.

Paving, flooring, and building bricks.

CLASS No. 207.

**49.—Neuville, Luis.**
### LISBON.

Refractory bricks.  See Class 202.


CLASS No. 208.

**50.—Boim & Co.,**
### PONTA DELGADA.

Dutch tiles.


**51.—Coelho, Francisco,**
### Meia Via, SANTAREM.

Tiles.


**52.—Costa, Antonio d'Almeida da & Co.,**
### OPORTO.

Dutch tiles—Bricks, tiles, and drain pipes.

Established in i869.
Employs—80 men.     Wages from 360 to 1,200 reis.
     · 15 women.        "      "    160 to 200    "
       26 children.     "      "    120 to 300
Annual production,        -        -                          28,600 $ 000 reis
Markets—Portugal, Brazil, and Spain.


**53.—Cuco, Jose Maria,**
### BEJA.

Tiles.


**54.—Joao Antonio,**
### EVORA.

Ventilating Tiles.


**55.—Lamego, Antonio da Costa,**
### LISBON.

Dutch Tiles.


**56.—Marcal, Joao Lopes,**
### EVORA.

Tiles.

**57.—Martins, Alberto Cypriano,**
                      **LISBON.**

Dutch Bricks.


**58.—Mira, Jose Paulo de,**
                      **EVORA**

Tiles.


**59.—Moedas, Jose,**
              **MOURA.**

Tiles.


**60.—Neuville, Luiz,**
                  **LISBON.**

Drain Pipes.  See Class 202.


**61.—Rio Junior, Joao do,**
                      **Villa Nova de Gaya, OPORTO.**

Dutch Tiles.

Established in 1802.
Employs—43 men.   Wages, 360 to 800 reis.
        10 women.      "     140 to 200   "
        20 children.   "     160 to 240   "
Raw material—Domestic and foreign, to the annual value of 13,500 $ 000 reis.
Annual production, 28,000 $ 000 reis.
Markets—Portugal, adjacent islands, Africa, Brazil, and France.
*Awards.—Medals at the Industrials of 1857 and 1861 and International of Oporto, 1865.*

---

## CLASS No. 210.

**62.—Boim & Co.,**
              **PONTA DELGADA.**

Glazed Stoneware, colored.


**63.—Borges, Joaquim Antonio,**
                      **VIANNA DO ALEMTEJO.**

Glazed Earthenware.


**64.—Campolini, Miguel,**
                  **OPORTO.**

Earthenware.

Annual production,                                          1,000 $ 000 reis
Markets—Portugal, adjacent islands, and England.

**65.—Candido, Coimbra,**
### OSSELLA.

Black Earthenware.

Employs two men, and all the labor is done by hand, the ovens being in the open air.
Raw material is from the locality.
Annual production, 100 $ 000 reis.


**66.—Carranquinha, Joaquim Antonio,**
### BEJA.

Earthen Pitcher.


**67.—Conqueje, Manuel,**
### PONTA DELGADA.

Common Earthenware.


**68.—Cunha, Jose Alves and Henriqueta Sezelina de Mendonca,**
### CALDAS DA RAINHA.

Earthenware known by the name of "Louca das Caldas."

Established iu 1866.
Employs—9 men.      Wages, 240 to 500 reis.
     5 women.      "      80 to 120  "
     3 children.     "      60 to 80  "
Most of the work being by hand.
Annual production,   -   -   -   -   1,000 $ 000 reis
Market—Portugal.


**69.—Fanfarrao, Joao,**
### Cervaes, BRAGA.

Earthenware.


**70.—Joao, Antonio,**
### EVORA.

Earthenware.


**71.—Lamego, Antonio da Costa,**
### LISBON.

Crockery and Earthenware.


**72.—Mafra, Manuel Cypriano Gomes,**
### CALDAS DA RAINHA.

Earthenware known by the name of "Louca das Caldas."

Established in 1854.
Employs—10 men.      Wages, 300 to 600 reis.
     7 women.      "      100  "
     6 children.     "      60  "
Award—Medal of Merit at Vienna, 1873.

**73.—Manuel, Leite Pereira & Irmao,**
PONTA DELGADA.

Glazed Stoneware.

**74.—Marques, Joao da Rosa,**
EXUREMOZ.

Earthenware.

Employs 10 women. Wages, 160 to 180 reis.

**75.—Marques, Pedro Antonio,**
AVEIRO.

Glazed Earthenware.

Established in 1775.
Employs—8 men.    Wages, 240 to 480 reis.
     2 women.    "    200  "
     1 boy.      "    120  "
Annual production,    -    -      1,200 $ 000

**76.—Martins, Alberto Cypriano,**
LISBON.

Earthenware. See Classes 206, 208, 210.

Established in 1820.
Employs 20 men.   Wages, 100 to 1,000 reis.
Market—Portugal.

**77.—Pimentao, Antonio Ayres,**
VIANNO DO CASTELLO.

Glazed Earthenware.

**78.—Portuguese Government,**
OVAR.

Red Earthenware.

**79.—Silva, Miguel da,**
EVORA.

Earthenware.

**80.—Scholfield, John Howarth,**
LISBON.

White and Colored Table and Decorative Stoneware.

Established at Sacavem in 1866.
Employs—46 men.    Wages, 280 to 1,000 reis.
     12 women.    "    120 to  600  "
     38 children.   "    80 to  300  "
Raw materials are from Portugal and England, to the annual value of 10,000 $ 000 reis.
Annual production,    -    -    -    28,000 $ 000 reis
Markets—Portugal, the Colonies, and Brazil.
*Awards.—Medal at Oporto. and Honorable Mention at Vienna.*

**81.—Victoria, Jose Goncalves da,**

### ARADA.

Earthenware.

Employs a man and a woman. All the labor is done by hand. The ovens being in the
open air.
Raw material used is from Bôco or the locality—all domestic.
Annual production,  -   -   -    -          80,000 reis
Markets—Aveiro, Oporto, and Coimbra.

---

### CLASS No. 213.

**82.—Vista Alegre Porcelain Manufactory,**

### VISTA ALEGRE.

Porcelainware for Table and Toilet.

---

### GLASS AND GLASSWARE.

---

CLASS 214.—Glass used in construction and for mirrors. Window glass of various grades of quality and of size. Plate glass, rough, and ground or polished. Toughened glass.
CLASS 215.—Chemical and pharmaceutical glassware, vials, bottles.
CLASS 216.—Decorative glassware.

---

### CLASS No. 214.

**83.—Cabo Mondego Mining and Industrial Company,**

### LISBON.

Cylindrical Glass composed of Carbonate and Sulphate of Soda.

Employs—60 men.    Wages, 200 to 600 reis.
       20 women.      "    100 to 120  "
       15 children.    "     70 to 100  "
*Awards.—Medals at Vienna and at the Districal of Coimbra.*

**84.—Michon, Andre,**

### OPORTO.

Glass cylinder for panes, plain and ground plate-glass, ovals, square glass
shades, and glass tiles.

Employs a steam-engine of 10 horse-power and 41 hands. Wages range from 320 to 3,500
reis.
Markets—Portugal and adjacent islands.
*Awards—Medals at Oporto, 1861 and 1865; London, 1862, and Paris, 1867.*

# FURNITURE AND OBJECTS OF GENERAL USE IN CONSTRUCTION AND IN DWELLINGS.

CLASS 217.—Heavy furniture.—Chairs, tables, parlour and chamber suits, office and library furniture, vestibule furniture. Church furniture and decoration.

CLASS 218.—Table furniture.—Glass, china, silver, silver-plate, tea and coffee sets, urns, samovars, epergnes.

CLASS 219.—Mirrors, stained and enamelled glass, cut and engraved window-glass, and other decorative objects.

CLASS 220.—Gilt cornices, brackets, picture frames, etc.

CLASS 221.—The nursery and its accessories; children's chairs, walking chairs.

CLASS 222.—Apparatus and fixtures for heating and cooking—stoves, ranges, heaters, etc.

CLASS 223.—Apparatus for lighting—gas fixtures, lamps, etc.

CLASS 224.—Kitchen and pantry—utensils, tinware, and apparatus used in cooking (exclusive of cutlery).

CLASS 225.—Laundry appliances, washing machines, mangles, clothes-wringers, clothes-bars, ironing tables.

CLASS 226.—Bath-room and water-closet, shower bath, earth closet.

CLASS 227.—Manufactured parts of buildings—sash, blinds, mantels, metal work, etc.

---

## CLASS No. 217.

**85.—Alcobia, Joao Thome,**
### • LISBON.

A washing-stand made of iron. See Class 224.


**86.—Barboza & Costa,**
### LISBON.

A Devotional Chair.


**87.—Manuel, Rodrigues de Gaspar,**
### FUNCHAL, Island of Madeira.

An Inlaid Wooden Table.


**88.—Santos Chaves, Augusto Prudencio,**
### LISBON.

Wash-stand, arm-chair with wire seat, flower-stand, all of iron.

Established in 1858.
Employs 30 workmen. Wages, 600 to 2,000 reis.
Raw materials are Domestic, or from England, at an annual cost of 12,000 $ 000 reis.
Annual production, -          30,000 $ 000 reis
Markets—Spain, Brazil, and Africa.
*Award—Medal of Honor from the Portuguese Royal Central Association of Agriculture.*

## CLASS No. 218.

### 89.—Marinha Grande Royal Glass Works,
#### LISBON.

Crystal and Glassware.

Established in 1769.
Employs 2 hydraulic motors and and one steam-engine of 20 horse-power; Siemens' gas ovens; old-style ovens, &c., &c., &c.

575 men. ⎫
76 women ⎬ Wages, 80 to 2,600 reis.
95 children ⎭

Raw materials used are from France, England, and Germany, to the annual total of 25,000 $ 000 reis.
Annual production, - - - 140,000 $ 000 reis
Markets—Portugal, Africa, and Brazil.
*Awards—Medals at Oporto*, 1865; *Paris*, 1867, *and Vienna*, 1873.

---

## CLASS No. 219.

### 90.—Santos & Irmao,
#### OPORTO.

Looking-glasses.

Established in 1859.
Employs—10 men. Wages, 300 to 600 reis.
5 children. " 120 to 200 "

---

## CLASS No. 222.

### 91.—Costa Basto & Co.,
#### Foundry of Bolhao, OPORTO.

Parlor Stove and Iron Pots and Kettles.

Established in 1847.
Employs—30 men. Wages, 300 to 1,800 reis.
9 children. " 100 to 300 "

Raw materials used are from England and Portugal, at an annual cost of 10,000 $ 000 reis
Annual production, . . . . . 30,000 $ 000 reis
Markets—At home.
*Awards.—Honorable Mention at London*, 1851; *Silver Medal at Oporto*, 1857 and 1861, and *International*, 1865.

---

## CLASS No. 224.

### 92.—Silva, Jose Goncalves,
#### OPORTO.

Wire Bird Cages.

Established in 1868.

**93.—Alcobia, Joao Thome,**
**LISBON.**

Tinware, Kitchen and Pantry Utensils, lacquered and plain.

Established in 1854.
Employs 30 hands.
Wages, 800 reis.
Annual production,  .  .  .  4 to 6,000 $ 000 reis
Markets—Portugal, adjacent islands, and Africa.
*Award.—Copper Medal, Oporto,* 1861.

**94.—Antonio, Baptista Moreira & Irmao,**
**Massarellos, OPORTO.**

Triped Iron Pots.

Established in 1840, under the title of "Foundry of Boa Viagem."
Employs a steam-engine of 4 horse-power and 7 men.  Wages, 320 to 500 reis.
3 children.  "  100 to 160  "
Raw material used, iron and coal, from England, to the annual value of 2,428 $ 000 reis
Markets—Portugal and Spain.

**95.—Pedro Maralha,**
**BEJA.**

Copper Vessel.

**96.—Schalck, H.**
**LISBON.**

Lead-foil covers for bottles.

**97.—Silva, Jose Goncalves e,**
**OPORTO.**

Six round Bird Cages.
Two fancy round Bird Cages.

---

## YARNS AND WOVEN GOODS OF VEGETABLE OR MINERAL MATERIALS.

CLASS 228.—Woven fabrics of mineral origin.—Wire cloths, sieve cloth, wire screens, bolting-cloth.
Asbestos fibre, spun and woven, with the clothing manufactured from it.
Glass thread, floss and fabrics.
CLASS 229.—Coarse fabrics, of grass, rattan, cocoa, nut, and bark.
Mattings—Chinese, Japanese, palm-leaf, grass, and rushes.
Floor-cloths of rattan and cocoanut fibre, aloe fibre, etc.
CLASS 230.—Cotton yarns and fabrics, bleached and unbleached.
Cotton sheeting and shirting, plain and twilled.
Cotton canvas and duck. Awning, tents.
CLASS 231.—Dyed cotton fabrics, exclusive of prints and calicoes.
CLASS 232.—Cotton prints and calicoes, including handkerchiefs, scarfs, etc.
CLASS 233.—Linen and other vegetable fabrics, uncoloured or dyed.
CLASS 234.—Floor oil-cloths and other painted and enamelled tissues, and imitation of leather, with a woven base.

## CLASS No. 228.

**98.—Panada, Joao Luiz,**
### LISBON.

Samples of Wire Work.

---

## CLASS No. 229.

**99.—Almeida & Silva,**
### OPORTO.

Several kinds of Mattings.

Established in 1872.
Employs—2 men.      Wages, 400 reis.
     2 children.      "      300  "
Raw material—Domestic, to the annual value of 400$000 reis.
Annual production,      .                                      1,000$000 reis
Markets—Portugal and Brazil.

**100.—Borges, Manuel da Cunha,**
### PONTA DELGADA.

Grass Mats.

**101.—Bruno da Silva,**
### LISBON.

Matting of several qualities.

Established in 1855.
Employs—5 looms, of his invention, that can make mattings 6 metres wide.
    12 men.      Wages, 500 to 700 reis.
    8 women.      "   .  200 to 300  "
    6 children.      "      300 to 400  "
Raw materials used are from Portuoal and Russia, to the annual value of 2,000$000 reis
Annual production,      .        .        .                      8,000$000 reis
Markets—Portugal, France, England, Africa, and Brazil.
*Awards.—Silver Medals at Oporto*, 1865, *and Paris*, 1872; *Bronze ones at Paris*, 1867, and
*Lisbon*, 1873; *Of Progress at Vienna*, 1873.

**102.—Dabney, R. L.,**
### FAYAL.

Straw Mat, with edging.

**103.—Department of Public Works,**
### Manufactured by the House of Correction, LISBON.

Mats.

**104.—The Portuguese Government,**
### Manufacturers—The Prisoners of the Central Jail, LISBON.

Door Mats.

**105.—Machado, Manuel,**
### PONTA DELGADA.

Straw and Corn-Husk Mats and other articles of the same materials.


**106.—Margarido, Manoel d'Oliveira,**
### OPORTO.

Mattings of several qualities.
A Covered Bottle.
A Covered Flask.

Established in 1865.
Employs 2 looms and 5 men.　　　Wages, 400 reis.
　　　　　　　　　2 women.　　　"　200　"
　　　　　　　　　2 children.　　"　120　"
Raw material used is from Portugal.
Annual production,　　　　.　　　.　　　　　　　2,500 $ 000 reis
*Award.—Diploma of Merit at Vienna,* 1873.


**107.—Melindre, Joaquim d'Oliveira,**
### OPORTO.

Mattings of several qualities.

Established in 1869.
Employs 2 looms and 6 men.　　　Wages, 500 reis.
　　　　　　　　　2 women.　　　"　200　"
　　　　　　　　　2 children.　　"　120　"
Raw material—Domestic. Annual value of the same, 1,200 $ 000 reis.
Annual production,　　　.　　　.　　　　.　　　　4,500 $ 000 reis
Markets—Portugal, adjacent islands, and Brazil.
*Award.—Diploma of Merit at Vienna,* 1873.


**108.—Silva, Manoel Dias da,**
### OPORTO.

Samples of different kinds of Matting.

Established in 1855.
Employs 2 looms and 7 men.　　　Wages, 500 reis.
　　　　　　　　　2 women.　　　"　240　"
Raw material—Domestic, to the annual value of 1,500 $ 000 reis.
Annual production,　　　.　　　　.　　　　　　5,000 $ 000 reis
Markets—Portugal and Brazil.
*Awards.—Copper Medals at Braga,* 1863; *second-class one at Oporto,* 1865; *Honorary Mention at Vienna,* 1873.


**109.—Mattos, F. C. Pereira,**
### FARO.

Rush Frails.


**110.—Santo Thirso, Antonio dos Reis,**
### AVEIRO.

Matting.

**111.—Santos, Antonio Marques dos,**
BRAGA.

Mats.

**112.—Santos, Jose Marques dos,**
OVAR.

Samples of Mattings.

---

## CLASS No. 230.

**113.—Bahia & Genro,**
OPORTO.

Drills.
Cotton Prints.
Cotton Flannels. See Class 233.

Established in 1855.
Employs a steam-engine of 4 horse-power.
    "   150 looms, &c., &c., and 100 men.    Wages, 320 to 500 reis.
                          300 women.     "    140 to 240  "
                          200 children.    "    100 to 140  "
Raw material from Portugal, England, Germany, and Brazil.
Annual production, -    -    -    -              120,000 $ 000 reis
Market—Portugal and adjacent islands.

**114.—Balsa Cotton Factory,**
Vallongo, OPORTO.

Samples of Yarn and Twisted Cotton.

Employs a hydraulic motor and a steam-engine of 25 horse-power each; spinning and
   twisting looms, with colouring apparatus.
Also, 18 men.     Wages, 300 to 960 reis.
     30 women.      "    160 to 200  "
     36 children.     "    100 to 200  "
Raw materials from Brazil.
Annual production,                       36,000 $ 000 reis
Market—Portugal.

**115.—Crestuma Spinning Co.,**
FEIRA AVEIRO.

Samples of Woven Thread.
Samples of Warpings.

Established in 1856.
Employs a hydraulic wheel of 35 horse-power, a turbine of 90, a steam-engine of 80;
   12,000 spindles, and all the corresponding machinery.
Also,  63 men.     Wages, 240 to 1,000 reis.
     ' 105 women.      "    100 to  200  "
      82 children.     "     40 to   90  "
Raw materials are from Brazil, Africa, and North America.
Annual production,    -    -    -    -    -    140,000 $ 000 reis
*Awards.—Silver Medal at Oporto,* 1861; *Diploma of Honor at London; Silver Medal at
Lisbon,* 1863, *and Gold Medal at Oporto,* 1865.

**116.—Dias, Rodrigo Antonio Ferreira,**

### OPORTO.

Drills.
Ducks.
Cotton Blankets.
Shawls, and Canton Flannel.

Established in 1856.
Employs—50 men.    Wages, 500 reis.
      20 women.    "    300   "

---

## CLASSES Nos. 230, 231, AND 232.

**117.—Fraternal Association of Weavers and Correlative Arts,**

### Alcantara, LISBON.

Cotton Prints.
Table Cloths.
Napkins.
Towels.
Paddings.
Cache-nez (Scarfs).

Established in 1859.
Employs—Manuel weavers and a Jacquard loom.
Also, 15 men.      Wages, 360 to 600 reis.
    5 women.      "      140 to 240   "
    1 child       "          140   "
Raw material—Domestic and some imported, at an annual cost of 4,000 $ 000 reis.
Annual production,  -  -  -  -  -  6,000 $ 000 reis
Market—Portugal.
*Awards.—Oporto*, 1861; *Lisbon*, 1863; *and Oporto*, 1865.

---

## CLASS No. 230.

**118.—Leite, Tito Jose,**

### OPORTO.

Twisted Cotton, of 2 and 3 threads, for embroidering and of several colors

Established in 1867.
Employs—9 men.      Wages, 320 to 600 reis.
    30 women.      "     160 to 240   "
    8 children.    "      80 to 120   "
Raw material used is imported, at the annual cost of 10,000 $ 000 reis.
Annual production,  -  -  -  -  -  15,000 $ 000
Markets—Portugal and Brazil.

---

## CLASSES Nos. 230 AND 231.

**119.—Lisbon Spinning and Weaving Co.**

### LISBON.

Cotton yarns, unbleached cotton, crash, bed-ticking, striped tent-cloth, striped cotton stuffs, cotton blankets, napkins, table-cloths; yarns, bleached, unbleached, and colored; sewing cotton, cord, lacings, &c. &c.

Established in 1838.

Employs a steam-engine, 250 horse-power.
     64 carding machines. 2,132 bobbins.
     354 looms and several other apparatuses.  -
     160 men.    Wages, 280 to 800 reis.
     400 women.    "   120 to 240  "
     240 children.    "   80 to 160  "
Raw material—Cotton, from Brazil and Portuguese possessions in Africa, to the annual
    value of 130,000 $ 000 reis.
Annual production,    -            -           -           350,000 $ 000
Markets—Portugal and its possessions in Africa.
*Awards.—Nine Gold and Silver Medals and Medals for Merit at the National Exhibitions
of 1849, 1861, 1863, and 1875; at London, 1851 and 1862; at Paris, 1855 and 1867, and
at Vienna, 1873.*

## 120.—Mello, Jose Carneiro de,

### OPORTO.

    Drills.
    Canvas.
    Serge.
    Cotton Flannel.
    Cotton Yarn.

Employs a steam-engine of 8 horse-power, a carding machine, a cylinder, a loom of
150 spindles, and one of 80. Also, 78 men and 400 women.

---

## CLASS No. 230.

## 121.—Montes, Manuel Alvares,

### OPORTO.

    Samples of Cotton Goods.

Established in 1865.
Employs manual labor.
Raw material—Foreign, at the annual cost of 20 to 25,000 $ 000 reis.
Annual production,             -        -    45 to 50,000 $ 000 reis
Market—Portugal.

## 122.—Oporto Spinning Co.,

### OPORTO.

    Samples of plain and twisted Cotton Thread.

Established in 1863.
Employs 2 steam-engines of 40 horse-power each and 260 hands, whose wages average
    from 100 to 800 reis.
Raw materials used are from Brazil and Portugal, at the annual cost of 150,000 $ 000
    reis.
Market—Portugal.
*Awards.—Medal at Oporto, 1665, and Medal of Honor at Vienna, 1873.*

## 123.—Rio Vizella Spinning Co.,

### OPORTO.

    Cotton Threads of different qualities in process and finished.

This establishment is going through a complete transformation on account of en-
larging its production.

**124.—Souza e Silva, Antonio Jose,**

Vallongo, OPORTO.

Several kinds of Blue and White Twisted Cotton.


**125.—Thomar Royal Spinning Co.,**

**THOMAR.**

Raw Warpings.
Raw Thread.
Raw woven Thread.
Blue Colored Thread.

Established in 1873.
Employs a turbine of 160 horse-power and a steam-engine of 200; 13,000 spindles and all the corresponding machinery.
Also, 68 men.      Wages, 160 to 300 reis.
    140 women.      "      100 to 240  "
    20 children.     "       60 to 80   "
Raw materials used are from Africa and America, and the annual value of them is 108,000$000 reis.
Annual production,                                              400,000 $ 000
Market—Portugal.


## CLASSES Nos. 230 AND 231.


**126.—Xabregas Cotton Manufacturing Co.,**

**LISBON.**

Dyed Lining Goods.
Unbleached Cotton.
Cotton Yarns.

Established in 1858.
Employs two steam-engines of 50 horse-power, carding machines, looms, &c.
    55 men.      Wages, 220 to 600 reis.
    43 women.      "      150 to 300  "
    90 children.     "       80 to 140   "
Raw material used is from Brazil and the Portuguese Colonies, at the annual cost of 70,000 $ 000 reis.
Annual production,                   -                   120,000 $ 000 reis
Market—Portugal.
*Awards.—Oporto* 1862 *and* 1865, *Lisbon* 1863, *and Vienna* 1873.


## CLASS No. 232.


**127.—Anjos & Co.,**

**LISBON.**

Cotton-printed Handkerchiefs and Medal Prints.

Established in 1812.
Employs manual labor, relief stamping machine and dyeing vats.
Raw material—Foreign, at an annual value of 100,000 $ 000 reis.
Annual production,      -      -      -      -      135,000 $ 000 reis
Markets—Portugal, its Colonies, Spain, and Brazil.

**128.—Anjos, Cunha, Ferreira & Co.,**

### LISBON.

Cotton prints, colored handkerchiefs, a sample book of the products of the factory.

Established in 1840. Enlarged lately.
Employs a steam-engine of 30 horse-power, 4 stamping machines, &c.
Also, 114 men.　　Wages, 280 to 2,650 reis.
　　36 children.　　"　100 to 240　"
Raw material used is imported from England, costing yearly—Cotton, 225,000 $ 000 reis,
　and Domestic and Foreign drugs, 55,000 $ 000 reis.
Annual production,　-　　　　　　　　　　400,000 $ 000 reis
Markets—Portugal, the Colonies, and Spain.
*Awards.—Lisbon 1848, London 1851, Oporto 1861, London 1863, Lisbon 1863, Oporto 1865
and Vienna 1873.*

**129.—Bolhao Cotton Printing Factory,**

### OPORTO.

Calicoes.
Umbrella Goods.
Handkerchiefs.

Established in 1852.
Employs stamping plates, calenders, cylinpers, vats, driers, &c., &c., &c.
Also, 25 men.　　Wages, 300 to 600 reis.
　　15 children.　　"　60 to 200　"
Raw material—English, to the annual value, of 30,000 $ 000 reis.
Annual production,　-　　　　　　　　　　45,000,000 reis
Market—Portugal.
*Awards.—Medal at the Oporto Industrial Exhibition.*

**130.—Etur, Augusto Frederico,**

### LISBON.

Cotton Prints.

Established in 1870.
Employs hand-motors, a stamping machine, dyeing tubs, &c., &c.
Also, 40 men.　　Wages, 300 to 700 reis.
　　30 children.　　"　60 to 240　"
Raw materials used are cotton goods from England and blue from India, to the annual
　value of 80,000 $ 000 reis.
Annual production,　-　　　　　　　　　　90,000 $ 000 reis
Markets—Portugal and Spain.
*Award.—Medal at Vienna, 1873.*

---

### CLASSES Nos. 232 AND 233.

**131.—Joao, Roiz de Deus & Co.,**

### TORRES NOVAS.

Different qualities of Linen and Cotton Goods.

Established in 1875.
Employs—10 men.　　Wages, 240 to 800 reis.
　　50 women.　　"　120 to 400　"
　　20 children.　　"　50 to 120　"
Material is imported from Germany, at an annual cost of 4,000 $ 000 reis.
Market—Portugal.

## CLASS No. 232.

**132.—Lisbon Cotton Dyeing and Printing Co.**

### LISBON.

Calico Prints for Dress and Furniture.

Established in 1875.
Employs 3 steam-boilers of 50 horse-power each, engines, and all necessary apparatuses
    for stamping, washing, dyeing, drying, and finishing.
    60 men.      Wages, 260 to 3,000 reis.
    20 children.     "    100 to   240   "
Raw material—From Portugal and England.
Annual peoduction,          -               400,000 $ 000   reis
Markets—Portugal and the Colonies.


**133.—Queiroz, Antonio Goncalves de,**

### OPORTO.

Samples of Striped Cotton.

Employs 9 men. Wages, 300 to 400 reis.
Markets—Portugal and Brazil.

---

## CLASS No. 233.

**134.—Albuquerque Dr. Caetano d'Andrade,**

### PONTA DELGADA.

Cotton Rag Quilt.


**135.—Almeida, Jacintho Pacheco,**

### PONTA DELGADA.

Linen Table-cloths and Towels.
Striped Linen Drill.


**136.—Bahia & Genro,**

### OPORTO.

Linen Goods.   See Class 230.


**137.—Baptista, Joao Guerreiro,**

### ALMODOVAR.

Linen in Thread and Woven Linen.


**138.—Brum, Caetano de,**

### PONTA DELGADA.

Samples of Linen Drill.

**139.—Camara, D. Hermelinda Gago da,**
PONTA DELGADA.

Linen Table Cloths, Linen Thread.

**140.—Canto, D. Anna Adelaide do,**
PONTA DELGADA.

Sewing Linen Balls.

**141.—Carvalho, D. Isabel Candida Alves de,**
MONDIM DE BASTO.

Two Samples of Linen Stuffs.

**142.—Carreiro, Anna,**
PONTA DDLGADA.

Linen and Cotton Bed Qnilt.

**143.—Castro, Joao Vaz Pacheco de,**
PONTA DELGADA.

Samples of Flax Yarn.

**144.—Collaco, Manuel Martins,**
CASTRO VERDE.

Napkins.

**145.—Dias, Rodrigo Antonio Ferreira,**
OPORTO.

Linen Duck and Canvas. See Class 230.

**146.—Falleiro, D. Barbara Rita Fernandes,**
CASTRO VERDE·

Linen Napkins·

**147.—Guimaraes, Antonio da Costa,**
GUIMARAES.

Linen Goods of different qualities, large and small Towels, Napkins, Bed Covers and Linen Thread.

**148.—Guimaraes, Balthasar Jose Pereira,**
PENAFIEL.

Linen Fabrics.

Annual production,     -                                  52,560 $ 000 reis
Markets—Portugal and Brazil.

**149.—Guimaraes, Manuel Mendes Ribeiro,**

GUIMARAES.

Linen Table Cloths and Napkins.


**150.—Guerra, Joaquim Baptista da Silva,**

OPORTO.

Bed-Covers.
A Hammock.   See Classes 245, 246, and 247.


**151.—Lanca, Francisco Pereira da,**

CASTRO VERDE.

Linen Bed Cover, Linens, Towels, etc.


**152.—Magalhaes, Francisco Thiago,**

Taboa, COIMBRA.

Linens.


**153.—Mello, Gil Tavares de,**

PONTA DELGADA.

Samples of Linen and Flax Goods.


**154.—Mello, Jose Carneiro,**

OPORTO.

Samples of Linen Goods.   See Classes 230, 231.


**155.—Mesquita, Pedro Jose,**

Taboa, COIMBRA.

Samples of Linens.


**156.—Montes, Manuel Alvares,**

OPORTO.

Samples of Linen Fabrics.


**157.—Moreira, D. Maria Jose,**

PONTA DELGADA.

Unbleached and Bleached Linen Drill.

**158.—National Rope Yard,**
### Junqueira, LISBON.

Canvas and Duck.   See Class 287.

Established in 1788.
Employs a movable steam engine of 6-horse power, manual and mechanical spinners
and other apparatus.
    80 men.      Wages 300 to 400 reis.
    20 children.    "    80 to 200  "
    80 women.    "   120 to 260  "
Annual production in canvas and duck,  -    -   .   -   21,000 $ 000 reis
Market—The products are exclusively destined for the uses of the Ministry of Marine
and the Colonies,
*Awards.—Silver Medal, Oporto, 1861, and a Copper one at Paris, 1867.*

**159.—Nobre, Jose Rodrigues Furtado,**
### ODEMIRA.

Spools, Skeins, and Spindles of Thread.
Samples of Linen Goods.

**160.—Nogueira, Manuel Augusto,**
### PONTA DELGADA.

Samples of Unbleached Canvas.

**161.—Pacheco, Antonio Vaz,**
### PONTA DELGADA.

Samples of Linens.

**162.—Pacheco, Francisco Jeronimo,**
### PONTA DELGADA.

Samples of Linens.
Linen Thread.
White Woollen Flannels.

**163.—Pacheco, Joao Vaz,**
### PONTA DELGADA.

Linen and Cotton Covers.

**164.—Resende, D. Barbara,**
### PONTA DELGADA.

A Linen and Cotton Counterpane woven in relief.

**165.—Rosa de Mattos,**
### PONTA DELGADA.

Samples of Linen and Flax.

**166.—Santos, Ascencio Jose dos,**
### VALENCA.

Several kinds of Linen and Crash Goods. '

These products are made, in general, by peasant women and are destined to their use. The flax is grown in the locality.

**167.—Silva, Jose Pinto da,**
### Cucujaes, OLIVEIRA D'AZERNEIS.

A piece of Linen.

**168.—The Portuguese Government. '**

Samples of Linens.

**169.—Teixeira, D. Maria Amalia,**
### PONTA DELGADA.

Sewing Linen Balls.

**170.—Torres Novas Spinning and Weaving Co.,**
### TORRES NOVAS.

Bleached Canvas of different qualities.

Established in 1845.
Employs a turbine, Brault, of 75-horse power, a vertical wheel of 40 and a steam engine of 70 horse-power, also 40 men, 70 women and 130 children.
Raw material—The linen in main part is imported from Russia, India, Egypt and Italy.
Markets—Portugal and Brazil.

## CLASS No. 234.

**171.—Viuva Barboza Marinho,**
### LISBON.

Oil Cloths.

## WOVEN AND FELTED GOODS AND MIXTURES OF WOOL.

CLASS 235.—Card wool fabricks.—Yarns, broadcloth, doeskins, fancy cassimeres. Felted goods.
CLASS 236.—Flannels.—Plain flannels, domets, opera and fancy.
CLASS 237.—Blankets, robes and shawls.
CLASS 238.—Combined wool fabrics.—Worsteds, yarns, dress goods for women's wear, delaines, serges, poplins, merinoes.
CLASS 239.—Carpets, rugs, etc. Brussels, Melton, tapestry, tapestry Brussels, Axminster, Venetian, ingrain, felted carpetings, druggets, rugs, etc.
CLASS 240.—Hair, alpaca, goat's hair, camel's hair, and other fabrics, mixed or unmixed with wool.
CLASS 241.—Printed and embossed woolen cloths, table covers, patent velvets.

## CLASS No. 235.

### 172.—Bibianno, Antonio Alves, Castanheira de Pera,
#### PEDROGAO GRANDE.

Black Cloths.

Established in 1868.
Employs 3 hydraulic iron wheels, 2 turbines, 2 steam-engines of 40 horse-power, mechanical and usual looms, carding machines, spinners, &c., &c.

| | | |
|---|---|---|
| 80 men. | Wages, 300 to 1,500 reis. | |
| 75 women. | " 120 to 300 " | |
| 50 children. | " 100 to 200 " | |

Raw materials used are domestic and foreign, to the annual value of 80,000 $ 000 reis.
Annual production,   -    -    -    -    -    150,000 $ 000 reis
Markets—Portugal and America.   •
*Award.—Silver Medal at the Districtal Exposition of Coimbra.*


### 173.—Campo Grande Woollen Fabrics Co.,
#### LISBON.

Cloths, Cassimeres, Melton, Men's Shawls.

Established in 1837.
Employs a hydraulic motor of 40 horse-power, mechanical spindles, carding machines,
etc., also,

| | | |
|---|---|---|
| 61 men, | Wages, 440 reis. | |
| 59 women, | " 200 " | |
| 32 children | " 120 " | |

Raw materials—Domestic and Foreign.
Annual production,    -     -       100,000 $ 000 reis
Market—Portugal.
*Award—Medal of Merit at Vienna, 1873.*


### 174.—Campos Mello & Co.,
#### COVILHAN.

Summer Cassimeres.

Established in 1836-
Employs steam engine of 60 horse-power and 3 hydraulic wheels, usual looms and mo-
chanical, spinning, twisting and weaving apparatuses, etc., etc.

| | | |
|---|---|---|
| 282 men, | Wages, 200 to 2,000 reis. | |
| 118 women | " 100 to 200 " | |
| 52 children, | " 80 to 200 " | |

*Awards—Medals at London, Paris, Oporto and Vienna.*


### 175.—Collaco, Manuel Matheus,
#### Castro Verde, BEJA,

Woollen Horse-Blanket.
Saddle Bags.


### 176.—Conceicao, Umbelina da,
#### Castro Verde, BEJA.

Saddle Bags.

Established in 1850.
Employs wooden looms, the work being by hand and two women.
Raw material costs 7,500 reis for every 15 kilolitres.
Annual production,     -     -       210 $ 000 reis

CLASSES Nos. 235 AND 237.

**177.—Constant Burnay,**
### LISBON.

Cassimeres.
Cloth.
Blankets.

Established in 1836 and rebuilt in 1875.
Employs a steam-engine of 30 horse-power and a dydraulic motor of 16.
  90 men.  Wages, 300 to 1,000 reis.
  150 women.   "  160 to 400 "
  25 children.   "  100 to 160 "
Markets—Portugal and its Colonies.

**178.—Costas & Carvalho,**
### OLIVEIRA D'AZEMEIS.

Woollen Cloths and Shawls.

Established in 1864.
Employs a hydraulic motor of 20 horse-power, 25 manual spinners and one mechanical
  and other necessary apparatuses, also
  42 men,  Wages, 200 to 1000 reis.
  25 women,  " 100 to 300 "
  18 children,  " 60 to 120 "
Raw material—Domestic and Foreign, to the annual value of    18,000 $ 000
Annual production,   -   -       27,000 $ 000
Market—Portugal.
*Awards—Honorable mention, Oporto, 1865·*

---

CLASS No. 235.

**179.—Custodio & Silva,**
### COVILHAN.

Woollen Cloths, Flannels, and Cheviots.

Established in 1851.
Employs a hydraulic motor of 14 horse-power and apparatuses for threading, carding,
  weaving, dyeing, &c., &c., and 38 men.  Wages, 360 to 600 reis.
        16 women and children.  " 60 to 200 "
Raw material—Domestic and Spanish, to the annual cost of 18,000 $ 000 reis.
Annual production,   -   -   -   -  22,000 $ 000 reis

**180.—Goncalves, Manuel Joao,**
### Castro Verde, BEJA.

Woollen Sash.

**181.—Guilherma, Maria,**
### Castro Verde, BEJA,

A first quality Woollen Blanket.
A second quality Woollen Blanket.

Annual production,             4,000 $ 000 reis
*Award·—Paris, 1867.*

CLASSES Nos. 235 AND 237.

**182.—Leandro, Manuel,**

Castro Verde, **BEJA.**

Serge.
Blanket.

CLASSES Nos. 235 AND 236.

**183.—Lordello Woollen Fabrics Co.,**

Lordello, **OPORTO.**

Cloths.
Mixed Cloths.
Cassimeres.
Montagnac.
Flannel.

Employs a steam-engine, 68 kinds of machines and 97 looms, and 9 men, 73 women and 26 children.

CLASS No. 235.

**184.—Mirrado, Jose Pedro Mendes,**

Macao, **SANTAREM.**

Samples of Woven Woollen Goods.

**185.—Neves, Balbina das,**

Brinxes, **SERPA.**

Coarse Woollen Cloth.

**186.—Padronello Woollen Fabrics Co.,**

**AMARANTE.**

Cassimeres.
Pilot Cloth.
Montagnac.
Melton.

Established in 1855.
Employs a hydraulic motor of 30 horse-power and a steam-engine of 18, usual spinners
    and a Jacquard loom, also,
    71 men.     Wages, 240 to 600 reis.
    54 women.     "     120 to 240   "
    38 children.     "     80 to 120   "
Raw material—Domestic and foreign, of the yearly value of     25,000 $ 000 reis.
Annual production,      -      -     47,000 $ 000 reis
Market—Portugal.
*Awards.—3 Silver Medals and a Copper one in National Exhibitions.*

**187.—Perdigao, Miguel S. R.,**

**S. Miguel de Machede, EVORA.**

Samples of coarse-woven Woollen Goods.

**188.—Portalegre Woollen Manufacturing Co.,**

**PORTALEGRE.**

Samples of Cassimeres, Dark Cloths, and cloths of different qualities.

Established in 1772.
Employs a Steam-engine from 50 to 60 horse-power, and
150 to 200 men.     Wages, 200 to 300 reis.
30 to 60 women.     "     80 to 120   "
15 to 30 children.  "     60 to 160   "
Raw material from Portugal, Spain, Buenos Ayres, and Cape of Good Hope, to the
annual value of 40 to 60,000 $ 000 reis.
Annual production,     .     -     90 to 100,000 $ 000 reis
Markets—Portugal.
*Awards.—Silver Medal at Paris,* 1855; *Oporto,* 1861; *Lisbon,* 1863; *and Society for the Promotion of the Fabril Industry.*

**189.—Silva, Jose Francisco da,**

**REDONDO.**

Samples of coarse-woven Woollen Goods.

**190.—Vicencia Roza,**

**AVEIRO.**

Samples of Woven Woollen Goods.

CLASS No. 237.

**191.—Albuquerque, Dr. Caetano d'Andrade,**

**PONTA DELGADA.**

Linen and Cotton Bed-Covers, colored.

**192.—Maria Barroga,**

**Safara, MOURA.**

One Quilt.

**193.—Bernardo Dauplas & Co.,**

**LISBON.**

Cassimeres, Shawls, Flannels, Mantels, Petticoats, Colored Night Caps,
Undershirts, Sashes.

Established in 1839.
Employs a steam-engine of 78 horse-power; 4,000 bobbins, with 11 complete carding ma-
chines; 50 manual and 36 mechanical looms; 200 braiding machines, and 144 for
making braid shoes; also, 330 men.     Wages; 450 to 800 reis.
370 women.     "     200 to 300   "
15 children.   "     100 to 200   "
Raw material used—wool, from Portugal, Spain, Germany, Cape of Good Hope, and
South America, at an annual cost of 100,000 $ 000 reis.
Annual production,     -     -     -     -     300,000 $ 000 reis
Markets—Portugal, its Colonies, and Brazil.
*Awards.—Bronze Medal at Oporto,* 1857; *Silver one at Oporto,* 1861; *of Honor at Oporto,* 1865;
*Bronze at Paris,* 1867; *Silver at Lisbon,* 1863, *and a Silver one at the Barcelona Exposition.*

**194.—Costa, Clemente Joaquim,**
### PONTA DELGADA.

Cotton Shawls colored.

**195.—Filippa Piteira,**
#### Brinxes, SERPA.

Blankets.
Mantillas.

**196.—Pacheco, Joao Vaz,**
### PONTA DELGADA.

Samples of Linen Fabrics for covering and dressing.

**197.—Pignatelli, Jose da Cunha,**
### GUARDA.

Blanket.

**197.ª—Ponte, Jose Caetano da,**
### ALMODOVAR.

Woollen Mantle.

**198.—Moreira, D. Maria Jose,**
### PONTA DELGADA.

Linen and Woollen Bed Covers, colored.

**199.—Resende, Francisca de,**
### PONTA DELGADA.

Linen and Woollen Fabrics, colored.

**200.—Simoes, Clara Rosa,**
### AVEIRO.

A Mantle of woven Linen and Rags.

— · —

CLASS No. 238.

**201.—Montes, Manuel Alvares,**
### OPORTO.

Samples of Combined Wool and Cotton Fabrics.  See Classes 230, 231.

**202·—Netto, Antonio Eugenio Bello,**
                                    **SANTAREM.**

Woollen stuffs for Mantles.

---

## CLASS No. 240.

**203.—Manuel Fernandes,**
                        **COIMBRA.**

Samples of Goat's Hair Fabrics.

---

## SILK AND SILK FABRICS, AND MIXTURES IN WHICH SILK IS THE PREDOMINATING MATERIAL.

CLASS 242.—Cocoons and raw silk as reeled from the cocoon, thrown or twisted silks in the gum.

CLASS 243.—Thrown or twisted silks, boiled off or dyed, in hanks, skeins, or on spools.

CLASS 244.—Spun silk yarns and fabrics, and the materials from which they are made.

CLASS 245.—Plain woven silks, lutestrings, sarsnets, satins, serges, foulards, tissues for hat and millinery purposes, etc.

CLASS 246.—Figured silk piece goods, woven or printed, upholstery silks, etc.

CLASS 247.—Crapes, velvets, gauzes, cravats, handkerchiefs, hosiery, knit goods, laces, scarfs, ties veils, all descriptions of cut and made-up silks.

CLASS 248.—Ribbons, plain, fancy, and velvet.

CLASS 249·—Bindings, braids, cords, galloons, ladies' dress trimmings, upholsterers', tailors', military, and miscellaneous trimmings.

---

## CLASS No. 243.

**204.—"Sericola Egyptaniense" Company,**
                                       **OPORTO.**

Silk Yarns.

---

## CLASSES Nos. 242, 243, 245 AND 246.

**205·—National Silk Spinning and Weaving Company, Successor to Cordeiro & Irmao,**
                                                              **LISBON.**

Nineteen frames with Samples of Silk Goods for Dresses and Upholstery. One frame with Cocoons, Raw Silk and Twisted Silk.

Established in 1852.

Employs a steam-engine of 6 horse-power, also band and mechanical looms and other apparatuses.

      28 men,     Wages, 400 to 700 reis

      143 women    "   160 to 400 reis.

Raw material—Domestic.

Annual production,   ·      ·      ·      100,000 $ 000 reis

Markets—Portugal and Brazil.

*Awards.—First Medals at Oporto, 1861, 1863 and 1865; second medal at Paris, 1867; Silver Prize at Oporto, 1869, and of Progress at Vienna, 1873, and decorated by the Portuguese Government for services rendered to the Industry.*

## CLASS No. 244.

### 206.—Brandao, Jose Marcal,
#### OPORTO.

Skeins of Colored-Twisted Sewing Silk.

Established in 1860.
Employs spindles and 12 men.  Wages, 440 reis.
      22 women.   " 200 "
      16 chidren.   " 120 "
Raw materials are raw silk, from China and Turkey.
Markets—Portugal and Brazil.
*Awards.—Oporto*, 1861; *Paris*, 1867, *and Vienna*, 1873.

### 207.—Silva e Alves, Antonio Jose Pereira da,
#### OPORTO.

Twenty-six Skeins of Silk, weighing 160 grammes.

Established in 1820.
Raw material—Domestic and foreign.
Markets—Portugal and Brazil.
*Awards.—Medal at National Exhibition of* 1865, *honorable mention in* 1861, *Bronze Medal at Faris*, 1867.

## CLASSES Nos. 245 AND 247.

### 208.—Fonseca, Manuel da Motta,
#### OPORTO.

Samples of Silk Serge.
Colored Satin Handkerchiefs.

Established in 1871.
Employs 7 small machines and 6 Jacquard looms.
Men's wages, 460 reis.
Women's wages, 120 to 240 reis.
Children's wages, 80 to 160 reis.
Raw material used to the annual value of    5 to 6,000 $ 000 reis
Annual production,   -      7,000 $ 000 reis

## CLASSES Nos. 245, 246, AND 247.

### 209.—Guerra, Joaquim Baptista da Silva,
#### OPORTO.

Samples of Poplins.
Satin Handkerchiefs.
Sample of Yellow and Blue Brocade.

Established in 1866.
Employs Jacquard looms and other apparatuses, also,
   26 men, 320 to 750 reis.
   20 women, 160 to 260 reis.
   25 children, 80 to 130 reis.
Raw materials used to the value of 30,000 $ 000 reis.
Annual production, 45,000 $ 000 reis.
*Awards.— Medals at Paris*, 1867; *Oporto*, 1865, *and Vienna*, 1873, *and decorated by the Portuguese Government for services rendered to Industry.*

## CLASSES Nos. 245 AND 246.

### 210.—Herderos de Manuel Custodio Moreira,
#### OPORTO.

Samples of Damask, Satin, Poplin and Silk Goods.

Established in 1823.
Employs 10 men and 2 children.
Raw materials are imported, to the annual value, 3,000 $ 000 reis.
Annual production, 5,400 $ 000 reis.
Markets—Portugal and Brazil.
*Awards.—Medals at Oporto,* 1865, *London,* 1851, *Oporto,* 1867, *and Lisbon,* 1863.

### 211.—Ramires y Ramires,
#### LISBON.

Samples of Silk Goods.
Threading and Knitting Factories.

Employs one steam-engine of 10 horse-power, 80 men, and 100 women.
Raw materials—Domestic and foreign.
Annual production—Threading,        30,000 $ 000 reis
            Knitting,        70,000 $ 000 reis
Markets—Portugal and Brazil.
*Awards.—National Medals at Oporto,* 1861; *Lisbon,* 1863; *International, Oporto,* 1865; *and Vienna,* 1873.

---

## CLASS No. 246.

### 212.—Araujo, Antonio Jose Barboza de,
#### BRAGA.

Variegated Silk.

---

## CLASSES Nos. 246 AND 249.

### 213.—Silva, Manoel Jose Francisco da,
#### BRAGA.

Gold Lustring.
Variegated Silks.
      "      Damask.
Wide Silk Galoons.
Narrow "    "

---

## CLASSES Nos. 246 AND 247.

### 214.—David Jose da Silva & Filho,
#### OPORTO.

Damask, of different qualities, Satins, and Gold Damask for upholstery.

Established in 1825.
Employs a Jacquard loom and 10 men.     Wages, 300 to 800 reis.
                8 women.      "     200 to 300   "
                2 children.    "     80 to 120   "
Raw material from China, Italy, and Portugal.
Market at home.
*Awards.—Medals at London,* 1851; *Paris,* 1855; *Oporto,* 1861; *Lisbon,* 1863, *and Oporto,* 1869

**215.—Vasconcellos, Jose da Silva Pereira,**

**BRAGA.**

Red Damask.
Black Velvet.

---

## CLASS No. 247.

**216.—Manuel Joaquim de Lima & Filho,**

**OPORTO.**

Black Velvet·
9 Parasol Silk Covers.

Established in 1850.
Employs 10 men,    Wages, 400 reis.
  4 women,     " 200 reis.
  2 children,     " 120 reis.

**217.—Pimentel & Queiroz,**

**OPORTO.**

Samples of Velvet, Satin, Silk and Taffeta.

Employs—2 men.    Wages, 400 reis.
  8 women.     " 240 "

---

## CLASSES Nos. 248 AND 249.

**218.—Nogueira, Francisco Jose,**

**OPORTO.**

Silk Ribbons.
Silk and Cotton Ribbons.
Plain Silk.
Silk Velvet.
Silk Fringe.

Established in 1853.
Employs 10 men
  6 women.
  3 children.
Raw materials—Domestic and Foreign.
Annual production, . . .       8,000 $ 000 reis
Markets—Portugal, Spain and Brazil.
*Awards—Medals at Lisbon and Braga*, 1863, *Oporto*, 1865.

---

## CLASS No. 248.

**219.—Motta, Augusto Antonio da,**

**OPORTO.**

Woollen, Silk, and Cotton Thread.

Established in 1864.
Employs 10 hands.   Wages, 200 to 800 reis.
Raw materials from England, to the annual value of 8,000 $ 000 reis.
Market—Portugal.

## CLASS No. 249.

**220.—Machado, Julio Rodrigues,**

### OPORTO.

. Silver and Gold Tassels and Ornaments for Church Vestries.

Established iu 1872.
Employs 12 hands.


**221.—Viuva Ferreira Campos & Co.,**

### OPORTO.

Several samples of Gold and Silver Braid and Galoons, small and large
Cylindrical Gold Beads, Gold Thread and Trimmings, etc., etc.

Established in Oporto in 1785.
Employs Jacquard looms, also,
    8 men.     Wages, 400 to 1200 reis.
    7 women.     "   150 to 300   "
    5 children.     "   120 to 240   "
Annual production,     .    .    .        12 to 20,000 $ 000 reis
*Awards.—Medals at London,* 1852, *Oporto* 1861.


**222.—Coelho, Jose de Souza,**

### PENAFIEL.

Samples of different kinds of Metal Galloons.


**223.—Guimaraes, Custudio Lopes da Silva,**

### PENAFIEL.

Samples of Metal-woven Galoons.

Established in 1872.
Employs 125 looms, weaving only 1 galoon at a time.
    15 men.     Wages, 140 to 550 reis.
    105 women.     "   80 to 220  "
    130 children.     "   30 to 80  "
Raw materials used are from Germany, England, and America.
Annual production,     - ,    -    -        20,000,000 reis
Markets—Portugal and Brazil.


**224.—Carneiro, Francisco dos Santos,**

### OPORTO.

Samples of False Braided Goods.

Established in 1852.
Employs 155 hands; wages, 120 to 600 reis.
Raw material to the annual value of 8,000 $ 000 reis.
Annual production,     -    -    -        12,000 $ 000 reis
Markets—Portugal, Spain, and Brazil.
*Awards.—Medals at Oporto and Lisbon, and Diploma of Merit at Vienna,* 1873.


**225.—Guimaraes, Custodio Jose da Silva,**

### OPORTO.

Samples of Galoons.

**226.—Braga, Manoel Jose Vieira,**
### BRAGA.

A Silk Emblem.

**227.—Alexandre Henriques,**
### OPORTO.

Samples of Elastic Webs.

**228.—Antunes, Jeronymo Jose,**
### BRAGA.

Samples of Elastic Webs of several kinds.

**229.—Costa, Jose Antonio da,**
### OPORTO·

Samples of Elastic Webs.

Established in 1869.
Employs—4 men.     Wages, 300 to 400 reis.
      1 woman.       "     200 to 300  "
      2 children.     "     100 to 160  ";
Raw material used is foreign, at the annual cost of 2,200 $ 000.
Annual production,    -     -     -     ·      3,500 $ 000 reis

**230.—Cardoso, Manoel Joaquim,**
### OPORTO.

Samples of Elastic Webs.

*Awards.—Silver Medal at Oporto,* 1851; *Honorable Mention at Oporto,* 1867.

---

## CLOTHING, JEWELRY AND ORNAMENTAL TRAVELING EQUIP-MENTS.

CLASS 250·—Ready-made clothing, knit goods and hosiery, military clothing, church vestments, costumes, waterproof clothing, and clothing for special objects.

CLASS 251.—Hats, caps, boots and shoes, gloves, mittens, etc., straw and palm-leaf hats, bonnets, and millinery.

CLASS 252.—Laces, embroideries, and trimmings for clothing, furniture, and carriages.

CLASS 253.—Jewelry and ornaments worn upon the person.

CLASS 254.—Artificial flowers, coiffures, buttons, trimmings, pins, hooks and eyes, fans, umbrellas, sun-shades, walking-canes, pipes, and small objects of dress or adornment, exclusive of jewelery. Toys ane fancy articles.

CLASS 255.—Fancy leather work, pocket-books, toilet cases, traveling equipments, valises and trunks.

CLASS 256.—Furs.

CLASS 257.—Historical collections of costumes, national costumes.

CLASS No. 250.

**231.—Calheta; Maria Pereira da,**

PONTA DELGADA.

White Coverlet, Knitted Hose.
Pillow Cases,       "
Night Caps.

**232.—Conceicao, Umbelina da,**

CASTRO VERDE.

Saddle Bags.

**233.—Dabney, S. W.,**

FAYAL.

Six pairs of Embroidered Stockings.

**234.—Florencia Serrana,**

AVEIRO.

A Peasant's Boddice with large silver buttons.

**235.—Paixao Junior, Antonio Augusto,**

COIMBRA.

French cloth Frock Coat.

**236.—Rego, A. P.,**

LISBON.

Naval Officer's Uniform, coat and pants.

---

CLASS No. 251.

**237.—Costa Braga e Filho,**

OPORTO.

Felt and Silk Hats.

Established in 1866.
Employs a steam engine of 15-horse power.
140 men.
 60 women.
Annual production,   -    -    -            120,000 $ 000 reis
Markets—Portugal, Spain, Brazil and South America.
*Awards.—First and Second Class at Rio de Janeiro, Oporto, 1865, Paris, 1867, Vienna, 1873.*
*Decorated by the Portuguese Government for services rendered to the industry.*

**238.—Bahia, Antonio Jose Rodrigues,**

BRAGA.

Hats of different qualities.

**239.—Bahia, Custodio Jose Rodrigues,**

**BRAGA.**

Hats of different qualities.

**240.—Dabney, R. L.,**

**FAYAL.**

Hat of Wood Shavings.

**241.—Ferreira, D. Joanna E.,**

**FAYAL.**

Ladies Hats of Wood Shavings.

**242.—Lima Carvalho,**

**FAYAL.**

Eight Straw Hats and Samples of Plaited Straw.

**243.—Maia, e Silva, Filho & Goncalves,**

**OPORTO.**

Hats of various kinds.

Established in 1854.
Employs 225 men, 85 women, and 45 boys.
Uses a machine of 35 horse-power.
Annual production,   -    -    -    190,000 $ 000
Markets—Portugal, Spain, Africa, and Brazil.
*Awards at several Exhibitions.*

**244.—Maria da Salga,**

**PONTA DELGADA.**

A white, Soft Rush Hat.

**245.—Official Commission of Ponta Delgada,**

**Island of S. Miguel, AZORES.**

Straw Hats.

**246.—Paula, Antonio Jose,**

**BARCELLOS.**

Cork Hats.

**247.—Pereiras Irmas,**

**PONTA DELGADA.**

Straw Hats.

**248.—The Portuguese Government.**

Broad Brimmed Hats.

**249.—Ramalho, Jose da Cunha,**

### PONTA DELGADA.

Straw Hats.

**250.—Santos & Irmao,**

### OVAR.

Hats of various kinds.

Established iu 1875.
Employs 36 men, 33 women and 6 boys·
Uses a steam engine from 25 to 40-horse power, and other different apparatuses.
Raw materials used to the annual value of 37,000 $ 000 reis.
Annual production, - - - - - 124,000 $ 000 reis
Markets—Portugal and Colonies, Spain, Brazil and Rio de la Plata.

**251.—Silva, Antonio Moreira da,**

### AVEIRO.

Woollen Hats.

Established in 1849.
Employs 50 men, 30 women, and 20 children.
Annual production, 20,000 $ 000 reis
Market—Portugal.
*Awards.—Industrial Exhibition of Oporto*, 1861.

**252.—Viuva de A. Roxo,**

### LISBON.

Hats of different kinds.

Established iu 1852.
Employs a steam engine of 2½ horse-power.
Annual production, 70,000 $ 000 reis, a great part of which is exported.
*Awards.—Medals at London*, 1862; *Oporto*, 1865; *Bordeaux*, 1865; *Lisbon*, 1865; *Paris*, 1867; *Vienna*, 1873.

**253.—Valenca, Domingos Fernandes,**

### AVEIRO.

Woollen Hats.

Established in 1871.
Employs 20 men, 7 women and 14 boys·
Annual production, 8,000 $ 000 reis

**254.—Almeida, Germano de,**

### LISBON.

Ladies' and Gentlemen's Boots and Shoes.

Established in 1866.
Employs—10 men.       Wages, 600 to 1,000 reis.
       9 women.       "        200 to   360  "
       2 children.      "        100 to   160  "
Raw materials used are domestic, French, and German.
Annual production,                                                              6 to 7,000 $ 000 reis
Markets—Portugal, Brazil, and Africa.


**255.—Areu, Manuel Joaquim da Silva,**

### BRAGA.

Different kinds of Boots and Shoes.


**256.—Barreiros, Francisco Isidoro,**

### BEJA.

Boots and Shoes,


**257.—Carvalho, Joaquim Jose de,**

### GUIMARAES.

Clog-Shoes and Slippers.


**258.—Bernardo Daupias & Co.,**

### LISBON.

Men's, Ladies' and Children's Woollen Shoes.


**259.—Dias, Antonio,**

### OPORTO.

Clog-shoes.

Established in 1870.
Raw materials used are Domestic.
Annual production,                                                              5,500 $ 000 reis


**260.—Ferreira, Jose Bento,**

### LISBON.

Calf-skin and Carpet Shoes, and Morocco Slippers.

**261.—Gomes & Filho,**

### LISBON.

Boots and Shoes.

Employs 50 men,      Wages, 360 to 800 reis.
      20 women,      "    160 to 400   "
       1 child,      "    100      "
Raw materials are domestic and foreign,
Markets—Portugal, Brazil and Africa.

**262.—Guimaraes, Custodio Jose da Silva,**

### OPORTO.

List Shoes.

**263.—Guimaraes, Custodio Lopes da Silva,**

### LISBON.

List Shoes.

Established in 1874.
Employs—45 men.      Wages, 240 to 850 rejs.
      270 women.      "    160 to  320   "
      130 children.      "    80 to  160   "
Materials used—Domestic and foreign, to the annual value of 58,000 $ 000 reis.
Annual production,   -   -   -   -   -   90,000 $ 000 reis
Markets—Portugal and Brazil.

**264.—House of Correction,**

### LISBON.

Shoes of different qualities.

**265.—Paiva, Manuel Joao da,**

### BRAGA.

Different kinds of Boots and Shoes.

**266.—Pereira, Luis Maria,**

### OPORTO.

Ladies' and Gentlemen's Boots and Shoes.

Established in 1836.
Employs—10 men.      Wages, 400 to 700 reis.
      3 women.      "    300      "
      1 child.
Annual production,            8,000 $ 000 reis

**267.—Santo Thirso, Antonio dos Reis,**

### AVEIRO.

Embroidered Clog Shoes.

**268.—Sequeira, Francisco Pinto,**
### OPORTO.

Boots and Shoes.

Established in 1864.
Employs 15 to 16 men.
Annual production,                                       4 to 5,000 $ 000 reis


**269.—Serra, Felippe Jose,**
### LISBON.

Ladies' and Gentlemen's Boots and Shoes

Established in 1866.
Employs—30 men.        Wages, 400 to 1,000 reis.
      12 women        "        240 to   300  "
Raw materials used are from Portugal, France, and Germany, to the annual value of 12,000 $ 000 reis.
Annual production,        -        -                     24,000 $ 000
Markets—Portugal, Africa and Brazil.
*Awards.—Medals at Industrial, Oporto, 1861, and International, Oporto, 1865.*


**270.—Silva, Julio Pereira da,**
### PENAFIEL.

Different kinds of Ladies' and Gentlemen's Clog-Shoes.


**271.—Silva, Miguel Manuel da,**
### VIANNA DO CASTELLO.

Boots.

Established in 1864.
Employs 36 men.        Wages 200 to 300 reis.
      12 children.        "        80 to 120   "
Annual production,        -        -        -        -     8,000 $ 000 reis
This manufactory furnishes several Infantry Army Corps.


**272.—Soares, Jose Nogueira,**
### PENAFIEL.

Clog Shoes.

Established in 1869.
Employs—5 men.        Wages, 300 to 600 reis.
     2 women.        "        160 to  300   "
Annual production,        -        -`        6,000 $ 000 reis
Market—Portugal and Brazil.
*Awards.—Diploma of Merit at Vienna, 1873.*


**273.—Souto, Rodrigo Alves Martins,**
### OPORTO.

Boots and Shoes.

Established in 1871.
Employs 8 men.  Wages, 600 to 800 reis.
    3 women.        "        200         "
Annual production,        -        -        2,000 $ 000 reis
Market—Portugal.

**274.—Souza, Jose da Cunha Alves de,**

### BRAGA.

Boots and Shoes.


**275,—The Portuguese Government.**

Clog Shoes and Slippers.


**276.—Vianna, Antonio Martins,**

### OPORTO.

List Shoes.

Established in 1872.
Employs—20 men.      Wages, 360 to 700 reis.
     50 women.      "      180 to 360   "
     10 children.      "      80 to 140   "
Raw materials used—Domestic.
Annual production,      -      18,000 $ 000 reis
Market—Portugal and Brazil.
*Awards—Honorable Mention at Paris, 1867, and Diploma of Merit at Vienna, 1873.*


**277.—Delaye, Hypolito,**

### LISBON.

Kid Gloves of different qualities.

Employs 10 men.      Wages, 1500 reis.
    50 women.      "      300   "
    25 boys.      "      120   "
Annual production in canvas and duck,      -      -      -      40,000 $ 000 reis
*Awards—Medal of Merit at Vienna, 1873; Medal of Merit, Society for the Promotion of the Fabril Industry. Decorated by the Portuguese Government.*


**278.—Jorge, Diogo, successor of Baron,**

### LISBON.

Kid Gloves of different qualities.

Employs 8 men,      Wages, 800 reis.
    72 women,      "      160   "
    2 boys,      "      120   "
Material used to the annual value of 12,000 $ 000 reis.
Annual production,      -      -      18,000 $ 000 reis.
Markets—Portugal, Brazil and Africa.
*Awards—Medals, London, 1851, Paris, 1855.*


**279.—Oporto Glove Company,**

### OPORTO.

Kid Gloves of different qualities.

Established in 1872.
Employs—10 men.      Wages, 400 to 2,250 reis.
    60 women.      "      100 to   800   "
    3 boys.      "      100   "
Annual production, -      -      -      10,000 $ 000 reis
Markets—Portugal and South America.

**280.—Silva, Bernardino Antunes da,**
### LISBON.

Kid Gloves of different qualities.

Established in 1872.
Employs ten men and one hundred women.
Annual production,        -        -        -        18,000 $ 000 reis
Market—Portugal.
*Award—Medal at Vienna,* 1873.

---

### CLASS No. 252.

**281.—Bivar, Manoel d'Almeida Coelho de,**
### PORTIMAO.

Laces.

**282.—Camara, Manuel da,**
### PONTA DELGADA.

A Table Cover.
Samples of Cotton Lace.

**283.—Carvalho, D. Anna Candida Leonor da Costa,**
### OVAR.

A Silk Cambric Handkerchief with embroidered Hems.

**284.—Coral, Joanna Maria Dias,**
### OVAR.

Embroideries.

**285.—Dabney, S. W.,**
### FAYAL.

Aloe Shawl.
Over Dress, Jacket and Sash.
Muslin Neck-ties.

**286.—Goes, Francisco Emilio de,**
### ALJUSTREL.

Samples of Laces.

**287.—John Davies,**
### FAYAL,

Two Pincushions.
Crivo Work.

**288.**—Nabinho, Jose da Fonseca,

OPORTO.

Samples of Woollen Cord.
Samples of Fine Woollen, Linen and Cotton Cord.
Samples of Corset Strings.

**289.**—Ferreira, D. Joanna B.,

FAYAL.

Black Lace with straw protections for Ladies' Hats.
White Lace.
A Petticoat, Jacket, and Sash of Lace with Straw protections.

**290.**—Lima, Anna Julia da Conceicao,

PONTA DELGADA.

Samples of Linen and Cotton Lace.

**291.**—Lima, Bernardo de Abreu,

PONTA DELGADA.

A Table Cloth.
Strips of White Embroidery.

**292.**—Magalhaes, D. Anna Maria Barboza,

AVEIRO.

Laces.

**293.**—Oliveira, I. F. d',

Island of Madeira, FUNCHAL.

Embroidered Caps, Collars, and Handkerchiefs.

---

CLASSES Nos. 252 AND 254.

**294.**—Santos Brites, Maria Gomes e Rosa Gomes dos,

OVAR.

Laces, Crochet Work, and Embroidery.
Artificial Flowers made of the pits of the fig-tree and of shells, of silk, wool, &c.

---

CLASS No. 252.

**295.**—Tavares, Rita de Jesus,

AVEIRO.

Linen Lace.

**296.—Teixeira, Carlotta Mathilde,**

**Island of Madeira, FUNCHAL.**

Samples of White Embroidered Cotton and Linen Goods, such as hand-kerchiefs, insertings, edgings, dresses, caps, &c.

**297.—The Portuguese Government.**

Linen Laces manufactured at Vianna do Castello.

**298.—The Primary School of**

**BARCELLOS.**

Embroideries.

**299.—Themundo (Maria Eduarda),**

**CASTRO VERDE.**

Laces.

**300.—Theresa de Jesus,**

**PONTA DELGADA.**

Shirts Fronts.

### CLASS No. 253.

**301.—Aurificia Company,**

**OPORTO.**

Engine-turned and Chiselled Silver and Gilt-silver Pieces.

This company owns also a saw-mill. See Class 601.
Established in 1865.
Employs—100 men.    Wages, 240 to 2,250 reis.
        40 women.      "   120 to  300  "
        40 children.   "    80 to  160  "
Uses a steam engine of 50 horse-power.
Raw materials from England, France, Germany, and Portugal, to the annual value of
100,000 $ 000 reis.
Annual production,                          200,000 $ 000 reis

**302.—Cerquinho, Francisco Augusto Vaz,**

**OPORTO.**

Gold and Silver Filagree Work, and other articles of the same metals.

Established in 1871.
Markets—England, France, Brazil.
*Awards—Medal of Progress at Vienna,* 1873.

**303.—Couto, Antonio Guilherme do,**

**S. Pedro da Cova, OPORTO.**

Silver Filagree Work.

**304.—Coutinho, A. & Filho,**
####### OPORTO.

Silver Filagree Work.

**305.—Leitao & Irmao,**
####### OPORTO.

Gold and Silver Filagree Work.

**306.—Lobao e Ferreira,**
####### OPORTO.

Gold Jewelry and Silver Purses.
Gold and Filagree Work.

**307.—Marques Junior, Manuel Martins,**
####### Fanzeres, OPORTO.

Silver Filagree Work.

**308.—Moutinho, Luiz Pinto,**
####### LISBON.

Silver Table Ornaments, Centre Pieces, and Ornaments for Images.

Markets—Portugal, Brazil, and Africa.

**309.—Moutinho de Souza, F., Successors,**
####### OPORTO.

Oold and Silver Filagree Work.

**310.—Nogueira, Antonio Marques,**
####### OPORTO.

Silver Filagree Work.

**311.—Seabra, Jose dos Santos,**
####### OPORTO.

Gold and Silver Filagree Work, and other articles of the same metals.

Markets—Portugal, Spain, England and Brazil.

**312.—Teixeira, Jose Rodriques,**
####### OPORTO.

Silver Jewelry and Silver Purses.

*Awards.—Bronze Medal at London,* 1851, *and Silver Medal at Oporto,* 1865.

## CLASS No. 254.

**313.—Carvalho, Maria da Conceicao,**
### PONTA DELGADA.

A frame with flowers made of the Pith of the Fig Tree.


**314.—Dabney, S. W.,**
### FAYAL.

An Eagle made of Pith of the Fig Tree.


**315.—Ferreira, D. Joanna, E.,**
### FAYAL.

Flowers for Millinery purposes.


**316.—Lima, Joao Bernardo de Abreu,**
### PONTA DELGADA.

A frame of Pricked Paper.


**317.—Pinho, D. Guilhermina d'Oliveira,**
### PONTA DELGADA.

Four bunches of Feather Flowers.
Twenty-six bunches of Rag Flowers.


**318.—Souza, D. Maria Magdalena de,**
### PONTA DELGADA

A Yacht and a Steamboat made of the Pith of the Fig Tree.
Bunches of flowers of the same material.
Flowers made of Stearina.


**319.—The Portuguese Government,**

Artificial Flowers manufactured at the House of Correction, Lisbon.


**320.—Schalck, H.,**
### LISBON.

Samples of Buttons and of Hooks and Eyes.

Established in 1847.
Employs—60 men.     Wages, 400 to 900 reis.
       80 women.     "     200 to 360   "
       80 children.     "     80 to 120   "
Uses a steam engine of 20 horse power.
Markets—Portugal, Spain, and South America.
*Awards.—Bronze Medal at Paris,* 1855; *Silver Medal at Oporto,* 1865: *Paris,* 1867 ; *Medal of Merit at Vienna,* 1873; *Bronze Medal, Society for the promotion of the Fabril Industry,* 1873. *Decorated by the Portuguese Government.*

**321.—Goncalves Ribas & Co.,**

### OPORTO.

Samples of Buttons.

Established in 1863.
Employs  10 men.   Wages, 700 reis.
    60 women.   "   240  "
    10 children.   "   120  "
Raw material used are from Portugal, France, England, and Germany, to the annua
 value of 12,000 $ 000 reis.
Annual production,    -            20,000 $ 000 reis
Markets—Portugal and Brazil.
*Awards.—Silver Medal at Oporto,* 1865.

**322.—Marques, Jose Antonio,**

### BRAGA.

Umbrellas used by the peasants.

**323.—Diogo, Manuel Antonio,**

### OPORTO.

Umbrellas.

Established in 1871.
Employs 15 men, 6 women and two boys.
Annual production,  -    -         16,000 $ 000 reis
Markets—Portugal and Spain.

**324.—Cunha, Augusto Mendes da,**

### GUIMARAES.

Horn Combs.

**325.—Passos, Augusto Fructuoso,**

### GUIMARAES.

Horn Combs.

---

## CLASS No. 255.

**326.—David, Jose d'Azevedo,**

### OPORTO.

Trunks and Hat Boxes.

Established in 1874.
Employs 3 men, wages, 300 to 600 reis.
Raw material used to the annual value of 800 $ 000 reis.
Annual production,  -    -      2 to 3,000 $ 000 reis
Markets—Portugal and Brazil.
*Awards—Silver Medal, Oporto,* 1865 : *copper medal, Oporto,* 1865.

**327.—Ramos, Joaquim Antonio,**
**BEJA.**

A Skin of Wine.
A Wine Leather Flask.

**328.—Rocha, Francisco Jose da Silva,**
**OPORTO.**

Wooden trunks covered with Leather, Valises and Travelling Bags.
Game Bag and Shot Belt.

CLASS No. 257.

**329.—Trindade, Joaquim Antonio,**
**BEJA.**

Peasant's Gaiters.

**330.—The Portuguese Government,**
**LISBON.**

A Peasant Woman's Dress.

**331.—Coutinho, Jose Maria da Camara,**
**PONTA DELGADA.**

A Cap of Linen Duck.
A Cap of Blue Cloth worn by the people of Azores Islands.

## PAPER, BLANK BOOKS, AND STATIONERY.

CASS 258.—Stationery for the desk, stationers' articles, pens, pencils, inkstands, and other apparatus of writing and drawing.

CLASS 259.—Writing paper and envelopes, blank-book paper, bond paper, tracing paper, tracing linen, tissue paper, etc., etc.

CLASS 290.—Printing paper for books, newspapers, etc.
Wrapping paper of all grades, cartridge and manilla paper, paper bags·

CLASS 261.—Blank books, sets of account books, specimens of ruling and binding, including blanks, bill heads, etc.: bookbinding.

CLASS 262.—Cards—Playing cards, cardboard, bindees' board, pasteboard, paper or cardboard boxes.

CLASS 263.—Building paper, pasteboard for walls, cane fibre felt for car wheels, ornaments, etc.

CLASS 264.—Wall papers, enamelled and coloured papers, imitations of leather, wood, etc.

## CLASS No. 259.

### 332.—Freitas, Feliciano Gabriel de,
**LISBON**.

Blue Writing Paper (Foolscap)
White Writing Paper (Foolscap)
Wrapping Paper.

Employs— 8 men.  Wages, 240 to 600 reis.
  12 women.   "  100 to 120  "
  6 boys.    "  50 to 80  "
Uses a hydraulic machine of 5 horse-power.
Annual production, -  -         4,000 $ 000 reis
Market—Lisbon.

### 333·—Lemos, Joao Goncalves de,
**LOUZAN**.

Writing Paper of different qualities.

Uses a steam engine and a hydraulic machine.

### 334.—Prado Paper Mill Company,
**THOMAR**.

Samples of Writing Paper.

Established in 1875.
Employs 100 workmen. Wages from 60 to 240 reis.
Uses hydraulic machines.
Raw materials—Domestic. Drugs, imported.

---

## CLASS No. 260.

### 335.—Galiano, Manoel Aspres d'Oliveira,
**OPORTO**.

Corn-Husk Cigarette Wrappers.

### 336.—Raul Mesnier,
**COIMBRA**.

Corn-Husk Cigarette Wrappers.

---

## CLASS No. 261.

### 337.—Lisboa, Jose Balbino da Silva, & Co.,
**LISBON**.

Specimens of ordinary and elegant Book-binding.

Established in 1856.
Employs—22 men. Wages, 300 to 1,600 reis.
  7 women  "  160 to 400  "
  4 children.  "  120 to 160  "
Raw materials are domestic and foreign, to the annual value of 10 to 12,000$000 reis.
Annual production, -  -  -  -  - ·12 to 15,000 $ 000 reis
Awards.—*Silver Medal at Oporto,* 1865; *one of merit at Vienna,* 1873; *and one from the Society for the Promotion of the Fabril Industry.*

## CLASS No. 262.

**338.—Lisbon National Printing Office,**

### LISBON.

Playing Cards.  See Class 265.

**339.—Santos Brites, Maria Gomes y Rosa Gomes dos,**

### OVAR.

A Paste-board Calvary.

---

## CLASS No. 265.

**340.—Lallemant Freres,**

### LISBON.

Plain and Fancy Typographical Works.  Satin impressions.

Established in 1855.
*Awards.—Medals at Oporto, 1865; Paris, 1867; Vienna, 1873.  Three Honorable mentions for services rendered to the Typographical Art.*

**341.—National Printing Office of Lisbon,**

Typography.
Common and Illustrated Books.
Liturgical Works.
Fine and Handsome Editions.

Type Foundry.  See Class 542.
Engraving Plates.
Types.
Variety of Cliche's.

Lithography.  See Class 423.
Plans, Maps, Specimens of Chromolythography.

Plain Cards·  See Class 262.
Cards prepared on the best Italian Paste-board.

Established in 1768.
Employs a steam engine of 6 horse-power.
*In the Typography* 18 manual and 9 mechanical presses and other auxiliary machines.
*In the Foundry,* 14 casting machines, 7 crenating machines, 6 turning machines, 8,000 punches, 37,000 matrices and other implements.
*In the Lithography,* 16 manual and 1 mechanical presses and other implements.
And 231 men, 16 women, and 37 children.
Raw matarial—Paper from Abelheira (Tojal), Alcmquer, Thomar, and Louzan. Lead from the Bracal mines in Portugal and Huelva in Spain. to the annual value of (paper not included), 48,000 $ 000 reis.
Annual production,       -       -       -       -                    130,000 $ 000 reis
Markets—Portugal and Brazil, in regard to types.
*Awards—Medals at London, 1862; Gold Medal at Oporto, 1865; Gold Medal and the Cross of the Legion of Honor at Paris, 1867, and Medal of Progress at Vienna, 1873.*

**342.—Nepomuceno, Manuel,**

### OPORTO.

Specimens of Typographical Work.
Books.

Established in 1855.
Employs—20 men.　　Wages, 500 to 1,000 reis.
　　6 children.　　"　　100 to　300　"
Raw materials used are domestic and foreign.
Annual production,　.　　　　　　　　　　7,000 $ 000 reis
Markets—Portugal and Brazil.

---

# MILITARY AND NAVAL ARNAMENTS, ORDNANCE, FIRE ARMS AND APPARATUS OF HUNTING AND FISHING.

CLASS 265.—Military small arms, muskets, pistols, and magazine guns, with their ammunition.
CLASS 266.—Light artillery, compound guns, machine guns, mitrailleuses, etc.
CLASS 267,—Heavy ordnance and its accessories.
CLASS 268.—Knives, swords, spears and dirks.
CLASS 269.—Fire arms used for sporting and hunting, also other implements for the same purpose.
CLASS 270.—Traps for game, birds, vermin, etc.

---

### CLASS No. 266.

**343.—Tavares, Francisco Antonio,**

### Azeitao, SETUBAL.

A Conical Ball for a smooth-bore Cannon.　29 pound.

---

### CLASS No. 269.

**344.—Carvalho e Mello, A. J., de,**

### BRAGANCA.

A Cane changeable into a Gun.

---

### CLASS No. 265.

**345.—Cardoso, Jose Pereira,**

### OPORTO.

Samples of Lead Shot.

*Awards.—Medals at the Exhibitions of Paris*, 1855 *and* 1867 ; *Lyons*, 1872 ; *Oporto*, 1857, 1861 *and* 1865.

## CLASS No. 269.

**346.—Ferreira, Joao Jose,**
### OPORTO.

Sporting Breech-loading Gun.

---

## CLASS No. 265.

**347.—Manuel Antonio da Silva & Filhos,**
### LISBON.

Samples of Lead Shot.

*Awards.—Bronze medals at the Exhibitions of London and Paris, 1867.*

---

## CLASS No. 270.

**348.—Pilao e Luzes, Antonio d'Oliveira & Joao Gomes Leite,**
### OVAR.

Fishing Nets.   See Class 594.

**349.—Oliveira, Gaspar Jose de.**

Fishing Nets.

---

## MEDICINE, SURGERY, PROTHESIS.

CLASS 272.—Medicines; officinal (in any authoritative pharmacopœa), articles of the materia medica, preparations, unofficinal.

CLASS 273.—Dietetic preparations, as beef extract, and other articles intended especially for the sick.

CLASS 274.—Pharmaceutical apparatus.

CLASS 275.—Instruments for physical diagnosis, clinical thermometers, stethoscopes, opthalmoscopes, etc., (except clinical microscopes, etc., for which see Class 324).

CLASS 276.—Surgical instrments and appliances, with dressings, apparatus for deformities, prothesis, obstetrical instruments.

CLASS 277.—Dental instruments and appliances.

CLASS 278.—Vehicles and appliances for the transportation of the sick and wounded, during peace and war, on shore or at sea.

---

## CLASS No. 272.

**350.—Drack Junior, J. Ribeiro Guimaraes,**
### LISBON.

Drack's Pectoral Syrup of Cherry Laurel.
Health's Restorative.   Pectoral Flour.
Drack's Anti-Scorbutic Elixir.

Drack's Horse-Radish Syrup, iodized.
Syrup prepared with the Sap of the Maritime Pine Tree.
Syrup of Quinine and Iodine of Iron.
Aubergier's Syrup of Lactucarium.
Dr. Dechoix's Aromatic Tincture of Arnica.
Dr. Dechoix's Aromatic Tincture with Camphor.
Norwegian Cod-Liver Oil.
Norwegian Cod-Liver Oil, desinfected.
Norwegian Cod-Liver Oil, ferruginous.
Norwegian Cod-Liver Oil, with iodine of iron.
Norwegian Cod-Liver Oil, with iodine of iron, desinfected.
Agua das Damas.
Bruguet's Oil.

Many of these medicines are the exclusive property of the exhibitor, and are only manufactured in his own laboratory.

## 351.—Ferraz, Jose Libertador de Magalhaes,

### COIMBRA.

Cod Livei Oil, purified with roasted coffee, after the exhibitors' formula.
Saccharuret of Pyro-phosphate of Iron and soda; a new manner of administering to the sick a salt of iron of remarkable solubility.
Elixir, after Richard's formula, modified by the exhibitor.
Sweet Almond Oil.
Castor Oil, extracted from seeds gathered in the environs of Coimbra.
Glycerine in its greatest degree of purity, after Merfit's method.
Soluble Phosphate of Iron of Leras, made according to Leras' process.
Syrup of Sap of Maritime Pine Tree.
Pectoral Syrup of Iceland Moss.   Exhibitor's formula.
Syrup of Hypo-phosphate of Lime.
Syrup of Hypo-phosphate of Soda.
. Cod-Liver Oil and Iron reduced by Hydrogen.   Exhibitor's process.
Cod-Liver Oil with Ioduret of Iron, prepared by the exhibitor.
Vermifugous Biscuits.   Exhibitor's formula.

This product has for basis the hydralcholic extract of the male fern.  It contains no santomine, nor does it contain calomel or any other mineral substances.  Exhibitor's formula.

An imitation of Eau de Cologne.   Exhibitor's formula.

The essential oils are extracted from aromatic plants gathered in the neighborhood of Coimbra.

Oppodeldoc and Arnica.   Exhibitor's formula.
Hygienic Injections.

*Awards.—Gold Medal at the District of Coimbra, 1869.*

## 352.—Figueiredo, Joaquim de,

### AVIZ.

Syrup.
Lactucarium.
Ergotine.

**353.—Franco, Pedro Augusto,**
                                        **Belem, LISBON.**

James' Pectoral Syrup.

Annual production,       -       -       -                20,000 $ 000 reis
James' Syrup was patented by decree of June 22, 1869.


**354.—Galiano, Manuel Aspres d'Oliveira,**
                                        **OPORTO.**

Anti-Scrofulous Syrup.
Watery Solutive Syrup.
Alcoholic Solutive Syrup.
Pomade.


**355.--Jesus, Manuel Vicente,**
                                        **LISBON.**

Pills of Unalterable Ioduret of Iron.

Annual production,   -                                    5,000 $ 000 reis
Markets—Portugal and Brazil.
*Awards.—Medals at Oporto,* 1865, *and Vienna,* 1873.


**356.--Lima, Guilherme A. E.,**
                                        **LISBON.**

Ricon's Injection.
Dentrific Elixir.
Dona Maria's Tooth Powders.
Dona Rosa's Tooth Powders.
Medicine for Deafness and Ringing of the Ears.


**357.—Nobreza, Frederico Augusto da Silva,**
                                **Figueira da Foz, COIMBRA.**

Vermifugous Lozenges.


**358.—Grajera, Dr. Antonio Maria Mendes,**
                                        **Reguengos, EVORA.**

Capsules of Apiol.
Pills of the Extract of Apiol and Iron.
Pectoral Balsamic Cigars.
Dolorifuguos Elixir.
Anti-Herpetic Pomade.


**359.—Rei, Jose Joaquim,**
                                        **LISBON.**

Ferruginous Syrup of Quinine.
Cod Liver Oil with Ioduret of Iron.
Flower of Youth.
Anti-Asmathic Elixir.
Indian Drops.
Sympathic Pomade.

**360.—Rodrigues, Jose Pereira,**
### LISBON.

Syrup of Quinine and Iron.
Syrup of the Sap of the Maritime Pine Tree.
Wine of Quinine.
Cod-Liver Oil with Proto-Ioduret of Iron.
Markets—Portugal and Brazil.

**361.—Salgueiro, Nuno Freire Dias,**
### OPORTO.

Compound Syrup of Balm of Tolu.

---

### CLASS No. 273.

**362.—Pires, Joao de Jesus,**
### LISBON.
Chocolate of Gluten.

**363.—Schurman, Adolpho,**
### LISBON.

Brustmehl's Pectoral Flour.
Brustmehl's Ferruginous Flour.
Flour, good in the Treatment of Coughs.

These flours are all prepared by the exhibitor, having been approved by the Industrial Institute of Lisbon.

---

### CLASS No. 276.

**364.—Andrade, Albano Abilio de,**
### OPORTO.

Ivory Bougies used as Surgical Instruments to Produce the Dilation of the Wrethra.

*Awards.—Silver Medal at the Industrial Exhibition of Oporto; First-Class Medal at the International, Oporto, 1865. Honourable Mention at Paris, 1867.*

---

## HARDWARE, EDGE TOOLS, CUTLERY, AND METALLIC PRODUCTS.

CLASS 280.—Hand tools and instruments used by carpenters, joiners, and for wood and stone in general. Miscellaneous hand tools used in industries, such as jewellers, engravers.
CLASS 281.—Cutlery, knives, penknives, scissors, razors, razor-straps, skates, and implements sold by cutlers.
CLASS 282.—Emery and sand-paper, polishing-powders, polishing and burnishing stones.
CLASS 283.—Metal hollow-ware, ornamental castings.
CLASS 284.—Hardware used in construction, exclusive of tools and implements. Spikes, nails, screws, tacks, bolts, locks, latches, hinges, pulleys. Plumbers' and gasfitters' hardware, furniture fittings, ships' hardware, saddlers' hardware, and harness fittings and trimmings.

CLASSES Nos. 280 AND 284.

**365.—Cardozo, Joao Thomaz,**
### Villa Nova de Gaia, OPORTO.

Cooper's Tools, Brands, Hatchets, for different purposes.
Door Locks.
Samples of Nails.

Established in 1840.
Employs—35 men.     Wages, 400 to 1200 reis.
         12 children.     "    100 to 200   "
Markets—Portugal and Brazil.
*Awards.—Honourable Mention at the Exhibition of Oporto, 1878; Silver Medal at Oporto, 1861; Gold Medal at Oporto, 1865.*

CLASS No. 280.

**366.—Oporto Industrial Institute,**
### OPORTO.

Tools for Working on Granite.

**367.—Santos, Manuel Moreira dos,**
### OPORTO.

Caulking Irons.

CLASS No. 282.

**368.—Alves Junior, Antonio,**
### VILLA REAL.

Pruning Knives.

**369.—Cunha, Augusto Mendes da,**
### GUIMARAES.

Scissors, Pruning Knives, Table Knives.

**370.—Guimaraes, Joaquim Mendes da,**
### GUIMARAES.

Scissors, for various purposes, with Silver Mountings.

CLASS No. 284.

**371·—Antonio da Camara,**
### PONTA DELGADA.

A Secret Lock.

**372.—Jacob Ben-Saude,**

### PONTA DELGADA.

Twelve samples of Copper Nails.
Twelve samples of Zinc Nails.
Seven samples of Iron Nails.
One sample of Round Nails.
One sample of Flat Nails.

**373.—Goncalves, Jeronimo Ferreira,**

### OPORTO.

Brass Tacks of various sizes.

**374.—Guerra, Antonio Jose de Souza,**

### OPORTO.

Brass Stop-Cocks for various uses.
Hinges, Water Plugs, Bells.

Annual production,                                    3,000 $ 000 reis
Market—Portugal.

**375.—Lemos & Antunes,**

### Figueira da Foz, COIMBRA.

Pulleys and Blocks.

**376.—M. J. Ferreira da Silva & Filho,**

### BRAGA.

Iron Nails of different qualities.

**377.—Pacheco, Francisco Gomes,**

### BRAGA.

Iron Nails of different sizes and for different purposes.

Established in 1850.
Employs 30 men and 10 children.
Raw material from England and Sweden.

**378.—Peixoto, Jose Rodrigo**

### PENAFIEL.

Brass Tacks of various sizes.

Established in 1846.
Employs— 4 men.        Wages, 300 to  500 reis.
             1 woman.        "     160 to  200  "
             3 children.      "      80 to  120  "
Raw materials imported to tha annual value of 800 $ 000 reis.
Annual production,      -      -      -      -        5,000 $ 000 reis
Market—Portugal.

**379.—Santos, Rocha & Moreira,**

## OPORTO.

Lead Pipes.

Employs 3 men, wages from 400 to 600 reis, and a steam-engine of 4 horse-power.
Annual production,         -        -       12,000 $ 000 reis
Market—Portugal.
*Awards.—Medals at the International Exhibitions of Oporto, 1865, and Vienna, 1873.*

**380.—Santos, Joaquim Antunes dos,**

## LISBON.

Iron and Wire Nails.

**381.—Schalck, H.,**

## LISBON.

Samples of Nails.

# FABRICS OF VEGETABLE, ANIMAL, OR MINERAL MATERIALS.

CLASS 285.—India rubber goods and manufactures.
CLASS 286.—Brushes.
CLASS 287.—Ropes, cordage.
CLASS 288.—Flags, insignia, emblems.
CLASS 289.—Wooden and basket ware, papier maché.
CLASS 290.—Undertakers' furnishing goods, caskets, coffins, etc.
CLASS 291.—Galvanized ironwork.

### CLASS No. 286.

**382.—Oliveira, Manuel de,**

## OPORTO.

Painters' Brushes.

**383.—The Portuguese Government.**

### Manufacturers---The Prisoners of the Central Jail, LISBON.

Scouring Brushes.

### CLASS No. 287.

**384.—Cruz, Joao Maria da,**

## SETUBAL.

Tow-Cord.
Flax-Thread.
Feather Grass Cord.

**385.—Barboza, Jose Antonio,**
### OPORTO.

Samples of Ropes, Lines, Thread, Twine, &c.

Raw materials are from Russia, India, &c., to the value of 8,000 $ 000 reis.
Annual production,    -      -      -        -     10,500 $ 000 reis
Markets—Portugal and Brazil.


**386.—National Rope Yard,**
### Junqueira, LISBON.

Ropes, Cords, Lines, Twine, &c., for shipping purposes.

Established in 1788.
Employs a movable steam-engine of 6 horse-power; manual and mechanical spinners,
and other apparatuses, and 50 men.    Wages, 300 to 400 reis.
                      80 women.    "    120 to 260  "
                      20 children.    "    80 to 200  "
Raw material used is Russian linen, to the annual value of 35,000 $ 000 reis.
Annual production in cords, 27,000 $ 000 reis. See Class No. 233.
Market—The products are exclusively destined for the use of the Ministry of Marine
and the Colonies.
*Awards.—Silver Medal at Oporto,* 1861, *and a Copper one at Paris,* 1867.


**387.—Oliveira, Balthasar Pinto,**
### OPORTO.

Samples of Ropes.

---

### CLASS No. 289.

**388.—Augusta, Maria da Piedade,**
### COIMBRA.

Tooth-Picks.


**389.—Avellar & Miranda,**
### LISBON.

Tooth-Picks.


**390.—Joaquim Maria,**
### BARCELLOS.

Tooth-Picks.


**391.—Jose Gaudencio,**
### COIMBRA.

Tooth-Picks.


**392.—Maria Jose,**
### COIMBRA.

Tooth-Picks.

**393.**—Jeronimo Martins & Filho,

**LISBON.**

Tooth-Picks.


**394.**—Silva, Joaquim da,

**COIMBRA**

Tooth-Picks.


**395.**—Baptista, Joao Guerreiro,

**ALMODOVAR**

Wooden Spoons made by Shepherds.


**396.**—The Portuguese Government,

**Several Manufacturers——LISBON.**

Willow and Wicker Basket Work.
Wooden Spoons.


**397.**—Ferreira, D. Joanna E.,

**FAYAL.**

One Dozen of Napkin-Rings.


**398.**—Araujo, Jose Antonio,

**BARCELLOS.**

Willow Baskets.


**399.**—Dabney, S. W.,

**FAYAL.**

One Set of Nest Baskets.


**400.**—Mattos, Antonio de,

**BARCELLOS.**

Basket Work.


**401.**—Tavares, Jose,

**OPORTO.**

Hand and Clothes Baskets.
Panniers.

**402.—Tavares, Laureano,**

### PONTA DELGADA.

Collection of Willow Baskets.
Pincushion of Aloe, Fibre and Silk.

---

## CARRIAGES, VEHICLES, AND ACCESSORIES.

(For farm vehicles and railway carriages, see Department of Agriculture and Machinery.) (Carriages exhibited in separate Annexe.)

---

CLASS 292.—Pleasure carriages.
CLASS 293.—Travelling carriages, coaches, stages, omnibuses, hearses, Bath chairs; velocipedes, baby carriages.
CLASS 294.—Vehicles for movement of goods and heavy objects, carts, waggons, trucks.
CLASS 295.—Sleighs, sledges, sleds, etc.
CLASS 296.—Carriage and horse furniture, harness and saddlery, whips, spurs, horse blankets. carriage robes, rugs, etc.

---

### CLASS No. 296.

**403.—Beirollas, Antonio Manuel,**

### GOLLEGA.

Horse Shoes.

**404.—Carvalho, Manuel,**

### GUIMARAES.

Horse Bits, Stirrups, and Spurs.

**405.—Cunha, Augusto Mendes da,**

### GUIMARAES.

Horse Bits.
Spurs.

**406.—Cruz, Luiz Ferreira de Souza,**

### OPORTO.

Axles for Carriages.

**407.—Guimaraes, Joao Carvalho,**

### GUIMARAES.

Horse Bits and Spurs.

**408.—Silva, Joao Baptista da,**

     **BRAGA.**

Horse Bits.

**409.—Silva, Joao d'Oliveira e,**

     **BRAGA.**

Portuguese Saddle and several kinds of Harnesses.

**410.—Souza, Luiz Augusto,**

     **EVORA.**

Harness Bells.
Signal Bells.

# DEPARTMENT III.

# EDUCATION

## AND

# SCIENCE.

# DEPARTMENT III.---EDUCATION AND SCIENCE.

*Location :*—MAIN BUILDING.

## EDUCATIONAL SYSTEMS, METHODS, AND LIBRARIES.

CLASS 300.—Elementary instruction, Infant schools and kindergartens, arrangements, furniture appliances, and modes of training.

Public schools, graded schools, buildings and grounds, equipments, courses of study, methods of instruction, text books, apparatus, including maps, charts, globes, etc.; pupils' work, including drawing and penmanship; provisions for physical training.

CLASS 301.—Higher education. Academies and high schools.

Colleges and universities. Buildings and grounds; libraries, museums of zoology, botany, mineralogy, art, and archeology; apparatus for illustration and research, mathematical, physical, chemical, and astronomical courses of study; text books, catalogues, libraries, and gymnasiums.

CLASS 302.—Professional schools, theology, law, medicine and surgery, dentistry, pharmacy, mining. engineering, agriculture and mechanical arts, art and design, military schools, naval schools, normal schools, commercial schools, music.

Buildings, text books, libraries, apparatus, methods, and other accessories for professional schools.

CLASS 303.—Institutions for instruction of the blind, deaf, and dumb, and the feeble-minded.

CLASS 304.—Education reports and statistics.

National bureau of education.

State, city, and town systems.

College, university, and professional systems.

CL ss 305.—Libraries, history, reports, statistics, and catalogues.

CLASS 306.—School and text books, dictionaries, encyclopædias, gazetteers, directories, index volumes, bibliographies, catalogues, almanacs, special treatises, general and miscellaneous literature, newspapers, technical and special newspapers and journals, illustrated papers, periodical literature.

---

## CLASSES Nos. 300 AND 306.

1.—Aranha, Pedro Wenceslau de Brito,
### LISBON.

Several works on Elementary Instruction and General Literature and Art.

---

## CLASS No. 300.

2.—Godolphim, Costa,
### LISBON.

A Book on Associations.

## CLASS No. 302.

**3.—Lisbon Industrial Institute,**
### LISBON.

Descriptive work of the Institute, its organization, regulations, &c. See
Class 320.

---

## CLASS No. 305.

**4.—Queiroz, G. Jose de,**
### LISBON.

General Statistics of the Commerce of Portugal, graphically arranged.

**5.—Department of Finance,**
### LISBON.

Commercial Statistics of Portugal.

---

## CLASS No. 306.

**6.—Ernesto Chardron,**
### OPORTO.

Dictionary of the Portuguese Language, by Frei. Domingos Vieira. 5
Volumes.

Ernesto Chardron is proprietor of the International Book Store, one of the bests in
Oporto, and has been established in said City only a few years. He is also an editor
of many works.

**7.—Ferraz, Jose Libertador de Magalhaes,**
### COIMBRA.

Work on Pharmacy.

**8.—Magalhaes & Moniz,**
### OPORTO.

Elementary, Literary and Scientific Works.

**9.—Mengo, Francisco da Silva,**
### OPORTO

Exhibits 142 Volumes of different Portuguese Works.

He is the present proprietor of the book-store—Moré. This book-store was established
in the city of Oporto in 1835. It is a very good establishment and very well thought
of throughout the country. During many years, and when it belonged to widow
Moré, it was superintended and administered by José Gomes Monteiro, one of the
most erudite men of the city of Oporto.

10.--Moraes Sarmento, Anselmo Evaristo de,

### OPORTO.

The newspaper "A Actualidade," of which he is Proprietor and Founder, and 24 *brindes*, (gift volumes).

This journal was established in 1874.
The subscribers have distributed monthly with the title of " *Brinde*," a volume of about 180 pages of authors of acknowledged merit.

11.—Oporto Industrial Institute,

### OPORTO.

Thirty-four volumes of various works, original and translated.

The volumes exhibited belong to the Oporto Industrial Institute Library and are edited by Cruz Coutinho, of the same City.

12.—Portuguese Civil Engineers' Association,

### LISBON.

"Review of the Public Works and Mines." Technical Journal on Civil and Mining Engineering, written by the Members of the Association.

13.—Prostes, J. C.,

### LISBON.

Albums of Portuguese Newspapers forming 2 volumes.

14.—Royal Association of the Portuguese Architects and Archeologists,

### LISBON.

First series of the Association's Journal; 10 numbers in folio and 11 large illustrations. Second series, 8 numbers in quarto with 13 illustrations.

*Awards.—Grand Medal at the Paris Exhibition*, 1867. See Class 402.

15.—Silva, Joaquim Possidonio Narciso da,

### LISBON.

Memoir on Archeology, with the signs that are seen engraved on the ancient monuments of Portugal. 1 volume, 46 pages, and 558 figures.
Notes on the Antropologic and Pre-historic Congress of Balogna. 1 volume.
Artistic dissertation on Portuguese Architecture. 1 volume.
Historic and Artistic account of the Religious Buildings of Portugal. 1 volume.
Historic Eulogy of the Civil Architect—Mr. Victor Baltard.
Historic Eulogy of the Architect—J. C. Sequeira.
New Parlours of the Royal Palace d' Ajuda.
Statutes of the Architect's Association. Reports of the same Association.

*Awards,—Silver Medal at Oporto*, 1861; *Diploma of Merit at Vienna*, 1873,

## INSTITUTIONS AND ORGANIZATIONS.

CLASS 310.—Institutions founded for the increase and diffusion of knowledge. Such as the Smithsonian Institution, the Royal Institution, the Institute of France, British Association for the Advancement of Science, and the American Association, etc., their organization, history, and results.

CLASS 311.—Learned and scientific associations. Geological and mineralogical societies, etc. Engineering, technical and professional associations. Artistic, biological, zoological, medical schools, astronomical observatories.

CLASS 312.—Museums, collections, art galleries, exhibitions of works of art and industry. Agricultural fairs, State and county exhibitions, national exhibitions. International exhibitions.

Scientific museums, and art museums.

Ethnological and archeological collections.

CLASS 313.—Music and the drama.

### CLASS No. 310.

**16.—Oporto Industrial Institute,**

### OPORTO.

History, Organization, and Course of Studies.

### CLASSES Nos. 311 AND 335.

**17.—Observatory of the Infante D. Luiz,**

### LISBON.

Annals of the Observatory, Maps of the Gulf of Guinea, Meteorological and Magnetic Maps, Photographs of the Sun.

Photographs of the Stains of the Sun.

Photographs of the Eclipse of the 29th of September, 1875.

Photographs of Instruments.

Photolytographs of the Meteorological Charts.

Deviation of the Magnetic Needle on Board.

## SCIENTIFIC AND PHILOSOPHICAL INSTRUMENTS AND METHODS.

CLASS 320.—Instruments of precision, and apparatus of research, experiment, and illustration.

Astronomical instruments, and accessories, used in observatories.

Transits, mural circles, equatorials, collimators.

Geodetic and surveying instruments. Transit, theodolites, needle compasses. Instruments for surveying underground in mines, tunnels and excavations.

Nautical astronomical instruments. Sextants, quadrants, repeating circles, dip-sectors.

Levelling instruments and apparatus. Carpenters' and builders' levels, hand levels, water levels, engineers' levels.

CLASS 320—*Cont.*

Instruments for deep sea sounding and hydrographic surveying.
Meteorological instruments and apparatus.
Thermometers, pyrometers.
Barometers.
Hygrometers and rain gauges.
* Maps, bulletins.
Blanks for reports, methods of recording, reducing, and reporting observations.

CLASS 321.—Indicating and registering apparatus, other than meteorological; mechanical calculation.

Viameters, pedometers, perambulators.
Gas meters.
Water meters, current meters, ships' logs, electrical logs.
Tide registers.
Apparatus for printing consecutive numbers.
Counting machines, calculating engines, arithmometers.

CLASS 322.—Weights, measures, weighing and metrological apparatus.

Measures of length; graduated scales on wood, metal, ivory, tape, or ribbon; steel tapes, chains, rods, verniers, rods and graduated scales for measuring lumber, goods in packages, casks, etc., gaugers' tools and methods.
Measures of capacity for solids and liquids.
Weights. Scales and graduated beams for weighing; assay balances, chemical balances. Ordinary scales for heavy weights; weighing locomotives and trains of cars. Postal balances. Hydrometers, alcoömeters, lactometers, etc.; gravimeters.

CLASS 323.—Chronometric apparatus.

Chronometers. Astronomical clocks. Church and metropolitan clocks. Ordinary commercial clocks. Pendulum and spring clocks. Marine clocks. Watches. Clepsydras, hour glasses, sun dials. Chronographs, electrical clocks. Metronomes.

CLASS 324.—Optical and thermotic instruments, and apparatus.

Mirrors, plane and spherical.
Lenses and prisms.
Spectacles and eye glasses, field and opera glasses, graphoscopes and stereoscopes.
Cameras and photographic apparatus.
Microscopes.
Telescopes.
Apparatus for artificial illumination, including electric, oxyhydrogen and magnesium light.
Stereopticons.
Photometric apparatus.
Spectroscopes and accessories for spectrum analysis.
Polariscopes, etc.
Thermotic apparatus.

CLASS 325.—Electrical apparatus.

Friction machines.
Condensers and miscellaneous apparatus to illustrate the discharge.
Galvanic batteries and accessories to illustrate dynamical electricity.
Electro-magnetic apparatus.
Induction machines, Rumkorff coils, etc.
Magnets and magneto-electrical apparatus.

CLASS 326.—Telegraphic instruments and methods.

Batteries and forms of apparatus used in generating the electrical currents for telegraphic purposes.
Conductors and insulatoss, and methods of support marine telegraph cables.
Apparatus of transmission; keys, office accessories, and apparatus.
Receiving instruments, relay magnets, local circuits.

CLASS 326—*Cont.*
Semaphoric and recording instruments.
Codes, signs, or signals.
Printing telegraphs for special uses.
Electrographs.
Dial or cadran systems.
Apparatus for automatic transmission.
CLASS 327.—Musical instruments and acoustic apparatus.
Percussion instruments, drums, tamborines, cymbals, triangles.
Pianos.
Stringed instruments other than pianos.
Automatic musical instruments, music boxes.
Wind instruments of metal and of wood.
Harmoniums.
Church organs and similar instruments.
Speaking machines.
Vocal music.

## CLASS No. 320.

**18.—Lisbon Industrial Institute,**
**LISBON.**

Topo-photographic Camera (A. Rocha's).
Level of Precision, with two telescopes, invented by Brito Limpo.
Egault's Level.
Lenoir's Level.
Casella's Level.
Chesy's Level.
Pantometer, with Telescope.
Ordinary Pantometer.
Alhidate.
Surveyor's Table.
Heliotrope.
Planimeter.
Benevides' Apparatus.
Electric Pendulum, &c.
Morse's Receiver.
Alarm Clock.
Conductor.
Horizontal Compass.
Vertical Compass.
Disconnector.
Benevides' Disconnector.
Lightning-rod.
Telegraph Paper Wheel.
Photographs of the Different Departments of the Institute.

This establishment was organized by the decree of the 30th of December, 1852.
Employs a steam-engine of 3 horse-power, and 16 hands.
*Awards.—Copper Medal at London*, 1862; *Silver, at Paris*, 1867, *and of Progress, at Vienna*, 1873.

**19.—Pereira Coutinho, D. Martinho da Franca,**
**LISBON.**

A Pyramidal Compass.
Goniographic, Goniometric, and Telemetric Compass.

These two instruments are invented by the exhibitor.

## CLASS No. 321.

20.—Bastos, Antonio Pinto,
### LISBON.

Bastos' Hydrometer, with description.

Established in 1866.
Employs—25 men.      Wages, 600 to 900 reis.
        8 children,   "      100 to 360   "
A machine of 3 horse-power, and mechanical lathes, drilling and planing machines.
Raw materials from England, Belgium, France and Portugal.
Annual production,          .                    .          15,000 $ 000 reis
Markets—Lisbon, Spain, England and South America.
*Awards.—Diploma of Merit at Vienna, 1873; Medal of Merit at Madrid, 1873.*

21.—Pereira, Verissimo Alvares,
### LISBON.

Hydrometer.

---

## CLASS No. 323.

22.—Oliveira, Justino Gomes de,
### OPORTO.

Two Watches.

---

## CLASS No. 325.

23.—Motta, Jose Maria da,
### LISBON.

Electric Bell, No. 2.
Electric Bell, No. 4.
Indicator, with four numbers.
Electric Pile of four Batteries.
Electric Pile of two Batteries.
Transmitting Buttons (wooden).
Transmitting Buttons, with cords.
Conducting Wire.

---

## CLASS No. 327.

24.—Araujo, Joaquim Gomes,
### BRAGA.

Four Guitars.

25.—Cabral, Affonso do Valle Coelho,
### OPORTO.

A Violin, imitation of "Garnerius."

**26.—Sanhudo, Jose Ferreira,**
OPORTO.

A French Guitar.
A Guitar (Banza).
A Small Guitar of six strings.
One Small Guitar of four strings.


**27.—Ribeiro, Domingos Candido d'Almeida,**
OPORTO.

A Violin imitation of " Garnerius."


**28.—Pereira, Custodio Cardozo,**
OPORTO.

One Contrabass (American bass).
One Euphonium (American baritone).
One Euphonium (American baritone).
One Baritone (American tenor).
One Tenor (American alto).
One Alto (American cornet).
One Trombone, C and B flat.
One Cornet, B flat, 5 crooks.
One Copper Field Bugle, C.
One Brass Field Bugle, E flat.
One Brass Field Trumpet.
One Post Horn.
One dozen guitar string D.
One dozen guitar string A.
One dozen guitar string E.

Established in 1861.
Employs 2 apparatuses, indispensables for the factory, and 18 men.  Wages, 600 reis.
Raw material—From England.
Market—Portugal.
*Awards.—Second-class Medal at Oporto, 1865.*

---

# ENGINEERING, ARCHITECTURE, CHARTS, MAPS, AND GRAPHIC
# REPRESENTATIONS.

(For Agricultural Engineering, See Class 680).

(For Mining Engineering, See Class 120).

CLASS 330.—Civil engineering.   Land surveying, public lands, etc.
River, harbour, and coast surveying.  Construction and maintenance of
roads, streets, pavements, etc.  Surveys and location of towns and cities, with
systems of water supply and drainage.  Arched bridges of metal, stone,
brick, or beton.  Trussed girder bridges.  Suspension bridges.  Canals,
aqueducts, reservoirs, construction of dams.  Hydraulic engineering and
means of arresting and controlling the flow of water.
Submarine constructions, foundations, piers, docks, etc.

CLASS 331.—Dynamic and industrial engineering. Construction and working of machines; examples of planning and construction of manufacturing and metalurgical establishments.

CLASS 332.—Railway engineering. Location of railways, and the construction and management of railways.

CLASS 333.—Military engineering.

CLASS 334.—Naval engineering.

CLASS 335.—Topographical maps. Marine and coast charts. Geological maps and sections.

Botanical, agronomical, and other maps, showing the extent and distribution of men, animals, and terrestrial products. Physical maps.

Meteorological maps and bulletins. Telegraphic routes and stations. Railway and route maps. Terrestial and celestial globes. Relief maps and models of portions of the earth's surface. Profiles of ocean beds and routes of submarine cables.

---

## CLASS No. 330.

### 29.—Direction of Mondego and Figueira Bar Works,
#### FIGUEIRA.

Memoir on the Works of Mondego Figueira Bar, with Maps and Charts.

### 30.—Administrative Board of Ponta Delgada Artificial Harbor Works,
#### PONTA DELGADA.

1,000 copies, in folio, in Portuguese, French, and English, giving an account of the Ponta Delgada Artificial Harbor.

Drawing and Printed description of the same, framed.

1,000 Pamphlets, describing the above, in French and English.

A map showing the plan, under construction, of Ponta Delgada Artificial Harbor.

A Photographic view of the said Port.

An Oil Painting, representing the said Port and Dock of Ponta Delgada.

### 31.—Silva, Silverio Augusto Pereira da,
#### AVEIRO.

Model of a Bridge in Wood and Iron, accompanied by a description on this System.

---

## CLASS No. 331.

### 32.—Lecrenier, Nicolau Jose,
#### LISBON.

Model of Rail, with description.

---

## CLASS No. 332.

### 33.—Bayao, F. A. Pinheiro,
#### LISBON.

Description of a project for a Portable Railroad, with Lithographic Designs.

CLASS No. 335.

**34.--Oporto Industrial Institute,**
**OPORTO.**

Typographical Chart of the Douro River.
Topographical Map of the Wine Region of the Douro.

These maps were surveyed by Baron Forrester.

---

CLASSES Nos. 304 AND 335.

**35.—Pery, Gerardo A.,**
**LISBON.**

Geographical, Physical, and Orographical Maps of Portugal.
Geography and General Statistics of Portugal and the Colonies.

---

CLASS No. 335.

**36.—General Direction of the Geodetical, Topographical, Hydrographical**
**and Geological Labours.**                    **LISBON.**

## GEOGRAPHY.

Report on the Geodetical Labours in Portugal.
Report on the Labours executed by the General Direction of the Geodetical Works, from July, 1865, to December, 1874.
Instructions and Regulations for the Geodetical, Topographical, and Hydrographical Labours.
Instructions concerning the Hydrographical Labours.
Collection of the Conventional Signs adopted for the Hydrographical and Topographical Labours.
Tables to Facilitate Various Geodetical and Astronomical Calculations.
Memoir on the Improvement of the Seaport of Lisbon.
Memoir on the National Pine Forests of Leiria.
Report on the Works for the Improvement of the Bar and Port of Figueira.   Atlas belonging to the said Report.
Notices to Navigators, from 1869 to 1874.
Album of the Chorographical Maps.
Album of the Geological Perspective of the Coast Line.
Portfolio, with Sundry Maps and other Works.

## CHARTS AND MAPS.

Map of the Fundamental Triangles of the Kingdom and of the Leveling of Precision.
Geographical Map of Portugal.   Scale, 1–500,000.
Sketch of Map, representing the Cultivated and Uncultivated Surfaces of Portugal.   Scale, 1–500,000.
Topographical Map of the City of Lisbon.
Sheets of the Chorographical Map of Portugal.   Scale, 1–100,000.
Hydrographical Chart of the Bar of Lisbon.
Hydrographical Chart of the Bar of Oporto.
Chart of the Berlengas, Farilhoes, and Harbor of Peniche.
Chart of the Port of Lisbon with the Plan of the Works for its Improvement.

Chart of the Light-Houses of Portugal.
Chart with a Plan for the Improvements of Figueira Bar.
Topographical Chart of the National Pine Forest of Leiria.
Topographical and Hydrographical Conventional Signs.

## GEOLOGY—BOOKS.

Description of the Quaternary Formation of the Hydrographical Basins of the Tagus and Sado.
Memoir on the Supply of Lisbon with Spring and River Water.
Memoir on the Cesareda Caves.
Description of some chipped Silex and Quartzites, from the terciary and Quaternary Formations of the Basins of the Tagus and Sado.
Memoir on the Sixth Session of the Congress of Anthropology and of Pre-historic Archeology of Brussels.
Memoir on the General Foresting of the Country.
Memoir concerning the existence of the Silurian Formation in the Baixo-Alemtejo.

## CHARTS AND MAPS.

General Geological Map of Portugal.
Sheets representing geologically a perspective of 108 kilometres of the Portuguese Coast Line.

## PHOTOGRAPHY—BOOKS.

Information Concerning the First Exhibition of the Photographical section.

## PROOFS.

Crayon Drawing on Lithographic Stone.   Typographical fac-simile, (Chemical Drawing).
Typographical Photo-Engraving, (Reduction).
Typographical chemical engraving. Fac-simile of an engraving on stone,
Photolithograph.   Fac-simile of a Diploma.
Reduction of an Engraving of the Illustrated News.
New Photolithographic Printing Process, (Reduction of Original.)

## PHOTOLITHOGRAPHY.

Fac-similes, reduced, of several Engravings (artistic design).
Reduction of a Hydrographical Design, done by pen.
Fac-simile, reduced, of a Hydrographical Design.
Fac-simile, reduced, of a page of an Ancient Book.
Fac-simile, reduced, in different scales of Designs and Typographical Impressions.
Fac-simile of a page of an Ancient Book.
Fac-simile, reduced, of a Diploma.
Fac-simile, reduced, of a Hydrographical Design.

## PHOTOZINCOGRAPHY.

Reduction of several Printed Pages.
Fragments of a manuscript letter of Father Sechi.   Typographic Heliography.
Geographical Design by Pen, Fragments of a Map of Portugal.
Remarkable Small Reduction of a Printed Page.
Fac-simile of artistic Design Engraved for Typography.

## CLASS No. 344.

### 37.—General Administration of the Mint and Stamped Paper,
**LISBON.**

Postage Stamps, Stamped Papers.
Collection of Current Coins.

---

## CLASS No. 347.

### 38.—Society for the Promotion of the Fabril Industry,
**LISBON.**

A frame, containing diplomas, statutes, and works of instruction. Special Treatises on several branches of Industry. Reports and Copies of the Statutes of the Association, translated into French.

This association was instituted by a royal decree on the 20th of March, 1860, which approved its statutes. It purposes to promote, by the means within its reach, the development of National Industry. With this purpose it created schools of primary instruction, promoted national exhibitions, and co-operated for the success of the Portuguese Industrial exhibits in the Universal Expositions. It keeps an excellent industrial library, subsidizes the workmen and finds employment for them when they need it.

# DEPARTMENT IV.
# FINE ARTS.

# DEPARTMENT IV.---FINE ARTS.

## SCULPTURE.

CLASS 400.—Figures and groups in stone, metal, clay, or plaster.
CLASS 401.—Bas-reliefs, in stone, or metal; electrotype copies.
CLASS 402.—Medals, pressed and engraved; electrotypes of medals.
CLASS 403.—Hammer and wrought work— *repousse* and *rehausse* work, embossed and engraved relief work.
CLASS 404.—Cameos, intaglios, engraved stones, dies, seals, etc.
CLASS 405.—Carvings in wood, ivory, and metal.

---

## CLASS No. 400.

**1.—Abreu, Severiano Jose de,**

### LISBON.

A Royal Crown, made of Stone, with diadems, adorned with Symbolical Flowers.

Established in 1854.
Employs—8 men.　　Wages, 500 to 1,000 reis.
　　　　3 children.　　　" 　　80 to　300　"
Annual production,　　　-　　　　-.
Markets—Portugal and Brazil.

6,000 $ 000 reis

**2.—Almeida, Jose Joaquim de Azevedo,**

### LISBON.

An Image of Jesus Christ in Stone.

Established in 1860.
Employs 34 men,　　Wages, 600 to 1600 reis.
　　　　3 children.　　　"　　160 to　300　"
Raw materials used are from Portugal and Italy, at the annual value of 5,000 $ 000 reis.
Annual production,　　　-　　-　　-　　-　　-　　14,000 $ 000 reis
Markets—Portugal, Brazil, and Africa.

**3.—Campolini, Miguel,**

### OPORTO.

Clay Figures, representing National Costumes.

*Awards.—Medal at Oporto, 1865, and at Paris, 1867.*

**4.—Costa, Antonio Almeida da & Co.,**

### OPORTO.

Eighteen Porcelain and Clay Figures.

Established in 1869.
Employs—80 men.　　Wages, 360 to 1,000 reis.
　　　　15 women.　　　"　　160 to　300　"
　　　　26 children.　　　"　　120 to　300　"
Raw material—Domestic, to the value of 4,000 $ 000 reis.
Annual production,　　　-　　-　　-　　-　　-　　28,600 $ 000 reis
Markets—Portugal, Spain, and Brazil.

**5.—Rota, Antonio Moreira,**

### LISBON.

A Sculptured Trophy in Marble.   See Class 102.


**6.—Rio Junior, Joao do,**

### OPORTO.

Clay Figures Representing Juno and Jupiter.

Established in 1802.
Employs—43 men.   Wages, 360 to   800 reis.
     10 women.   "   140 to   200   "
     20 boys.   "   160 to   240   "
Raw materials used to the annual value of 13,500 $ 000 reis.
Annual production,  .   -   -   -   -   -   28,000 $ 000 reis
*Awards.—Medals at the National Portuguese Exhibitions o*  1857 *and* 1861, *and International*
*of* 1865.


**7.—Silva & Santos,**

### OPORTO.

Clay Figures, representing National Costumes.

Established in 1869.
Employs two men.   Wages, 600 reis.
Raw material—Domestic, to the annual value of 300 $ 000 reis.
Annual production,   -   -   -   -   900 $ 000 reis
Markets—Portugal, Spain, France, England, and Brazil.

---

### CLASS No. 402.

**8.—General Administration of the Mint and Stamped Paper,**

### LISBON.

Medals in Frames.   See Class 344.


**9.—Mollarinho, J. Arnaldo Nogueira,**

### OPORTO.

A Frame with Copper and Silver Medals.


**10.—Royal Association of the Portuguese Architects and Archeologists,**

### LISBON.

Proof of the Die ordered to be engraved for the Medals to be confered on
the members who may render important services in the studies of
Architecture and Archeology.

—

### CLASS No. 404.

**11.—Mendes, Malaquias Jose,**

### OPORTO.

Proofs, in Sealing Wax, of Monograms and Cyphers.

CLASSES Nos. 405 AND 442.

**12.—Commercial Aasociation of Oporto,**
## OPORTO.

Twenty-one Specimens of Wood Carvings belonging to the Interior Decorations and Furniture of the Building of the Association.
Specimen of Ornamental Work in Granite.

---

## PAINTING.

CLASS 410.—Paintings in oil on canvas, panels, etc.
CLASS 411.—Water colour pictures; aquarelles, miniatures, etc.
CLASS 412.—Frescoes, cartoons for frescoes, etc.
CLASS 413.—Painting with vitrifiable colours  Pictures on porcelain, enamel, and metal.

---

## CLASS No. 411.

**13.—Sequeira Thomas,**
## LISBON.

A Water colour in frame representing the Distribution of Soups at Lisbon at the time of the French Invasion, by Domingos Antonio de Sequeira.

---

## ENGRAVING AND LITHOGRAPHY.

CLASS 420.—Drawings with pen, pencil, or crayons.
CLASS 421.—Line engravings from steel, copper, or stone.
CLASS 422.—Wood engravings.
CLASS 423·—Lithographs, zincographs, etc.  ,
CLASS 424.—Chromo-lithographs.

---

## CLASS No. 422.

**14.—Brito Aranha, Pedro Wenceslau de,**
## LISBON.

Six Frames, containing Wood Engravings, by Joao Pedroza.

---

## CLASS No. 423 TO 432.

**15.—General Direction of the Geodetical, Topographical, Hydrographical, and Geological Labours,** **LISBON.**

Several Photographic Works.  See Class 335.

## CLASS No. 423.

**16.—Reis & Monteiro,**

### OPORTO.

Proofs of Lithographic Work.

Established in 1870.
Employs—15 men.      Wages, 700 to 1,500 reis.
          8 children.   "      160 to   240   "
          and a mechanical press, 4 manual presses, a Gulloche machine, 1 paper cut-
          ting machine, 1 for card cutting, a hydraulic machine, &c., &c.
Materials are from France, Germany, and England.
Annual production,                .              .                         12,000 $ 000  reis
Markets—Portugal and Brazil.

**17.—Braga, Antonio Pereira da Silva,**

### OPORTO.

A Frame with the Lithographs of the Armorial Bearings of different
Families in the Province of Minho.

## PHOTOGRAPHY.

CLASS 430.—Photographs on paper, metal, glass, wood, fabrics, or enamel
surfaces.
CLASS 431.—Prints from photo-relief plates, carbon-prints, etc.
CLASS 432.—Photo-lithographs, etc.

## CLASS No. 430.

**18.—Biel, E. & F. Bruett—Formerly Fritz,**

### OPORTO.

Photographs and Phototypes.

Established in 1854.
Employs 9 persons.  Wages from 500 to 3,000 reis.
Machines, those of Voigtlander and Sohn, in Braunschweig, Ross, Steinheil, Busch, the
     largest objective having an aperture of 7 inches.
Imports—Albuminous paper from Trapp & Munich in Troedberg.  The Phototype
     presses being from Boivier, of Paris.
Annual production,      -                  -                      -           20,000 $ 000 reis
Markets—Portugal and Brazil.
Awards—Silver Medal at Oporto 1861.

## CLASS No. 430.

**19.—Braga, Antonio Pereira da Silva,**

### BRAGA.

Photographic Views of Buildings in the city of Braga.

**20.—Camacho, J. T.,**
### Island of Madeira, FUNCHAL.

Collection of Photographic Views and Portraits.

**21.—Souza Fernandes,**
### OPORTO.

Photographs, Portraits, Costumes, and Amplifications of Microscopic Subjects.

Annual production,    -   -   -   -   -    1,000 $ 000 reis
*Awards.—Diploma of Merit at Vienna, 1873; Medal at the Photographic Exhibition of Brussels, 1875.*

**22.—Ferreira, Manuel Jose de Souza,**
### OPORTO.

Album of Photographic Views of the City of Oporto.

**23.—Fonseca, Antonio Correa da,**
### OPORTO.

Photographic Portraits of various sizes.

Established in 1873.
Employs 7 persons. Wages, 500 to 1200 reis.
Uses a Plague Machine and another for Stereoscopic Views.
Materials used to the annual value of 4,000 $ 000 reis.
Annual production,    -   -   -        7,000 $ 000 reis
Market—Portugal.

**24.—Nunes, Henrique,**
### LISBON.

A Frame, containing four Photographic Miniatures.

Established in 1860.
Employs four persons.
*Award at the Portuguese International Exhibition oj 1865.*

**25.—Relvas, Carlos, Amateur Photographer,**
### GOLLEGA.

Photographs and Phototypes.
Nos.
  1—Eight Cartes Albums, instantaneous.
  2—Eight Cartes Albums, portraits.
  3—Carlos Relvas' Studio at Gollega.
  4—Royal Palace of Pena, Cintra.
  5—Royal Chapel, Batalha.
  6—General View of the Monastery of Batatha.
  7—Gaya and the Douro, Oporto.
  8—Environs of Villa Real.
  9—Cottage at Vizella.
 10—Eight Phototypes—Portraits.
 11—Porch of the Unfinished Chapels, Batalha.
 12—Porch of the Monastery of Santa Maria de Belem.

13—Park of the Royal Palace of Pena, Cintra.
14—Olive Tree, 7½ metres in circumference, Barroca.
15—Carlos Relvas' Studio, Gollega.
16—Reproduction of an Engraving.
17—Reproduction of an Engraving.
18—Reproduction of an Engraving.
19—Seven Cartes Albums, carbon prints.
20—"Paladin" C. Relvas' Racer.
21—Positive by Transparency on Glass.
Two packets, with 24 stereoscopic proofs on albuminous paper.
The proofs from No. 1 to 9 were made on albuminous paper and nitrate of silver. No. 10 to 18 are phototypes obtained by means of the roller and lithographic ink. Nos. 19 and 20 were obtained by the carbon process.

*Awards.—Medal at the Exhibition of the French Society of Photography, 1870; Medal of Progress at Vienna, 1873; Silver Medal at the National Exhibition of Madrid, 1873; Rappel de Medaille at the Exhibition of the French Society of Photography, 1874; Silver Medal at the Exhibition of the Photographic Society of Vienna, 1875.*

**26.—Rochini, Francisco,**

### LISBON.

A Frame, containing 13 Photographs.

Established in 1861.
Employs the Apparatus of J. H. Dallmeyer, London; Rapid Rectilinear, and Triple Achromatic Lens.
*Awards.—Diploma of Merit at Vienna, 1873.*

---

## INDUSTRIAL AND ARCHITECTURAL DESIGNS, MODELS, AND DECORATIONS.

CLASS 440.—Industrial designs.
CLASS 441.—Architectural designs; studies and fragments, representations and projects of restorations from ruins and from documents.
CLASS 442.—Decoration of interiors of buildings.
CLASS 443.—Artistic hardware and trimmings; artistic castings, forged metal work for decoration, etc.

### CLASS No. 443.

**27.—Cruz, Luis Ferreira de Souza,**

#### OPORTO.

Two pieces of cast iron for decorative purposes.

### CLASS No. 442.

**28.—"Aurificia" Company,**

#### OPORTO

Samples of Carved Wood, Veneers, and Mouldings.

Established in 1865. It does Silver Work likewise.
Employs a high and low-pressure steam-engine of 50 horse-power and
    100 men.     Wages, 240 to 2250 reis.
    40 women,    "    120 to 300  "
    40 children.    "    80 to 160  "
Raw materials used are from Portugal, England, France, and Germany, to the annual
    value of 120,000 $ 000 reis.
Annual production,  -     -              200,000 $ 000 reis
Markets—Portugal, Brazil and Spain.

## 29.—Commercial Association of Oporto,
### OPORTO.

Stucco Ornaments for Interior Decoration of the House of said Association. See Class 405.

---

## DECORATION WITH CERAMIC AND VITREOUS MATERIALS.

---

CLASS 450.—Mosaic and inlaid work in stone.
CLASS 451.—Mosaic and inlaid work in tiles, tessaræ, glass, etc.
CLASS 452.—Inlaid work in wood and metal, parquetry, inlaid floors, tables, etc.
CLASS 453.—Stained glass.
CLASS 454.—Miscellaneous objects of art.

---

### CLASS No. 454.

## 30.—Venancio, Domingos,
### OPORTO.

Four Medalions representing different monuments, reproduced after the
Galvano Plastic System.

# DEPARTMENT V.

# MACHINERY.

# DEPARTMENT V.---MACHINERY.

*Location :*—MAIN BUILDING.

## MACHINES AND TOOLS FOR WORKING METAL, WOOD, AND STONE.

CLASS 510.—Planing, sawing, veneering, grooving, mortising, tongueing, cutting, moulding, stamping, carving, and cask-making machines, etc., cork-cutting machines.

CLASS 511.—Direct acting steam sawing machines, with gang saws.

CLASS 512.—Rolling mills, bloom squeezers, blowing fans.

CLASS 513.—Furnaces and apparatus for casting metals, with specimens of work.

CLASS 514.—Steam, trip, and other hammers, with specimens of work, anvils, forges.

CLASS 515.—Planing, drilling, slotting, turning, shaping, punching, stamping, and cutting machines. Wheel cutting and dividing machines, emery wheels, drills, taps, gauges, dies, etc.

CLASS 516.—Stone-sawing and planing machines, dressing, shaping, and polishing, sand blasts, Tilghman's machines, glass-grinding machines, etc.

CLASS 517.—Brick, pottery, and tile machines. Machines for making artificial stone.

CLASS 518.—Furnaces, moulds, blowpipes, etc., for making glass and glass-ware.

---

## CLASS No. 515.

1.—Oporto Industrial Institute,

Manufacturer—Jose Baptista,

OPORTO.

A Turner's Lathe and Appurtenances.
Specimens of Work.

---

## MACHINES AND IMPLEMENTS OF SPINNING, WEAVING, FELTING, AND PAPER MAKING.

CLASS 520.—Machines for the manufacture of silk goods.

CLASS 521.—Machines for the manufacture of cotton goods.

CLASS 522.—Machines for the manufacture of woollen goods.

CLASS 523.—Machines for the manufacture of linen goods.

CLASS 524.—Machines for the manufacture of rope and twine, and miscellaneous fibrous materials.

CLASS 525.—Machines for the manufacture of paper and felting.

CLASS 526.—Machines for the manufacture of india-rubber goods.

CLASS 527.—Machines for the manufacture of mixed fabrics.

## AËRIAL, PNEUMATIC, AND WATER TRANSPORTATION.

CLASS 590.—Suspended cable railways.

CLASS 591.—Transporting cables.

CLASS 592.—Balloons, flying machines, etc.

CLASS 593.—Pneumatic railways, pneumatic dispatch·

CLASS 594.—Boats and sailing vessels. Sailing vessels used in commerce. Sailing vessels used in war. Yachts and pleasure boats. Rowing boats of all kinds. Life-boats and salvage apparatus, with life rafts, belts, etc. Submarine armour, diving bells, etc. Ice boats.

CLASS 595.—Steamships, steamboats, and all vessels propelled by steam.

CLASS 596·—Vessels for carrying telegraph cables, and railway trains, also coal barges, water boats, and dredging machines, screw and floating docks, and for other special purposes.

CLASS 597.—Steam capstans, windlass, deck-winches, and steering apparatus, fans.

## CLASS No. 594.

**8.—Pilao e Luzes, Antonio d'Oliveira & Joao Gomes Leite,**

OVAR.

Model of a Fishing Boat.

www.ingramcontent.com/pod-product-compliance
Lightning Source LLC
Chambersburg PA
CBHW030354270326
41926CB00009B/1096